Visual Studies

This book presents a transcultural and generative introduction to the field of visual studies. Aimed primarily, but not exclusively, at students and scholars in the social sciences, it explores the multiple meanings of images and visual culture in human life.

Divided into three parts, the first section departs from a framework of the look as a medium for understanding imaging practices and offers a critical analysis of the changing ways in which vision has been understood across epochs and cultures and the politics attached. The second section opens with an expanded understanding of images, addressing their affective, sensory and performative roles. It then discusses semiotic tensions between the icon and the index and the role of social interaction in the visual field and ends with an analysis of immersive viewing in a creative juxtaposition between distinct, culturally situated, imaging practices. Building on the previous sections, the third part provides a series of applications in specific terrains, such as on the significance of faces, on cameras and their environments, the visual culture of death, x-ray imagery and the meaning and role of shadows. Insisting on the role of the look as a medium for studying the visual field, this book reminds us of the importance of images not only as representations of the world but also as proper co-travellers and companions of our journeys on the earth.

The book serves as an ideal introductory text for courses across the social sciences by directing the reader's attention to the generativity and interactivity of imaging practices.

Paolo S.H. Favero is Professor of Visual Cultures and Anthropology at the Visual and Digital Cultures Research Center (ViDi), University of Antwerp, Belgium.

Asko Lehmuskallio is Professor of Visual Studies and Director of the Visual Studies Lab at Tampere University, Finland.

Visual Studies
A Social Scientific Perspective

Paolo S.H. Favero and
Asko Lehmuskallio

LONDON AND NEW YORK

Designed cover image: Maija Tammi: One of Them Is a Human #1, Erica. Archival pigment print, 60 × 65 cm, framed. Photograph by Miikka Pirinen.

First published 2025
by Routledge
4 Park Square, Milton Park, Abingdon, Oxon OX14 4RN

and by Routledge
605 Third Avenue, New York, NY 10158

Routledge is an imprint of the Taylor & Francis Group, an informa business

© 2025 Paolo S.H. Favero and Asko Lehmuskallio

The right of Paolo S.H. Favero and Asko Lehmuskallio to be identified as authors of this work has been asserted in accordance with sections 77 and 78 of the Copyright, Designs and Patents Act 1988.

All rights reserved. No part of this book may be reprinted or reproduced or utilised in any form or by any electronic, mechanical, or other means, now known or hereafter invented, including photocopying and recording, or in any information storage or retrieval system, without permission in writing from the publishers.

Trademark notice: Product or corporate names may be trademarks or registered trademarks, and are used only for identification and explanation without intent to infringe.

British Library Cataloguing-in-Publication Data
A catalogue record for this book is available from the British Library

Library of Congress Cataloging-in-Publication Data
Names: Favero, Paolo S. H., author. | Lehmuskallio, Asko, author.
Title: Visual studies : a social scientific perspective /
Paolo S.H. Favero and Asko Lehmuskallio.
Description: Abingdon, Oxon ; New York, NY : Routledge, 2025. |
Includes bibliographical references and index.
Identifiers: LCCN 2024045216 (print) | LCCN 2024045217 (ebook) |
ISBN 9781350128910 (hardback) | ISBN 9781350128903 (paperback) |
ISBN 9781003084549 (ebook)
Subjects: LCSH: Visual anthropology–Study and teaching. |
Social sciences–Study and teaching.
Classification: LCC GN347 .F42 2025 (print) | LCC GN347 (ebook) |
DDC 301–dc23/eng/20241231
LC record available at https://lccn.loc.gov/2024045216
LC ebook record available at https://lccn.loc.gov/2024045217

ISBN: 9781350128910 (hbk)
ISBN: 9781350128903 (pbk)
ISBN: 9781003084549 (ebk)

DOI: 10.4324/9781003084549

Typeset in Sabon
by Newgen Publishing UK

Contents

Preface   *vii*

1 Introduction   1

2 Looking, Seeing, and Historical Notions of Vision and the Eye   5
   2.1 *The Look as a Medium* 5
   2.2 *A History of Vision* 16

3 Tools for Analysing Images   43
   3.1 *What Exactly an Image Is* 44
   3.2 *The Tension Between the Icon and the Index* 63
   3.3 *The Role of Social Interaction* 75
   3.4 *Immersive Viewing, From Byzantine Icons to Virtual Reality* 92

4 Applications of Visual Studies   112
   4.1 *The Significance of Faces* 112
   4.2 *Cameras, Environments, and 'Good' Images* 119
   4.3 *The Visual Culture of Death* 126
   4.4 *X-Rays Between Science and Popular Culture* 139
   4.5 *Shadows: Between Light and Darkness* 145

5 Conclusions   155

References   *157*
Index   *170*

Preface

This book represents an outgrowth from the discussion of how to encapsulate our perspectives on visual studies in a manner that opens the field well to students of the social sciences at the undergraduate level or pursuing an MA or PhD. Rather than introduce a sampling of perspectives, we have opted for a coherent treatment that directs the reader's attention to the generativity and interactivity of imaging practices. We hope this will be useful for readers approaching the field from other angles, too.

The volume builds on work conducted by the authors over many years, and it obtained its final form through a range of intense, highly rewarding meetings and rich exchanges of e-mail, social media messages, pictures, and drafts. While we cannot list all of the numerous individuals, of various stripes, who have come to influence the authors' thinking over the years, we would like to acknowledge a few institutional settings through which we have come into regular contact with them. Paolo S.H. Favero is indebted primarily to his junior and senior colleagues at the Visual and Digital Cultures Research Center of the University of Antwerp (ViDi), to his partners in the Visual Anthropology Network of the European Association of Social Anthropologists (VANEASA) and in the Images of Care Collective, and to colleagues dispersed across many countries' institutional departments covering fields from anthropology and sociology to art. Asko Lehmuskallio would like to thank his colleagues at the Visual Studies Lab at Tampere University for fruitful and engaging discussions, including those conducting collaborative research at partner universities (for example within TRAVIS: Trust and Visuality, Everyday Digital Practices), alongside those at the Media & Communications Department of London School of Economics and Political Science who hosted him as Visiting Professor. Furthermore, his colleagues co-organising and visiting the biennial Helsinki Photomedia conference have been important and influential companions over the years, as have members of the European Communication Research and Education Association's Visual Cultures section, which the two authors founded alongside Edgar Gómez Cruz.

The authors have divided up the work on the various portions of the book in such a way that the astute observer will be able to identify which of us has taken the lead in writing which chapter. Yet, we have sought to bring our respective positions and experiences into direct dialogue with the aim of creating a new amalgam. We have commented on each other's work accordingly, and we have opted for 'we' in the writing in order to stress that we proceed from similar general perspectives toward images and the study of the visual. Both of us received our initial training in cultural/social anthropology (in Sweden and Germany) but have since then moved to media and communication departments, carrying with us an interest in how images make life. We both also have experience with the practice of making images. Yet our approach is not, however, technical. Our way of approaching the subject is instead exploratory, generative, and synthesising. It inspires, creates room for, and indeed invites a cornucopia of analyses of the visual bound together by spirit rather than technical form.

While many of the chapters and sections were written specifically for this book, some have a grounding in, extend, or incorporate elements of previously published work. In order of appearance in this book, these roots have informed the discussion thus: parts of Section 2.1 were published in Lehmuskallio's 2019 article 'The Look As a Medium: A Conceptual Framework and an Exercise for Teaching Visual Studies', and Section 3.3's focus on screens zooms in on and extends material he published in a 2021 piece on video-mediated communication amid COVID-19 concerns for *Inquiries into Art, History, and the Visual*. Portions of the argument centred on dialogue between VR/XR/MR and Byzantine icons were presented by Favero in the 2019 *Anthrovision* paper 'A Journey from Virtual and Mixed Reality to Byzantine Icons via Buddhist Philosophy' and in the 2018 book *The Present Image: Visible Stories in a Digital Habitat*. Section 4.2 builds on work addressed in Lehmuskallio's chapter for the 2020 book *The Camera As Actor*. The section following that, 'The Visual Culture of Death', features a brief autobiographical revisiting of Favero's 2022 paper 'It Begins and Ends with an Image' printed in *Anthropological Journal of European Cultures*. This elaborates upon the earlier treatment. Finally, the same chapter's text on x-rays and on shadows consists of revised forms of two previously published contributions by Favero to edited volumes: his 2024 'Deep Visions and Superficial Desires: X-rays As Science and Popular Culture' and 2020 'Notes on Blackness, Darkness, and Shadowlands', respectively.

1 Introduction

In a small flat in South Delhi, a young woman walks up to her home's personal shrine. She lights a small lamp (a *diya*) and with one hand draws circles in the air in front of the image of a blue-skinned deity. With the other hand she insistently rings a bell. Then she bends before the icon, touches the surface on which it stands, and dips one finger into a tray containing sandalwood powder to draw a single line on the forehead of the deity. She does the same with her own forehead and leaves the room. Simultaneously, a woman in a north Italian cemetery walks past a tomb. She stops, as if she is collecting her thoughts and memories, while staring at the portrait of a man. She mutters something, bringing her fingers to her mouth in what looks like a gentle kiss. Her hand reaches out to the photograph. It lingers on the image for a few seconds. Then, with a gentle caress, she draws it back. She brings her fingers toward her mouth, as one might do upon receiving a kiss. She too turns around, and she walks away.

In 2018, the US military was forced to review its security policies after secret information leaked out to social media via the fitness tracker app Strava. By visualising georeferenced uploads from careless soldiers monitoring their training sessions, the company had inadvertently made public the exact position of top-secret military bases in the most remote areas of Syria and Afghanistan. In other quarters, meanwhile, erasure complicates things – Bedouin land claims in Israel have been made more difficult as traces characterising life in historical settlements get wiped away. While some of these erasures have been conducted on land, they have also been enacted by means of reduction in the resolution of satellite views of the locations. This rewriting of visual resolution renders it hard to decipher the signs of these settlements, such as wells, terraces, and graves.

In a London clinic a psychiatrist is exposed to a virtual-reality installation simulating a panic attack. The installation is designed to train doctors in developing an embodied, empathic understanding of what patients go through during these attacks and what they are often incapable of expressing in words. At the same time, somewhere in Europe, two

DOI: 10.4324/9781003084549-1

scholars hundreds of kilometres apart spend hours sitting in front of their computer- and phone-cameras working to complete together this very book. On the desk of the one located in Belgium there is a small wooden plank displaying a phrase by Persian poet Rumi. It says: 'Darkness is your candle'[lii]. And in the background of the other's office, there is a song playing. It is by Finnish musician Joose Keskitalo and it recites: 'Now it is your time to see visions, as the night has anointed you'[liii]. Each against their own poetic backdrops they share words, images, and visions. Their common presence strengthens the sense of togetherness along the journey.

As these glimpses may have expressed, images and visual culture at large touch many, if not all, facets of human life. We could say that, across time and space, they are at its very heart. Images provide life. They are constitutive of communities. They craft civilisations, yet they assume different meanings, depending on the specific cultural and historical settings in which they are inserted, watched, produced, and re-mashed. It matters little whether the images are created by digital or analogue means – they accompany us in life in any case, throughout life. They stitch us into our communities and our history. And, indeed, images form the entry to much broader terrain, that of visual culture and the senses.

Visual studies, as an academic field examining visual cultures, implies attending to far more than the role of particular pictures, no matter how relevant and central those instances might be. It means paying attention to that aspect of human life that responds, if we follow Blaise Pascal's manner of speaking, to the reasons of the heart. Pascal said that humans 'know truth, not only by the reason, but also by the heart' (1897: p. xc), hence anticipating where social scientists would turn much later when underscoring the role of the body, of ritual, of performativity and affect in understanding images and sociality.

Our manifold ways of being in the world are constructed at the intersection of complementary and intertwined ways of being and of operating. On one hand we are linguistic creatures, stitching together linear arguments of cause and effect, narratives of temporality that satisfy some aspects of our needs. However, we are also affective creatures, armed with an array of seemingly non-rational skills in realms such as sensation, intuition, spatial consciousness, and empathy. These make us into what we are. There is little doubt, though, that from Plato, via Descartes, onward, Western civilisations, in particular, have prioritised rational reasoning, a focus on language, logical sequences, and modes of organising these into ever more complex wholes. Paying attention to visual culture makes us aware of the multitudinous ways in which we inhabit the world in a constant dialogue between linguistic and embodied knowledge, knowledge that is felt, understood, and worked out *in situ* and *in actu*. David MacDougall once suggested that the visual offers 'pathways to the other senses and to social experience' (1997: p. 289), thereby providing us not only with a different way to understand others or ourselves but also with awareness that there are, again as MacDougall might say, different things to understand about the world and its various environments.

This book's aim is to introduce the reader to the terrain that characterises visual studies, defined above as the study of visual cultures. Devoting particular attention to students and scholars in various areas of social science, we start with two key assumptions. One is that visual cultures are constitutive of human life; cultural meanings and notions about society are fundamentally communicated and transmitted through the visual. Secondly, we find that, while vision has a physical substrate, it is in important ways socially and culturally constructed and situated. This means that understandings of vision, and of what is considered to be visual, are not the same everywhere. As we, to the best of our capacity, provide a range of examples across a vast tapestry of places and times, this book inevitably addresses the intrinsically political nature of the visual, its way of constituting a field where power battles are fought, while we always bear in mind that power remains polymorphous and at times difficult to point at. In the course of our enterprise here, we also address the multisensoriality of the visual field – the ways in which the visual is never about seeing on its own but also about hearing, touching, smelling, feeling, sensing. Seeing is only one of the ways in and through which organisms, and increasingly also machines, move about and exist in their environments. We, the authors of this book, are united by an interest in studying what Hal Foster pointed toward when recommending attention to 'how we see, how we are able, allowed, or made to see, and how we see this seeing or the unseen therein' (1988: p. ix). Foster's call is still today one of the most vibrant expressions of the interests that give direction to visual studies, addressing both cultural and 'natural' dimensions in efforts to tease out the roles of biology, desire, politics, tensions, and fictions between vision and the other senses, in whatever way they may be respectively ordered.

While a broad expanse connected with the visual intrigues us, we offer the readers a highly specific take on images, vision, and visuality. Grounded in a blend of practice theory, work related to visual culture and visual social science, and insights gathered from our own research and practice-based engagements with visual media, this book foregrounds the interrelations among situated, sensing bodies, with a range of complex mediations and a panoply of images, taking numerous forms. It is informed by the two authors' attention to literature on vision and visuality within both the social sciences and the humanities but speaks simultaneously to an interest in experiments and results in related academic disciplines, alongside those developed within artistic practices. The visual is far too central for any single academic discipline (or arts practice, for that matter) to cover all of its various facets.

This book does not provide an overview of all possible approaches to studying images and visual culture or even of those conventionally employed within the social sciences, nor can it. Quite a few useful contributions of that sort already exist (e.g., in work by the following scholars, among others: Aiello & Parry, 2019; Burnett, 1995; Edwards & Bhaumik, 2009;

Kromm & Bakewell, 2010; Manghani, 2013; Manghani et al., 2006; Margolis & Pauwels, 2011, 2017; Niederer & Colombo, 2024; Rose, 2022; Sturken & Cartwright, 2009). We believe that, instead, scholars and students are well served in getting a deeper (and, one would hope, critical) feel for the kind of perspective we consider beneficial for understanding the world of images and vision. This approach necessarily leaves many fascinating and illuminating analyses beyond the scope of our introduction, but we still hope it may ignite sparks of curiosity and further engagement among those joining us for the journey. We invite readers to embark on a path of discovery of the beauty and mystery, of the magic and power, and of the intelligibility and unintelligibility of the visual world. It is our hope that this book will function also as a stepping stone to exploring the skills carefully cultivated and at stake among those subjects who craft, create, and otherwise work with images.

We hope thus to be able to spark in our readers a curiosity centred on the worlds of images and visual cultures. This holds especially true perhaps for those of you who might not have paid attention yet to such an angle in your work and practice. Allow yourself to question the extent to which some attention to the visual may even assist you practically through new awareness of topics and events that you address via other methodological and analytical approaches, means, and tools. For those of you interested in stimulating attention to this dimension, also among students and colleagues, you will find, embedded in the various chapters that make up this book, invitations for exercises and drills. These are designed to trigger active reflection on questions bound up with vision, its role for social organisation, and the 'work' that images do in the world. They should also aid in contemplating why visual technologies are so central for the world's varied cultures, organisations, and societies.

With the part of the book that follows, we will start unpacking what lies on this terrain by means of two explanatory chapters. The first of them addresses the phenomenon of looking and seeing (and hence of mediation), while the second one will guide you through a brief history of scientific, philosophical, and artistic attempts at grasping the functioning of the eye. Following up on that, the third section will explore different tools at our disposal for analysing images. In the fourth section we will offer the readers a set of concrete applications of the toolkit described in the first part of the book on various specific terrains, such as that of faces, cameras, death, x-ray imagery, and shadows.

2 Looking, Seeing, and Historical Notions of Vision and the Eye

Much of the discussion along our route pays particular attention to the role of mediation. This, we suggest, is of fundamental importance for letting a panorama of theory unfold that can enrich understandings of images, vision, and the act of looking. The first part of this chapter will focus on looking as a mediated activity. This entails attention to both images and their contextual uses – and, thereby, consideration also of the web of relations between images and those looking at them. With the second part of the chapter, we outline some of the historical debates and understandings pertaining to vision; we will show that neither seeing nor the act of looking is to be taken for granted. Rather, each has been understood very differently, at times in a way quite alien to the portrayals that we can find today in textbooks for the natural sciences or humanities. We will also point toward the role of the visual orderings that specific cultural techniques supply, contrasting central geometrical perspective against other ways of conveying pictorial space to the viewers of an image. Our argument suggests that central geometrical perspective has solidified into a norm thanks to the sheer quantity of pictures created with single-lens cameras in photography and filmmaking. Today, it is adopted as a model underlying many computer-generated graphics too.

2.1 The Look as a Medium

Our interactions with and within the environment are structured in important ways by our ability to see. How individual houses, our local surroundings, and entire villages or towns and cities have been (and constantly, continually are) structured favours specific actors with views and lines of sight that other actors do not have. The same is true of digital environments: the success story of computing would be very different had we not had large screens to interact with or, at the other extreme, tiny photographic cameras embedded in mobile devices that enable us to connect at a distance. Consider Figure 2.1, showing a young person applying make-up in front of a mirror and an array of mobile phones at the Mobile World Congress in Shanghai. How does this person see their face? What forms of mediation does this photo suggest? And in which

DOI: 10.4324/9781003084549-2

6 *Visual Studies*

Figure 2.1 A young person applies make-up in front of a mirror and an array of mobile phones at the Mobile World Congress in Shanghai.

Source: Hector Retamal / AFP.

ways is the environment structured in order to be able to mediate the person's look 'properly'?

Seeing is only one of the senses allowing us to orient ourselves in our social and physical environments. It does not exist in isolation, of course – we hear, feel, touch, smell, and more while seeing. Inspired by this observation, with the book we intend to pay particular attention to the social role and embeddedness of our ability to see, an ability which is always multimodal, integrating other forms of perception too. Seeing, from this standpoint, plays a central role in so many of our social interactions that we might not even 'see' this fact, although an important variety of interpretations and practices comes into play over the broad span of cultures across time and space. Different cultures set their hierarchies of the senses in different ways (Howes, 2003, 2005), and ways of defining them, interpreting their significance, and structuring them may seem quite alien when compared to what we are used to in mainstream Western 'late modernity'. How this structuring works is itself intensely debated, and Western distinctions of senses do not hold everywhere (see Howes, 2003; Ingold, 2000; see also Ingold, 2011; Pink, 2010).

Visual-studies scholarship tends to focus either on visual media themselves, such as photographs, film, paintings, drawings and technical diagrams, and infographics, or on the ways in which visual media are used, understood, and moved about with the aid of human and technical infrastructure. Building on a practice theory perspective, our approach helps us step onto the visual terrain through a focus on our ability to see and, hence on the look as a medium. This angle will guide our attention to both images and their contextual uses by stressing the interrelations of images and those looking at them. Acknowledging that multifaceted relationship is particularly relevant for remaining sensitised to the fact that a given picture sometimes may be seen very differently by different people, not just in how it is interpreted but also in what is actually visually perceived. Two people looking at the same visual medium may not see the same image – they might be quite literally looking at different images, as will be explained below. A focus on the look and the ways in which it is mediated, encourages attending to what is seen and in which ways.

A 'look as medium' approach allows us to unpack the phenomena under study and to refine our analysis of related work on visual cultures, across three lines of enquiry:

1) *Vision*: The look itself becomes understandable only via its mediations.
2) *Visual media*: Humans create visual media specifically to be looked at, or to be looked through.
3) *Images*: The images we get to see depend significantly on the ways in which we look.

This triad assists both in focusing on particular empirical phenomena to be studied and in arranging the body of related literature amassing around questions of vision, visual media, and images. In the history of research into matters of vision, the look is studied and understood via its mediations, never as 'pure' perception. Visual media again are specific artefacts that humans in diverse times and cultures have crafted in order to be looked at. Images, from this perspective, emerge only within socially structured interactions. Our ways of looking influence what we are able, or privileged, to see.

While we might regard seeing as a natural ability that one may possess (or not, in cases of blindness, some temporary nerve/eye/brain damage, etc.), we posit that seeing is intimately tied to cultural forms of attention and skilled ways of seeing. It differs from person to person. The sets of skills that seeing requires are learnt within situated communities of practice, with the aid of material guides (books, models, software, etc.), in interaction within one's environments, all guided by specific ontological understandings of the world. This process is, in essence, situated within an ongoing dialectic between what often are called nature and culture – but where these two constitute a continuum rather than the extremes of a dualistic opposition.

2.1.1 Vision: The Look Made Understandable via Its Mediations

What people look at, for how long, and with what kinds of intentions and associated thoughts have long puzzled humans. What are they looking at?

Why? What interest is involved in looking at that? Such questions have surely been posed countless times, throughout history, in a wide variety of places.

To disentangle these questions, we need to understand how vision works, just as much as how looking, or the look, becomes understandable, asking questions such as these: What is a look? How do you actually know what other people look at or even are able to see? What is it that you yourself look at or can see in any given moment? We contend that these questions are fruitfully approached by focusing on the mediations – that is, the means by which vision, looks, and looking become understandable. In other words, for closer examination of what a look is, we must approach it via its various media.

The way we understand a medium for purposes of this discussion is aligned with a medium-theory stance oriented toward processual descriptions of how an act – whether looking or any other – is accomplished. In taking this perspective, we do not employ the word 'medium' primarily for newspapers, radio, television, social media, or 'the Internet', as some streams of media and communication scholarship do. We are more interested in the medium as an 'in-between' that affects how particular acts and practices unfold. Hence, in keeping with our interest in practice theory, we foreground actions and practices in analysis of social and cultural life and follow our interest in how various distinct elements within these practices influence them.

Within this logic, 'medium' denotes an in-between that is needed for an action to unfold. While a medium may take various forms, media (several types of medium) are, for a specific situational action, limited in practice. Instead of assuming the existence of a particular universal look, we approach looking via its mediations. This focus on the unfolding of a look serves a dual role: on the one hand, we can pay attention to the ways in which the medium of a look plays a role in what kinds of images are seen (for example, by paying attention to the roles whereby screens, other displays, windows, and further media influence how images get to be seen). On the other hand, we can deliberate how the look itself, which is not visible *per se*, gets mediated such that it becomes perceivable. Rather, the look is part of our visual perception and, accordingly, a part of what we do not have direct access to. As Tim Ingold, a scholar writing about skill, traces, and perception, has noted, 'the one thing we cannot perceive is perception itself' (2000: p. 243). This is a critical proposition well worth reflecting upon, and the reason perhaps for history having shown such a wide variety of stances to perception in general and our abilities to see in particular.

To understand the look as a medium, we need to trace how it situationally mediates images and how it becomes observable in itself. Considering specific empirical phenomena gives us a window to this, and in the history of visual perception several empirical phenomena, in their turn, have been foregrounded for meditating on the look. In our approach, the act of looking is understood as directing one's eyes *and* attention to seeing someone or something. In interpersonal conversation, we might, for example, while listening to what our conversation partner is saying, follow the path of the interlocutor's eye movements, focusing on the motions of the pupil across the white of the eye (the sclera), for an understanding of what each person is looking at. Considering eye movements alone is not sufficient for understanding the look, however; one also requires an understanding of the kind of attention involved in directing one's eyes toward something to be seen (Bundesen & Habekost, 2008). On one hand, an examining look might pay close heed to details of a particular face, the lips of a discussion partner, or the various areas of the surface of a painting under scrutiny, and one might trace the attention by following the direction of eye movements. But attention is slippery and not necessarily captured from following those movements. For example, casting one's eyes upward and pointing one's head toward the blue sky above may accompany thinking about a difficult question, such that the person pondering fails to see the movement of the passing clouds or a flock of birds that are in the line of sight. These would be immediately visible if they were attended to. Hence, modes of attention are integral to understanding a look.

While the noun 'look' often refers also to someone's appearance, especially when used in combination with a qualifying adjective (e.g., in comments that someone has a beautiful, stylish, personal, or frightened look), this usage hints at how our ways of looking may be captured, seduced, or taken hold of in a very particular manner, and also how we are visible social beings, who act in specific ways because of the looks that we receive. One's appearances may be arranged, and ordered, so as to spark specific interrelations among those seeing and those being seen. These might in turn provide for direct observations of how one appears, or for performances of these appearances (e.g., in theatre, in rituals, or when someone is 'undercover' or lying). For instance, the concepts of the 'male gaze', the 'Oriental gaze', and the 'spectator gaze' were developed in the 1970s and 1980s to address how specific visual media are geared for idealised spectators, who may take up and replicate in their actions a specific kind of looking (Rose, 2022). These qualifying looks remain of great interest for many scholars of visual cultures, especially since debate continues with regard to how a particular act of looking may or may not be bound up with broader visual orders (Seppänen, 2006). Looking binds the act of the look to that of being seen, and hence also to a 'right', which is often politically contested (cf. Mirzoeff, 2011). Accordingly, the ways in which appearances are ordered to be looked at are important too. Looking, as a right, is always tied in with ethics issues cohering around who has the right to see whom – when and in what kinds of situations – and who may become visible at any given point in space and time.

It is because the look is approached via its mediations that we proceed, as mentioned earlier, from an understanding of the medium that does not rely principally on the ontological separation of one media type from another (categories of photographs, television, film, and newspapers, for example). Instead, given our focus on mediations, we pay attention to the situational attachments and infrastructural interrelations within and through which one 'thing' mediates while another does not. This framing expands the scope of what may be considered a medium. Though such a notion of the medium may seem counterintuitive at first, it finds support also among well-regarded media and communication scholars, such as John Durham Peters (2015: p. 182), who writes:

> Our data media have won just as much of a planet-steering role as have more basic nature-engineering media such as burning, farming, herding, or building. Every medium, whether our bodies or our computers, is an ensemble of the natural and the artificial, and WikiLeaks, corn syrup, whale oil, squids, Facebook, jet lag, weather forecasts and bipedal posture are some of the parts that belong to media theory.

The look can easily be added to this list, but understanding the look as a medium is useful not because that list might possibly be expanded *ad infinitum* but because the idea of look as medium offers a particularly good lens for studying both Western and non-Western visual cultures.

The interrelations between the look and its mediations, framed in terms of the body and technology, are spelt out in *Optical Media*, in which Friedrich Kittler posits that 'we knew nothing about our senses until media provided models and metaphors' (2010: p. 34). This suggests that our understanding of our perception is tied to the media we have at hand for reflecting on it and that, in fact, the history of our attempts to understand vision is just as much a history of the technologies we apply to study vision. Optical devices, such as *camerae obscurae*, have offered commentators numerous models and metaphors for understanding how human vision works. Nevertheless, as Jonathan Crary (1992) has shown, this interrelation is not straightforward. For instance, French philosopher and scientist René Descartes found benefit in the *camera obscura* for explaining how the human mind works, via a 'conception of the human mind as an inner space in which both pains and clear and distinct ideas passed in review before an Inner Eye [...]. The novelty was the notion of a single inner space in which bodily and perceptual sensations [...] were objects of quasi-observation', per Richard Rorty (as cited by Crary, 1992: p. 43). Long before Descartes, around the year 1020, the *camera obscura* provided Ibn al-Haytham (known also as Alhazen) with the elements for producing a theory for the functioning of the eye. And many centuries later, Karl Marx and Sigmund Freud, in turn, utilised the *camera obscura* metaphor to explain what Crary termed 'a model for procedures and forces that conceal, invert, and mystify truth' (1992: p. 29). In all cases, the *camera obscura* served as a medium for reflection on how vision and human understanding operate, though the conclusions from these reflections were very different, since Marx and Freud focused on very different kinds of societal forces. Examples abound: the blind man's stick figures prominently in meditations on vision, as in the work of Descartes

(1988), Ingold (2000), and Merleau-Ponty (1993), just as much as the figure of looking at the (blue) sky, contemplated by Merleau-Ponty (1993), Gibson (1979), and Zuckerkandl (1969). As in the case of the camera obscura, the medium employed for thinking about vision and the look in the latter set of examples does not determine how the process of vision is understood, but it does serve as a medium for reflecting on the role of looking itself.

Although we regard the look as understandable via its mediations, the understanding generated is necessarily partial. Interpretations may differ with the broader analytical framework within which specific observations are enacted and connected to each other. The mediations do not fixate semantic meanings.

2.1.2 Visual Media: Creations Specifically for Being Looked At

While our environments are filled with materials – human-made and natural alike – that can or may be looked at, humans have long given direct attention to specific forms of media as visual media. Some examples are paintings, television screens, and mirrors. In fact, anything that has been specifically created in order to be looked at is included in the concept visual media. As we orient our entire sensory apparatus toward that which we apprehend, thereby hearing, feeling, smelling, tasting, touching, and seeing whatever is the focus of our attention at this particular point in time, the specificity of visual media lies in them having been created to be looked at. These media bear an imprint of an aesthetic difference (Bredekamp, 2015: p. 35), a surplus that is not purely functional. Early hand axes already bore traces of said aesthetic difference around 200,000 years ago. One found in West Tofts, with a fossilised clam at its very centre, clearly exemplifies this, displaying purposeful decoration (p. 36).

Archaeology provides us with numerous fascinating examples. Alongside found objects that have been modelled to embody an aesthetic difference exist our own bodies, especially our faces, which became particularly important surfaces for visual media quite early in humanity's development. Our bodies are sites of both seeing and displaying images. Hence, they must not be forgotten in discussions of visual media. Several examples of decorated skulls stand in support of the contention that the human head, its frontal area in particular, has long been considered to offer valuable surfaces for meaningful images (Belting, 2014). While the face has played an important role as a visual medium for many millennia, it grew important for symbolic articulations and as a marker of identity only once freed from the task of functioning as a vital organ for prehension (that is, of grasping physically), as Leroi-Gourhan (1993) has shown. Our erect locomotion as bipeds, the use of the hands for technical manipulation, and the discovery and invention of techniques connected with the crafting of physical artefacts afforded the facial organs' development of audible articulate speech and visible facial expressions. With time, our faces became shorter and the roots of our front teeth shrank, making our faces less suited to acts of prehension and simultaneously widening the spectrum of possible symbolic expressions.

With these changes in mind, some authors have found the human face to be an image *par excellence*, since it is a temporary result of a co-evolution process that has emerged as a particularly noteworthy visual medium for dense symbolic expression, allowing us to use our faces for creating a wide variety of images. The diversity of emotions that can be expressed with our faces and the multitudes of social attributes that we may carry on them to display a connection to specific groups or modes of thought together provide ample examples of the face's immense potential to act as a visual medium. The fashion industry, the beauty industry, music videos, theatre, and cinema thrive especially because of the range of images our faces may provide.

Today, we encounter diverse visual media, many of which continue to carry images of faces, such as those stamped into coins; cast as statues; or inscribed in portrait paintings, photographs, film posters, or digitally networked selfie photographs. Belting (2011) refers to these exteriorisations of facial images to other media as images in effigy, while images that we carry with us on our bodies are images *in corpore*. The distinction between the former (e.g., a painted portrait or a photograph) and the latter (e.g., a situational grimace on one's physical face) is especially valuable for our efforts to identify the intrinsic differences borne by visual media. While an image on the physical body might last merely a few seconds before the facial expressions get lost (consider when we react facially to something we find particularly pleasing or disgusting), images in effigy, captured from the same situation in a split second with a photographic camera on glass-plate film, may last several hundred years if the image is processed correctly and then stored appropriately. The image conveyed may be largely the same between the two cases, but the differences in visual media point to very different orders of life span between distinct visual media.

2.1.3 Images' Dependence on the Ways in Which We Look

Focusing on the look as a medium leads us to the question of what kinds of images this perspective allows us to see – i.e., what we actually mean by an image. A common assumption surrounding images is that they are polysemous and may be interpreted differently on the basis of the specific situation in which they are seen and the cultural background of those looking at them. Hence, a photograph showing two people, a naked adult and child seated in an ancient smoke sauna, might be interpreted in Finland as an image dense with symbolic meanings: the sauna has deep historical significance connected to the moment of birth and to leaving the world, and the act of visiting the sauna together also is central for the celebration, maintenance, and strengthening of social ties. This image, however, might be interpreted in a very different vein by someone without knowledge of these local customs and traditions: it could be interpreted as a problematic picture, one that inappropriately displays nudity, signals a troubling intimacy between adults and children, and depicts architectural solutions that may not comply with modern safety regulations. In research following similar lines, Lutz and Collins (1993) have studied how photographs published in *National Geographic* may be understood as an intersection of several kinds of looks, depending on whose interpretations one solicits. Attending to these distinct ways of seeing is particularly valuable since work of this sort allows us to understand the wide variety of interpretations that a specific image may call forth.

While images may be interpreted differently, research highlighting this variety still exhibits a tendency to assume that everyone involved is seeing the same images. Studies of how our eyes operate for seeing, however, attest to several cases in which the same visual media are looked at yet quite different images get seen. We find a classic example in work by Yarbus (1967), who engaged in development of eye-tracking technology in the 1960s to understand the interrelations between eye movements and vision. He was able to trace the location of the pupil against the sclera's whiteness and thereby estimate where exactly a person's gaze was directed. Studies of this kind called into question the presumption that human vision functions in the manner of a *camera obscura* or a photographic camera as other scholars had argued. They have been instrumental in drawing attention to the foveal area of the visual field, the relatively small spot on the retina's inner surface that allows us to see sharply. Yarbus took note of the various locations of the pupil in relation to the sclera when his research subjects were looking at a specific visual medium. Sequentially connecting these locations, commonly called fixation points, his project produced lines between them that suggest movement between one fixation point and another, known today as saccades. Whilst the camera medium encouraged understandings of the look wherein each image is viewed holistically, without any strict order (one need only think of the notion of releasing the shutter of a camera, leaving it open for a specified amount of time, and then closing it in order to record a photographic image), the use of eye-tracking technology revealed very specific successive motions and patterns in looking at pictures. Furthermore, Yarbus noticed that, even when the subject's eyes were fixed on one small part of a visual medium, such as a face in a painting, the pupil did not remain still in any single location. It continuously moved about within a smallish area, leaving traces that are known as micro-saccadic movements. Such observations highlighting temporality assist us in pointing out that viewers actually see even so-called still images – images presented via visual media that do not move, as in the case of a printed photograph hanging on a wall – as moving images. This alone can prompt one to question the utility of a strict division between still and moving images, since images cannot be seen at all without movement.

More significantly, Yarbus asked his research subjects to look at a copy of a famous Russian painting, Ilya Repin's *Unexpected Visitor*, both freely and after having been assigned specific tasks. He noticed that the fixation points, along with the type of movement between them, changed significantly with the tasks given. For example, when subjects were asked to guess the ages of those depicted or were instructed to remember the positions of people and objects in the room portrayed, the recorded traces revealed a focus on separate areas of the visual medium. This suggests that the subjects saw, in these separate moments, two different images despite looking at the same visual medium.

This phenomenon later received more specific attention, most famously perhaps from Mack and Rock (1998), who coined the term 'inattentional blindness'. The term denotes the inability to perceive a visual stimulus in plain sight that arises from situational inattention. Simons and Chabris (1999) devised the 'gorilla test' to demonstrate how involvement in task-based activities leads to sustained inattentional blindness over a longer time. This test reveals viewers' general incapacity of seeing a dancing gorilla when they are focused on counting the exact number of passes of a ball between members of a specified team. The gorilla test has received a reasonable amount of public attention, with versions of it having been created for such purposes as public service announcements aimed at motivating motorists to pay attention specifically to cyclists. It shows how specific ways of directing one's eyes and attention play a significant role in what ultimately gets seen.

The ways in which we look, for how long, at what, and with what kinds of interests all have an impact on the images we seek and, hence, see. Images emerge only within interactions, and they take time to unfold. They are not seen directly and at once, irrespective of what so many related publications claim. Rather, they emerge alongside particular forms and modes of interaction. You can test this out yourself: look at whatever visual medium you have in front of you, then close your eyes for a minute, think about whatever is most precious to you, and look at the visual medium again. Do you notice a different kind of image emerging within this interaction?

Accordingly, a particularly important medium to consider is the look itself, which affects what we actually get to see. While the look itself becomes understandable only via mediations (e.g., meditating on the role of the *camera obscura*, the blind man's stick, a gaze directed toward the blue sky, or the use of eye-tracking technology with aims of understanding processes related to seeing), we must take into consideration also that we direct our look itself differently as our attention and the situation-dependent task at hand dictate. As related research implies, the latter means that in practice we might be looking at the same visual media but are sensitised to very different kinds of images, so those that we are sensitised to are what we end up seeing.

2.1.4 Looking as a Skilled Practice

While situational tasks and cultural background influence what gets seen and how the seen is interpreted, both represent parts of human activity that require learning. Learning to pay attention to the mediations that render the look understandable, to distinguish on the basis of differences in visual media, and to understand the look as a medium of images all involve skills that do not come easily. They must be learnt, and sometimes painstakingly too, although our physical substrate for vision is undeniably important in this regard, as those with visual impairments surely will point out.

This education in visual perception has been addressed particularly in ethnographically based efforts to understand how specific people see their environment and why they do so in particular ways. Cristina Grasseni, in fieldwork among breeders of dairy cattle in the Italian Alps, paid attention to how the research participants were able to identify a particular person's bovine on sight and how they developed criteria for assessing the animals' beauty. She pointed out that a focus on the 'educated capacity for looking at cattle' was for her 'a necessary premise to access their worldview' (Grasseni, 2004: p. 42). This entails that studying specific ways of looking enabled her to gain some understanding of how her research subjects approached their worlds.

Her research interlocutors were enculturated into communities of practice early in life. Breeders' children, for instance, played games such as cow-spotting, and the adults frequently engaged with other skilled practitioners in their social networks (e.g., accomplished breeders). But Grasseni recognised the importance of something more in addition: devices that codify expression and help guide visual attention. She listed:

> blueprints for the 'ideal cow', specifying the defining characteristics of the breed (including a model of the ideal Italian Brown available online); diagrams highlighting each trait to be considered for morphological evaluation; sketches highlighting the preferrable manifestation of a trait; computerized programs whose algorithms compute the incidence of each trait towards the overall score (e.g., the udder weighs against 40 per cent of the total score); amateur and professional videos made by breeders at cattle fairs [...]; eloquent and colourful adverts for bull semen; registers of bulls, heifers, calves, and embryos, listed in order of their 'genetic indexes'.
> (p. 44)

These devices orient and structure attention, thereby supporting social cooperation over time and space. While communities of practice necessarily rely on other people if they are to thrive, Grasseni's work attests to how these employ diverse artefacts, also including multiple media, to learn and for knowing what to look at.

Diana Eck (1998) too has worked on understanding ways of looking in an ethnographic context. In her case, the attention centred on *Darsan*, a particular way of seeing the divine, in the setting of an Indian village (see also Babb, 1981). Her work illustrates ways in which our conceptions of seeing as something we actively do – whether because of a situational task or because of our enskilment into a specific way of looking – are themselves cultural constructs. In her research, Eck noticed that her informants spoke about seeing divine images as 'taking darsan', whereas she might have thought of the participants as actively looking at a deity in an image. This taking of *Darsan* was understood in a broader religious context, in which a deity is thought to present itself in a manifestation so as to be seen. In this reciprocal way of looking, one encounters an act initiated not by the viewers but by the deity who grants the seeing. Situational agency is accorded not to the person looking at an image of the divine but to the divinity that makes itself seen. The medium of the look is in this case taken over by an agent granted access to what is situationally seen. Such understandings of the look differ markedly from that of an active subject proactively searching for meaning in images. Later on in this book we will also address the multisensory nature of Hindu icons, in combination with their ontological value as emanations, which further challenge overly simplistic understandings of images as pure representations. While this is particularly evident in contexts of considering the appearance of deities, we argue that these kinds of practices of looking may emerge in nonreligious contexts too.

Eck's case study is of particular importance in allowing us to reconsider the mediations that render looking understandable, be they *camerae obscurae*, eye-tracking technology, or any of the numerous other devices mentioned that codify expression and take part in guiding visual attention. Just as these devices have functioned in generating a broad spectrum of understandings linked to how vision and the human mind operate, it may be worth reconsidering understandings of who sees whom when one is attending to powerful images, such as those that Eck examined. Thinking in terms of the look as a medium affords pointing to multiple understandings of seeing and the interconnected nature of images, vision, and the eye. In the wide variety of practices related to seeing, it is not always the person looking at someone or something that carries agency in the unfolding situation.

With the following chapter, we embark on exploring the multiple ways in which vision and images have been understood, along with alternative ways in which one may regard them. Starting with an exercise that we invite you to undertake to heighten your sensitivity (either on your own or with colleagues / your students), we proceed to look at the history of looking at vision (and the senses), the eye, and images.

2.2 A History of Vision

2.2.1 Setting the Stage: What Happens When We Focus on an Image

A tried-and-true meditation exercise calls on the practitioner to stare at an image briefly but intensely, at regular intervals. The meditators start by keeping their eyes open in front of an object. When repeating the exercise in preparation for this book, we chose a tree. In this case, participants are asked to stare at the tree for a few moments and then to close their eyes. With eyes shut, they are invited to mentally reconstruct whatever they saw, bit by bit. When doing this after having stared at the tree, one might see the trunk first, then the crown, then some leaves. A sense of green mixed with the brown of the trunk permeates our, by now, memory-driven field of vision. The image is wholly mental. We then reopen our eyes and look anew – for, say, half a minute. When we again close them, new details emerge. We now see how the leaves make up the crown, we see that there is ivy growing on the trunk of the tree, and we see the texture of the birch bark with the shapes that the sun draws on its corrugated surfaces. We even notice the shadows and the depth they create. Once that image has found its way into our awareness, we open our eyes once more and admit some additional evidence. We close them and the picture is fleshed out even further: we see a fuller scene, perhaps with the pond in front of the tree, the tree mirrored in it, the sky. We close our eyes yet again and continue the exercise. The image that gains room in our consciousness is crafted at the junction between what the eye sees and what the mind sees – neither fully 'there' nor entirely 'here'; it resides in between, within our interaction. Our exercise confirms what Belting suggested when stating that images 'neither exist only on the wall (or on the TV) nor only in our heads. They cannot be extricated from a continuous exercise of interaction, which has left so many traces in the history of artifacts' (2005: p. 51).

Another thing we realise when engaging in this exercise is that our seeing merges with what we sense with the rest of the body; the continuous exercise of interaction is an embodied activity. Our nostrils take in the smell of the forest, and our skin reports back the gentle breeze that enwraps our entire body as we sit in front of the tree. As time goes by, the image of the tree keeps growing within us, *in corpore*, in both size and density of information. And as it grows, it morphs continuously into something new also. The whole time, it is something known yet simultaneously unknown. It is in this progressive flow of presence and absence that our perception of the tree is shaped. The act of 'seeing' hence is constructed across the physical and the mental, across the dimensions of visual stimuli's perception and the memory of them, coupled at times with the anticipation thereof. Also, it builds on the overlap of boundaries between the senses. Smell, sound, touch, and that ambiguous perception of space that is so difficult to put into words all contribute to our sense of what we are seeing. Differently from what we are taught to believe, each sense is not a distinct affordance of our bodies; they all operate jointly when orienting our bodies.

Many questions arise when we sit and meditate visually in front of a tree. How much of the image of the tree that is shaped in our consciousness is actually connected to what we see and, thereby, to 'pure' visual perception? And how much is instead connected to what we recall and hence to memory? And what is the role of anticipation? Perhaps we are actually hallucinating when we see, as some neuroscientists suggest (see, for example, Seth, 2021). Is our vision guided primarily by the eye or, rather, by the mind? If the mind is its director, how sure can we ever be that what we see is truly what stands before us? As the ancient Greek and Buddhist philosophers did, many contemporary neuroscientists are exploring the extent to which an image might be nothing but an emanation from a mind, as opposed to an act of grasping something that preexists in awareness. Is there ever something that we can call seeing objectively? Or are we always enmeshed within multi-sense imaginative interactions with the environments in which we find ourselves?

As we continue with the journey, we aim to deepen our reflections on these questions that are obviously related to forms of attention and mediation of the look. The meditation exercise with which we opened this section brings to the surface many details that challenge our certainty about those senses we tend to consider our primary link to truth, or at least 'truth' as connected to modes of seeing. The English language offers ample evidence of this underpinning with its use of expressions such as 'I see what you mean' or 'having a clear point of view' to express rational understanding.

Seeing has become such a deeply rooted part of our cultures that many concepts related to knowledge are tightly interwoven with that ability etymologically and beyond, including idea, theory, and the word 'concept' itself. In post-classical Latin, 'idea' refers to form, image, or likeness; we find 'theory' linked through Middle French to contemplation and vision, alongside post-classical Latin's notion of speculation, and 'concept' in Middle French denoted an idea and internal image. All these roots are important sources for our understanding of these notions today, too.

The image of the tree in meditation raises some doubts, however, about the seemingly obvious interrelations of seeing, knowing, and vision, thus providing an additional vantage point for contemplating the look as a medium. Since the image that emerges in our awareness is not a finite and stable one, how can what we see serve as evidence of truth? And why are many of our knowing-related concepts interwoven tightly with our visual faculties? As we can now 'see', images are always emerging as parts of interactions within consciousness as ephemeral items, reminding us that vision – and perception at large – is relative, always emergent, and never fixed.

Beyond this, the exercise elucidates something more: that vision is connected to attention, as we pointed out with regard to Yarbus, and to movement (in that our eyes keep searching, scanning, or navigating the world seemingly in front of them). It also is bound up with memory (an act perhaps of scanning or navigating the world inside us, as well as that which we are reminded of when we enter a familiar environment) and to modes of anticipation (as the phenomenon of inattentional blindness attests). There is also the lesson that vision merges with the other senses in a choreography of sensations that can be hard to separate. Smell, sound, touch, thermoception, and spatial awareness combine with it to generate that unique experience of meditating in front of a tree, the attention to one's environment in the situation of running for a bus that is about to leave or toward the end of a long running session (cf. Hockey & Collinson, 2006), or the images and visions that emerge when we try to make sense of a previously unfamiliar environment.

Experimenting with such exercises seems promising for nudging us to rethink our mundane ways of looking and of thinking about ways of looking. Another reflection technique we often employ with students is one we call 'looking into each other's eyes' (see Lehmuskallio, 2019: pp. 15–19), which starts with two participants being asked to sit facing one another and staring for one minute into the other's eyes, with an open mind, without there being any further intentions or motives behind the act of looking itself. The task is to explore the emerging and evolving interaction, to focus on the above-mentioned unending exercise of interaction that Belting emphasised as having left 'so many traces in the history of artifacts' while having done the same in the history of our embodied responses to looking and being looked at. For the minute of looking, the instructor stands silently and observes what occurs, noting how the energy and rhythm within this exercise change as time passes. When the time has elapsed, the instructor asks the students to share their experiences. How did they feel? What did they pay attention to? What did they notice during the interaction? Students normally begin by addressing the overall experience in words such as 'embarrassing', 'weird', 'intense', and 'disturbing'. It might well have left them 'fragile'. The instructor writes these words on a classroom blackboard as more and more students join the conversation. After a few minutes of talking and writing, the board is full but the need for discussion remains. Instructors can simply gesture to the nest of words for evidence of the multifaceted, multidimensional nature of the act of looking, of the specific ways in which we almost naturally organise our interactions of looking into meaningful wholes that we find comfortable, for escaping the 'heat' or intensity we might experience when, for example, looking into each other's eyes for a prolonged span of time. To unpack this complexity, the instructor might use the set of words as material for generating a tentative set of categories that could encompass the various experiences of the students and might also suggest embarking on further iterations of the experiment. For instance, there is a variation that starts with one of the two students mediating the interaction further with a mobile camera phone held between the partners. After this engagement, both do so, with one's image stream later being displayed much larger than life-size on a projection screen. On a second blackboard, in connection with the ensuing discussion, we probably will then find labels related to politics, corporeality, media, feelings, law, and senses, all pointing to the complexity of the seemingly simple act of looking into another person's eyes.

Also, the act of making explicit the various mediations of the look that emerge from employing several distinct variations of seeing and being looked at helps us reconsider how the various visual technologies around us structure our ways of seeing – and how we might see the seeing herein. Screens, mobile camera phones, renderings of one's face in various sizes through visual mediation, etc. all point to the importance that technical arrangements within our immediate environments have for our ways of interacting with each other.

Exercises of this sort can thus function as a gateway to peeling back the layers for probing definitions of vision and visual culture, in combination with the roles that various kinds of mediations play for our understandings of them. They indicate the variety of perspectives characteristic of works by authors of various stripes, some of whom have attended to the ways in which particular people see and understand the world while others' attention has coalesced more around the kinds of visual media that allow images to be seen in the first place, be they used for purposes of depicting our worlds or in aims of studying the act of seeing. For the moment, let us suggest that visual culture is that terrain on which matters of perception, representation, and materiality meet within a continuous exercise of interaction (and the politics attached to it). Having suggested this, we can start digging further into the historical context that has made reflections on such matters possible.

2.2.2 Unveiling Vision: A Concise History of Western Conceptions

Vision is indeed a tricky sense. Those of us raised in parts of the world influenced (not solely, of course) by Western thought tend to believe that this is the most reliable of our senses. Yet, as the reflections above hint, it is also one of the most slippery and uncontrollable ones. It carries the burden of a promise of complete objectivity but fails to deliver on this. Vision has to deal with an inherent tension: it is a site of pursuing our longing for truth and clarity while it simultaneously gets accused of providing humans with merely shadow images that cannot be relied upon. In a famous articulation of the attendant distrust of vision, Michel Foucault even suggested that 'visibility is a trap' (1995: p. 200) ensnaring us within polymorphous techniques of power that we cannot escape.

In contrast against our other modes of sensing the environment, vision stands apart in its scale. While human touch and smell extend only to what is in relatively close proximity to us, eyesight lets neurotypical subjects see things that lie far outside their physical reach, much further away than the limits of what we can hear. When looking at the night sky, we can see stars that are so far away that we could never reach them within our lifetime. We can see them, but we cannot smell or taste them from such a distance. This scale advantage comes at a price: vision functions through an overload of information production. Neuroscientists have found that the eye refocuses 50 to 60 times per second during ordinary activities. Hence, our eyes work in constant motion, alternating between the act that we address in English with the word 'looking', implying active choice, and that of 'seeing', understood to be more passive. The eye, as Simon Ings has portrayed it, is 'always on the hunt' (2008: p. 153). The understanding of vision emerging from this metaphor, which builds on the notions of Theon of Alexandria (335–495 CE), is of the eye acting as a bow that shoots arrows in all directions in order to gain an understanding of what to see. In this logic, the images we see depend to an important extent on the ways in which we look.

But how does the eye function deep down? And how is it that an organ occupying such a small part of the human body can capture the vastness of the world in front of us?

2.2.2.1 *The Classical World*

2.2.2.1.1 EXTRAMISSION VS. INTRAMISSION THEORIES

The latter question has been central to the work of many scholars, from Antiquity to the present day. Until the seventeenth century, views of the eye as active in the discovery of the world in front of it tended to prevail, though confusion as to how vision and sight operate seemed to reign, at least in comparison with today's accounts. Later on, doubts surfaced with regard to whether the eye truly is an active agent from which rays emanate toward the external world or whether seeing functions the other way around. Might the eye be on the receiving end, collecting information as it arrives, with any activeness in proceedings being of less importance for the result? At this point, scholars, informed also by the advances made in the study of optics, apparently arrived at some agreement on the latter view, known as intramission. This persisted until extremely recent discoveries by neuroscientists revealed a more nuanced picture, shedding greater (and critical) light on the functioning of the brain, attention, and consciousness (Prakash et al., 2021; Seth, 2021).

Many of the early theories were based on the so-called principle of extramission. For example, Plato, living around the fourth century BCE, suggested that the eye conquers the things it sees. In an idea that at first blush may seem odd (at least until we think about our own rhetoric of 'capturing' and 'taking' photos), the notion of extramission entails the eyes emitting a fire, an energy of some sort, or a kind of substance. This energy could reduce the objects it encounters in size and bring them into the eye in some fashion, as if vision were a form of hunting or fishing (think back to the metaphor of the bow cited above). Within this conception, the world is made up of pure, universal forms – independently existing archetypes or forms to which all elements and objects that make up the world must adhere, to at least some extent. Democritus, who lived between 460 and 370 BCE, likewise held this view. He suggested that objects make copies of themselves that contract in size until they can be sucked up by the pupil. Democritus believed that objects emanate a thin pellicle (the *eidola*, etymologically an early term for 'image') that enters the mind after travelling through the eye. Another exponent of this theory was Empedocles (born slightly earlier, in 483 BCE, in Agrigento), who connected it with the classical notion of matter as composed of four elements: earth, air, wind, and fire. For him, vision was related to fire, and it was through this 'fire within' that light radiated from the eye and to the outside world. Empedocles envisioned the eye as illuminating the world with its own spirit, 'as when a human being going out at night lights up a lantern' (Ings, 2008: p. 156). The notion of extramission, after having dominated the state of the art of knowledge about vision for an extended time, grew outmoded fairly rapidly amid strides in optics, and was displaced by theories of intramission. Today, however, it is undergoing a resurgence of sorts through the above-mentioned theories developing in the realm of the neuroscience of perception, which broadly addresses the importance of human anticipation of what we will see with regard to grasping what we actually get to see. In the picture that is crystallising, the brain's prediction of visible signals strongly influences vision. It aids us in functioning better in the world rather than being bothered about truthfully representing a world out there.

Let us return to the ancient Greeks, among whom Galen (born in 129 CE, several centuries after Democritus) added spiritual connotations to theorising on vision. According to him, the optic-nerve route was hollow and capable of conducting what he conceptualised as 'visual spirits'. Following a logic inspired by theories of extramission, Galen suggested that a flow starting at the brain moved through the optical nerves, all of them hollow. This flow was centred on the *pneuma*, a 'vaporous substance which is formed in part by the inspired air and in part by the vaporization of the arterial blood' and, for him, was at once 'vital' and 'psychic' (Ierodiakonou, 2014: p. 10). For Galen, the category of the 'psychic' was at the core of the capacity to perceive colours and shapes, engage in cognition, and participate in the acquisition of knowledge. In his view, the *pneuma* constituted 'the first instrument of the soul that resides in the brain' (p. 9). Held up by contemporaries as an expert in conducting cataract surgery (he made rudimentary strides in removing the layers of cataracts from the lens of the eye), Galen concerned himself also with the material aspects of viewing. He expressed particular interest in the lens of the visual organ itself, that thin cover that he identified to be at the very centre of the eye.

While several centuries would pass before the notion of intramission supplanted extramission theories, Aristotle (385–323 BCE) lent early support to this novel approach to vision. Observing that objects are visible only insofar as they are lit up (as, for example, around a fireplace at night or if the things seen have luminous capacities themselves), he identified the eye as a receiving rather than emanating organ. His intuition was indeed noteworthy – in the words of Ings, he 'managed to explain the way in which distant objects too can be perceived instantly and also why objects are visible only during day time and not during night time' (2008: p. 159). When we look back, it is fascinating to notice how scholars of the past tackled major scientific questions by proceeding from very simple observations. Plato took his observations on shadows as a starting point and explanation aid, Aristotle approached his theories by considering light, al-Haytham too derived important insight from experimenting with light (as he worked with shadow images in his room), and mediaeval Muslim polymath Abu Yusuf al-Kindi identified the principle of focusing while engaged in the act of reading. All these examples speak to specific media's centrality for understanding visual perception. We recommend that the reader engage in such playful experimentation with several forms of mediation, to cultivate fuller understanding of vision, looking, and seeing.

Mere decades after Aristotle's death, Euclid expanded his theorising on vision into the domain of mathematics, producing an understanding of vision founded on a system of straight lines and angles. Euclid anticipated what Renaissance perspective would later make into a ruling regime for arranging our sense of vision and visuality, or a 'scopic regime' (Jay, 1988) as discussed further along, a symbolic form (see Panofsky, 1927) that organises so many of our colloquial understandings in this area.

2.2.2.1.2 REPRESENTATION

Greek civilisation wrestled for a very long time with the question that opened this chapter: how can such a small organ as the eye actually bring the immense vastness of the world into the consciousness of a human being? It was in the midst of these debates in ancient Greece that a key notion, one with the power to fuel thought for so many generations to come, would take root: the notion of representation. Following in the footsteps of Plato's intuition, an understanding grew prevalent wherein the way in which things appear is different from how they actually are. This understanding prevailed much earlier in writings elsewhere, in relation to such notions as *Maya* (which in Hindu traditions is understood to be a veil that obfuscates reality); however, a more familiar example is the classic one of Plato's conclusions that focusing on interplay between light and shadow often leads to contradictions and illusions. This observation also strengthens our argument pertaining to why a focus on our sensorial percepts alone might be misleading. However sophisticated our understanding might be in some respects, that focus persists in a considerable body of critical writing on the 'effects' of images presented in advertisements, children's television, and so-called mass media in general. Indeed, the truth must lie somewhere in the middle, beyond the dualism.

In his *Republic*, Plato presents an oft-cited dialogue between his brother Glaucon and Socrates. As the recounted conversation progresses, Socrates depicts the experiences of people forced to spend their whole lives in a cave. Chained to the wall, they engage with the world only through the shadows cast by the objects that pass behind them as these interact with the light from outside. For Socrates, this is a perfect metaphor for the way in which humans are caught in a world of flawed perceptions, and for us it assists in understanding which media Socrates used to try to make sense of visual perception. People see merely the surface of things, not the pure form, the latter being regarded as more valuable and truthful than that which is visible at first sight. 'Form' is what philosophers and critical thinkers should engage with. And form is, with the help of modes of attention, logical reasoning, and a distrust of images, capable of getting beyond the illusion – i.e., reaching past the shadows seen by the cave-bound inmates. Only form is capable of connecting with 'reality', whatever that might mean precisely. In the allegory, those inmates who may eventually manage to escape the cave finally become able to see the sun, only then recognising that they had, until that point, only seen shadows and not 'reality'. Plato applied this metaphorical characterisation for the way in which the human condition is trapped in a 'phenomenal state'. If confined within their senses, humans would be unable to grasp the true sense of reality, the realm of pure form. In the allegory, vision is hence associated not with knowledge but with deception. This association continues to be utilised by both political activists and religious doctrine to suggest that we should never really trust what we see.

In Plato's framework, the senses produce an illusionary perception of the world. This idea relies, further, upon culturally situated associations between darkness, shadows, and ignorance on one hand and linking light, truth, and wisdom on the other. It is crucial that Plato found liberation from the illusion possible. This could be achieved by subordinating perception to the workings of the mind – i.e., through acts of measuring, counting, and weighing. These mechanisms let us divert our attention from percepts to cultural techniques of dealing with them, per Plato's *Republic* (2000). Plato hence put in place the fundaments for another key assumption in Western epistemology, the Cartesian divide between the mind/soul and the body. We must remember at the same time the wide range of non-Western epistemologies addressing representation (and images) beyond dualistic categories, though. And several traditions of so-called Western thought made such windows available too[1]. Aristotle's notion of the phantasm is probably one of the best examples. A disciple of Plato who nevertheless rejected the latter's clear distinction between reality and illusion, Aristotle, born in 325 BCE, diverged from Plato in finding the phantasm, sometimes also referred to as the shadow, not to be a simulacrum devoid of any grounding in reality. For him, the phantasm ought to be understood as a sensory instrument used by human beings to grasp abstract concepts. Later on, Jacques Lacan added another dimension to the Aristotelian conception. For Lacan, the phantasm domesticates our perception. It helps us make sense of, understand, and accept the world that surrounds us (see Jovanovic, 2001). From both Plato's and Aristotle's perspectives, the phantasm served as a medium for thinking about vision.

2.2.2.2 The Role of Mediaeval Islam

A large amount of our knowledge of Antiquity, at least the Greek portion of it, comes to us via Arabic translations, which in turn were translated (some time later) into Latin, alongside other languages. Mediaeval Islam provides us with several important theoretical accounts of vision (see Belting, 2011; McQuire, 1998; Mirzoeff, 1999). In that milieu, notions similar to those promoted earlier by Galen took root. During the Golden Age of Islam, from approximately the eighth to the fourteenth century CE, Baghdad emerged as the seat of a cosmopolitan project aimed at making science and art flourish. Headed by the Caliphate, its leadership strongly encouraged research in many areas, with the study of vision among them. One key figure emerging during that epoch was al-Kindi. In an attempt to bring the psychology, physics, and geometry of vision under the same mantle, his scholarship supported a form of extramission theory. He held that the eye functioned like an emanator of rays, an assertion he intuitively felt able to prove with reference to how, when one reads a page, the eye always focuses on a single detail at a time, leaving the rest out of focus. His reasoning about this phenomenon, which for good reason we listed above among examples of how the faculty of visual perception grows understandable to thinkers via their attention to mediations of the look, indicated that it could be visualised as a cone of emanation that the eye carries with it as it moves around. The more one attends to the borders on the outskirts of the cone, the less sharp one's vision becomes. Ings pointed to an additional inherent shift sparked by al-Kindi's intuition. According to him, Al-Kindi identified light as quintessential to the functioning of vision. His theory was a proper 'philosophy of radiation' (Ings, 2008: p. 163) that seems to have inspired future thinkers and artists no less influential than da Vinci.

The most influential piece of work from the world of mediaeval Islam, however, is probably the treatise *The Book of Optics*, which al-Haytham wrote around the year 1021. A philosopher, mathematician, and astronomer born in Basra in 965 CE, he was a civil engineer working as 'wazir' for this city. Uninterested in his official work duties, he had a secret passion for science. To escape his assignments, among them participation in the construction of the Aswan Dam, he feigned having gone mad. He locked himself in his house and, at least according to the official chronicle of his life, spent the next 12 years in the dark. There, in relative darkness, he conducted experiments on the workings of light. Exploring the behaviour of light when it is projected from one room to another by means of small holes in the walls, he noticed that light does, in fact, emanate in straight lines, as the famous drawing in Figure 2.2 by Johann Zahn shows.

Working on the basis of his observations, al-Haytham produced a detailed theory of the functioning of the eye, paralleling that of Galen. Characterising it as the main organ managing the play of rays of light, he articulated the same intuition that the eye is connected to the brain through an optic-nerve pathway (though involving only one core nerve). He visualised this as a pyramid with the eye at one vertex and the visible field at the base.

Al-Haytham had detected the 'shadow image' left in human consciousness whenever one closes one's eyes after having been looking with eyes open at an intense source of light. Addressing this phenomenon as an expression of intramission, he realised that it is light that impinges on the eye, not the other way around. He ascertained also that rays must cross the eye if a human being is to be able to see. Having developed the conceptualisation in the figure, he continued his investigations by measuring the extent to which direct rays

26 *Visual Studies*

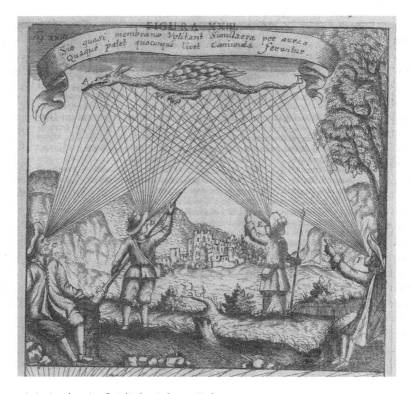

Figure 2.2 Oculus Artficialis by Johann Zahn.

are perceived as stronger than refracted ones. The first person documented to have demonstrated the details of these behaviours of light, al-Haytham had devised a lamp experiment involving an arrangement of several separate light sources spread over a large area. With this, he also explored how light could be transformed into an image, thereby offering yet another example of the importance of exercises and tests for understanding vision. al-Haytham invented a tool that would revolutionise how people approached the world of images, thus affecting the visions of many generations to come.

2.2.2.2.1 THE *CAMERA OBSCURA*

From his successful projection of an entire image from outdoors onto an indoor screen, al-Haytham can be regarded as the creator of the first known *camera obscura*. This is a device traditionally attributed to 'Western civilisation' not least because of observations by Aristotle, who had noted how sunlight passing through wickerwork forms an image of the sun on the surface opposite (Osborne, 2001). The term, which literally means 'dark room', refers to the optical phenomenon occurring when a set of visual reflections and emanations from a scene in the outside world gets projected, left to right and upside-down, through a small hole onto the walls of a small dark chamber, thus casting a set of moving images on its surface.

What al-Haytham invented received this name centuries later from Europeans, who refined the mechanics and developed a visual medium that proved hugely influential for both creating and displaying images. An especially important factor in the delay hinged on the fact that many of the earlier Greek writings were not preserved anywhere apart from the halls of mediaeval Islam. According to Nicholas Mirzoeff (1999: p. 36), this disinterest stemmed from a culturally situated lack of attention to the physiology of the eye, notwithstanding its importance to earlier scholars. He concluded:

> it took them 600 years to reach the same conclusion because they were not really interested in the question. What the eye did was irrelevant, what mattered was the intellect or the soul. The senses were part of the fallible human body, whereas the soul was divine. The key question, then, was how information was conveyed to the soul via the eye. The processes by which the soul interpreted this visual information were to all intents and purposes unknowable precisely because they belonged to the divine sphere.

The *camera obscura* came to prominence partly through da Vinci (1452–1519 CE), who engaged with it to increase the precision of his landscape paintings. Further operationalised over the decades via the addition of various kinds of lenses, it marked a true revolution for drawing and painting. It also functioned as an important tool for safely studying solar eclipses and as a gadget exploited for generating awe and fascination. Coupling the lens with the use of light-sensitive materials eventually led to the creation of the first photographic cameras, for producing, or freezing, the images within a *camera obscura*, which otherwise would drift and change. Irrespective of his many achievements, al-Haytham remained unaware of the functions of the body's nerves, so he never managed to explain why humans do not see images in the way his *camera obscura* displayed them: if the eye functions on the basis of the same principles, why weren't humans seeing an upside-down world? Solving these riddles requires greater knowledge of the various components and aspects of the functioning of the eye.

2.2.2.3 A Visual Renaissance

2.2.2.3.1 THE RETINAL IMAGE

Further discussing the principles connected with the *camera obscura*, Dutch scientist Kepler, who meticulously studied the work of al-Haytham, offered a proper, and probably the first, theory of the retinal image. For Kepler

(1571–1630), the pupil of the eye was ultimately nothing but a *camera obscura* in itself. Capitalising also on physicist Felix Platter's work on the functioning of the eye, Kepler realised that the light hitting the eye gets refracted at the level of the pupil, then again at that of the aqueous humour (the watery fluid inside the eye that we now call the crystalline lens). While being aware that the brain and retina are connected through the optic nerve, Kepler never ventured into the murky waters of attempting to figure out why images are not perceived upside-down. David C. Lindberg (1981: p. 203) summed up Kepler's insights in the following words:

> [V]ision occurs when the image of the whole hemisphere of the world that is before the eye [...] is fixed on the reddish-white concave surface of the retina. How the image or picture is composed by the visual spirits that reside in the retina and the nerve, and whether it is made to appear before the soul or the tribunal of the visual faculty by a spirit within the hollows of the brain, or whether the visual faculty, like a magistrate sent by the soul, goes forth into the administrative chamber of the brain into the optic nerve and the retina to meet this image as though descending to a lower court – this I leave to be disputed by the physicists.

It is interesting to notice Kepler's application of legal metaphors in expressing his stance on the subject. For him, the eye was a magistrate, a supreme judge, capable of ordering our vision. The parallel to how the camera has been etymologically connected to modes of decision-making is strong (Lehmuskallio, 2020). This metaphor was adopted also by da Vinci, who famously wrote, as paraphrased by Mirzoeff, that Renaissance, or geometrical perspective:

> is a rational demonstration whereby experience confirms that all objects transmit their similitude to the eye by a pyramid of lines. By a pyramid of lines, I understand those lines which start from the edges of the surface of bodies and, converging from a distance meet in a single point; and this point, in this case, I will show to be situated in the eye, which is the universal judge of all objects.
>
> (1999: p. 39)

Mirzoeff suggests here that the centrality of these metaphors provides us with evidence of how artists and philosophers in mediaeval Europe engaged with the functioning of the eye and the principles of vision. According to him, they were not genuinely interested in understanding the physiology of the eye so much as concerned with benefiting from it. He states (on p. 42):

> Artists and visual theorists alike were concerned with establishing a place from which to see, and thus create the effect of perspective, rather than fully understanding the physiology of perception which they took to be unknowable.

This attitude, which meshed with a growing sense of image creation as an act of control and possession of the world, proved fundamental to the Western world in the centuries that followed. A range of visual technologies, each needing to be used in accordance with highly specific techniques (including photographic cameras), consolidated an understanding of possessing the world by depicting it: theories of vision reflected an interest in applicability and control, a desire of ordering the world.

2.2.2.3.2 THE IMPORTANCE OF LIGHT

Descartes (1596–1650) gave further momentum to this debate in his famous *Discourse on the Method* (1637). With this work, the French philosopher shifted the focus of Western scholarship on vision from the functioning of the eye itself to the study of light. Let us remind the reader, however, that this change in emphasis had already become important for parts of the mediaeval Islamic world and also echoed an interest present among other thinkers of the preceding millennium. Albeit often tangentially, light had always featured in the reflections of thinkers and artists fascinated by the functioning of vision. Ancient Egypt offers us an excellent example: in roughly 1500 BCE, worshippers of Ra saw light as a sign of the existence of their god. The idea that light 'was the vision of god and things existed because Ra could see them' (Ings, 2008: p. 156) resonates with the thinking of those ancient Greek poets and philosophers for whom the human eye functioned likewise: emanations of visual rays render things visible. We could also cite how al-Kindi noticed the way in which light bounces around on the objects that make up the world. Nevertheless, Descartes took these intuitions further. To him, light was 'a material substance with concrete being' (Mirzoeff, 1999: p. 43); it had mechanical properties. Light was not spiritual but utterly material, and it literally touched objects. In his words:

> I would have you consider the light in bodies we call 'luminous' to be nothing other than a certain movement, or very rapid and lively action, which passes to our eyes through the medium of the air and other transparent bodies, just as the movement or resistance of the bodies encountered by a blind man passes to his hand by means of his stick.
> (Descartes, quoted by Mirzoeff, 1999: p. 117)

He reiterated that 'it is the soul which has sensory awareness, and not the body. For when the soul is distracted in ecstasy or deep contemplation, we see that the whole body remains without sensation, even though it has various objects touching it' (ibid.).

A central figure in the establishment of conventional Western dualistic reductions and of the separation of matters of the mind from matters of the body – a reductionism criticised by several waves of scholars (e.g., Ahmed, 2004; Akmolafe, 2017; Haraway, 1985; Shiva, 2010) – Descartes nevertheless contributed to future generations' enquiry in a healthy manner with regard to several factors related to perception (cf. Ingold, 2000). His thoughts on one of these, vision as dialectic, in particular were echoed many centuries later in the notions of, among many others, John Berger (1972: p. 8), who noted:

> We never look at just one thing; we are always looking at the relation between things and ourselves. Our vision is continually active, continually moving, continually holding things in a circle around itself, constituting what is present to us as we are.

Descartes also brought attention to several key facets of representation. While Kepler, alongside many others, had been unable to explain the inversion of the image in the eye, Descartes reasoned that this happens because of the brain recomposing what the eye can gather, assembling these constituents, and putting the things seen in some kind of order. Visual perception, in this understanding, is situated in the brain and not in the retina; seeing is 'an inspection of the mind' (Mirzoeff, 1999: p. 43). In an era defined by notions of resemblance, Descartes hence recognised that the way we see and produce images is not a perfect mirror of the outside world. Rather, he suggested, it should be thought of as a kind of code that the mind learns to interpret. He explained this with the example of a circle. For the human eye to perceive a circle in a drawing, the artist may have to represent not a perfect circle but, for instance, an oval, depending on the viewing position one holds. Imagine, for instance, a wheel of a cart angled at 45 degrees from a viewer. As the flat surface of the drawing or painting is viewed, that oval gets seen as a circle when considered in perspective. Descartes realised that, under the 'rules' of perspective, objects need not be exact copies of 'what is out there'. In essence, he pushed back to the brain the reassembling of the information that the eyes gather by looking at the world. He articulated the notion thus (ref.: pp. 120–121):

> [I]n accordance with the rules of perspective [engravings] often represent circles by ovals better than by other circles, squares by rhombuses better than by other squares, and similarly for other shapes. Thus it often happens that in order to be more perfect as an image and to represent the object better, an engraving ought not to resemble it. Now we must think of the images formed in our brain in just the same way, and note that the problem is to know how they can enable the soul to have sensory awareness of all the qualities of the objects to which they correspond – not to know how they can resemble these objects.

Descartes significantly influenced our way of understanding the physics of perception. His thoughts in this regard interwove with the pervasive separation between the mind and the body that has exerted such a profound influence on ways of understanding perception to this day; however much we do not share that dualistic view. Similarly to key thinkers before him, Descartes resorted to legal metaphors for explaining the function of perception, with the soul being the 'interpreting judge of sensory perception' (p. 43). His vision, therefore has a politics embedded in it, which is vital for understanding twentieth- and twenty-first-century studies of visual cultures.

2.2.2.4 Geometrical Perspective as a Hegemonic Approach to Images and Vision

As the notion of 'rules' mentioned above suggests, Descartes saw geometrical perspective as a natural law, something that perfectly represents the 'natural' functioning of the eye. Still today, it is not uncommon to equate central perspective produced via single-lens photographic cameras with human vision. This implication of equivalence persists even in a fairly wide range of studies of perceptual psychology. Martin Jay (1988) identified this Cartesian perspectivism as a scopic regime, a dominant theory of vision, in terms of which he attempted to pinpoint the major ways of ordering visual culture. Later, he pinpointed two regimes alongside this one as, in his view, influential for Western culture: Baroque reason and Dutch descriptivism (see Jay, 2012). Aligning and consolidating itself with Renaissance perspective, Cartesian perspectivism reflected the West's growing obsession with rationality, lines, and mathematics (as opposed to colours, senses, touch, etc.). Although subject to dispute, central geometrical perspective, and Cartesianism left an indelible imprint on how images would be interpreted in the future. They together became what, in Gramscian terms, one could call a hegemonic way of approaching the world of vision and images. This progressively marginalised other kinds of approaches to visuality, especially in the domain of 'technical' images such as photography and cinema. Renaissance perspective permitted ordering the world visually from a single standpoint, such that it could be drawn/painted, then carried as an image elsewhere in order to show how things 'are' where the original depiction was created. Given its political significance, we therefore must unpack the principles of geometrical perspective a little more.

Recall al-Haytham's novel depiction of vision as a pyramid with the eye at one of the vertices and the visible field at the base. Inspired by it, many European painters, architects, and mathematicians of the fifteenth through sixteenth centuries started assiduously working to develop a mathematical/geometrical formula capable of translating depth into a flat surface. Most notable in this respect was Leon Battista Alberti, who in the fifteenth century articulated the theory of the set of converging lines on which much of post-Renaissance art was built. Inspired by the ideas of architect Filippo Brunelleschi, Alberti suggested that any picture is best viewed as a window through which the depicted world can be seen. This conception was arranged via a double pyramid with the vanishing point at one extreme and the observer at the other (see Figure 2.3).

32 *Visual Studies*

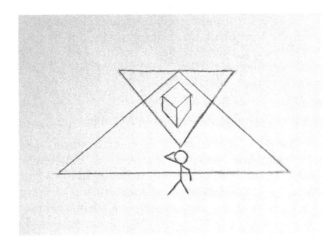

Figure 2.3 The double pyramid of lines.

Source: Drawing by Paolo Favero.

The metaphor of the window came to dominate in Western painting (cf. Sheikh, 2013). Albrecht Dürer made this principle visible in a drawing where he shows how a painter should sit in front of a window with an inset metal grid (for discussion of the importance of the grid in creating visual orders, see Siegert, 2015). Though offering mathematical precision for helping to translate the environment seen or envisioned (as in biblical narratives) into a flat image, the grid brought the cost of isolating the painter from the depicted world. This separation became such a powerful cultural force that, according to many theorists of visual culture, only overtly anti-hegemonic practices of translating space into images could contribute to overcoming it. In this understanding, central geometrical perspective is understood as exercising powerful agency in mediating the kinds of images one gets to depict and to see, affecting the ways in which looking as a practice of depiction and of seeing images is organised.

The vast majority of Renaissance painters opted to follow this principle, changing perspectival projection techniques accordingly. Artists abandoned previous forms of translating space through specific orders. Building on representations of space that are hierarchy-based (with prominence accorded to the relative importance of the characters composing the image), ordering at this time grew into one of the most important methods for conveying depth. At its core, 'Western perspective' constitutes an attempt executed by means of a geometrical ordering to render time and space on a two-dimensional surface, irrespective of whether the scene depicted actually existed as such or, for instance, portrays a religious or mystical event.

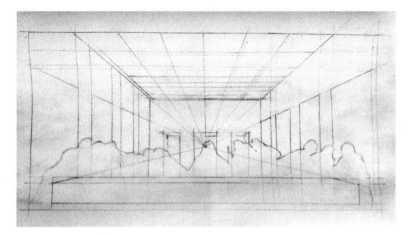

Figure 2.4 Sketch of Leonardo da Vinci's perspective for 'The last supper'.

Source: Drawing by Suor Maria Silvia Favero.

Quick on the uptake, da Vinci swiftly adopted this mode of rendering space. His *The Last Supper* is probably the single masterpiece that best symbolises this idea. See Figure 2.4.

The figure of Jesus is central both horizontally and vertically. Aligned with the horizon, he occupies the location from which all lines emanate. Everything in the room in which he sits, along with the Apostles, is ordered in accordance with him. And, true to this centrality, he invites the viewers to position themselves centrally, becoming one with him. Geometry thus promotes an act of faith here.

As portrayed in Dürer's famous drawing depicting the grid, geometrical perspective enables painters to measure a particular view and to implant that measurement in a visual reproduction of the scene in front of them. In doing this, it generates the separation alluded to above, between the observer and the observed, the self and the world. Before we dive more deeply into the politics of this, let us pause for a moment to note the cultural situatedness of the technique. Renaissance perspective held nothing 'natural'; it was one possible way, among many, to render depth on a flat surface. Painters in other parts of the world (and in pockets of the West too) used alternative techniques, rooted in the use of colour, of atmospheric elements (e.g., depicting the humidity of the air), of materiality, etc. to convey a sense of depth and space. As scholars of scopic regimes have noted, Cartesian perspectivalism has not been alone among scopic regimes in the West either, with the above-mentioned Baroque reason and Dutch descriptivism constituting only two examples (readers interested specifically in these two scopic regimes are directed to the discussion offered among others by Alpers (1984) and Buci-Glucksmann (1994). We could also cite navigation-linked images as a far-reaching scopic regime – bound up with vital processes of trade, travel, and commerce and imbued with implicit assumptions (e.g., related to what is at the map's centre and what seems safely warpable on its periphery). Their force is particularly evident with regard to Mercator projections, bringing their own grid to bear with lines of latitude and longitude that have afforded scaling up and expediting processes of colonisation and imperialism especially since the invention of techniques for finding longitude on sea. As our discussion unfolds, we will reflect also on new perspectives, such as how contemporary trends in virtual and augmented reality constitute a challenge to central geometrical perspective.

Extending an expansive reach, geometrical perspective reduced vision, in essence, to the model of a single eye, hence neglecting the depth that the presence of the second eye for most people generates in human perception of space while also overlooking the importance of embodied physical movement in space for seeing any image. Because of the ways in which geometrical perspective favours particular ways of rendering pictorial space, mathematician, theologian, and monk Pavel Florensky went so far as to claim that it is based on an empirical lie. He suggested that it reduces vision to a form of 'monocularism' making humans 'as monocular as the Cyclops' (Florensky, 1977: p. 262). Disregarding the extent to which the second eye, in neurotypical subjects, functions as a critical judge helping grant depth and greater value to what is seen, this form of perspective seemed to flatten sensory reality to a formula. It reduced the depth of visual perception within a given environment to a rectangular canvas. Simultaneously, it functioned as a form of abstraction – it supplied painters with a set of rules that they could overlay on any kind of scenario, letting them depict the world on a surface. In doing so, as with any other form of abstraction (numbers, money, pixels, etc.), perspective allowed for comparison. Yet not everyone wished to pay the cost bundled with these benefits.

As we hinted above, geometrical perspective did not go uncontested. Under its rule, the West witnessed the use of *vraisemblance*, anamorphism, and numerous other adaptations of perspective, as manifested in Rome's Church of St Ignatius of Loyola with its optical illusions, which will be examined in greater depth below. While by far the majority of scientists subscribed to the principles of geometrical perspective, many artists did not. In the seventeenth century at the court of Louis XIV (the *Roi Soleil*, who founded, among other institutions, the French Academy of Painting), numerous artists still adhered to Democritus's theory that the eye emits rays that enable it to perceive objects. Many also believed that the human body (and any object to be depicted) could not be truly approached via the recommended instruments of geometrical perspective. Following the Platonic tradition, they held that forced or inaccurate representations could lead to disease, various types of personal-level disturbance, political disobedience rooted in anamorphism, and social unrest stemming from certain adaptations of perspective (such as the optical illusions visible in the Church of St Ignatius of Loyola). This attests to the extent to which notions of magic remained part of their lifeworld, an understanding wherein images expressed an intimate connection with furthering morality or corruption of morals. Taking a position on popular and mass culture analogous to that of many contemporary artists, several scholars and artists argued that perspective, while surely useful for attracting the masses, would not be a suitable tool for any 'real', 'divinely inspired' artist. The latter should, they claimed, explore the world with other means. As discussed above with regard to theories of vision, theories of perspective addressed phenomena that are seen, visually ordered, and depicted as having varying relations to 'reality', 'essence', or 'truth'. Forms of mediation such as Renaissance perspective and the grid provided tools for speaking about 'reality' or 'truth', however contested that might be.

Relativising perspective's principles, Mirzoeff suggested that it was no more than a 'powerful formula for visual standardization: a mathematical vision which could be continually projected onto the real in a social context in which mathematics was increasingly offered as the universal measure of knowledge' (1999: p. 19). In other words, it is one way to address space pictorially, one way of interpreting the world visually, a 'symbolic form' in Erwin Panofsky's terms. Perspective must be examined, therefore, as a Western/European human-centric convention whose particularity is to centre a scene at the eye of the beholder. We get into the politics of this below, after glancing at other ways of conveying space that we can find when journeying across time and places.

2.2.2.5 Parallel Visualities

It is crucial to remind ourselves of how other civilisations, various subcultures, etc. have dealt with pictorial depth. This is an exercise in decolonising our thought, in learning to appreciate how even in the field of visual studies there are always different and at times contrasting ways of approaching any single phenomenon or practice. In the case of pictures we can notice how distinct techniques have been applied in distinct cultural settings for conveying space and, hence, an experience of reality. One example we could begin with is that of Japanese, Chinese, and various other scrolls. Rather than build on geometrical perspective, these tend to wrap their viewers within the image, both horizontally and vertically. Conventionally surrounded by these pieces in the space of a room, viewers can, in relation to the images, occupy one place and many places one after another. There is no privileged point of view here, and the act of viewing stands in stark contrast against that of Renaissance perspective, which favours a single privileged viewing position and shows far less interest in meandering and exploring different viewing positions. The effect is visible, for instance, in the famous Namban folding screens on view at the National Museum of Ancient Art in Lisbon. Figure 2.5. presents this. Dating back to the watershed events of the sixteenth to seventeenth century, these screens depict the arrival of Portuguese

36 Visual Studies

Figure 2.5 Namban art in the Museu Nacional de Arte Antiga, Lisbon.

vessels at the port of Nagasaki in 1534. Implemented via a series of separate screens on a golden background, the paintings offer a sequence of mutually distinct scenes that can be viewed from multiple angles. Rather than simulating depth within a picture, these screens (just as Chinese scrolls often do) play with the relationship between a viewer and the position of the image in order to stimulate the perception of depth. An example of another sort can be found in the context of Mughal paintings where colours (graded tones) and symbols convey a sense of tangible depth to the viewer (Sheikh, 1997). There, a sky would be a blue surface where spots of gold symbolise the stars, and colour differences between the walls give a hallway depicted on a flat surface a three-dimensional feel.

Pictorial imagery, Gulam Mohammed Sheikh suggests, has to be made believable rather than 'scientifically reproducing optical sights' (2013: p. 147). By expressing what is, in essence, identifiable as an outdoor vision (Sheikh, 2013), some forms of Indian and 'Oriental' painting promote an act of meandering scanning (Lannoy, 1975), actual movement of a viewer across the pictorial space. Sheikh continues: 'The prolonged sequence of time involved in appraising the pictorial space is antithetical to the notion of arresting a climactic moment' (2013: p. 147) in his critique of Western pictorial illusionism, promoting an argument that we perhaps could apply equally well to photography. Geometrical perspectivism directs the eye, guides it, and in a way 'arrests' the way in which pictures should be looked at. Sheikh noted especially how the imagery he studied allows a liberation of the eye in some respects.

Similarly to the above-mentioned Mughal approach to painting, Etruscan and Roman means of playing with pictorial space immersed viewers in the images. The Etruscans, who inhabited the central parts of Italy from 700 BCE to roughly 300 BCE and who eventually were absorbed by the Roman Empire, experimented with this mainly in the context of funerary practices. Their tombs were designed in such a way that the body of the deceased was entirely surrounded by images of the world just abandoned. Displayed on the walls of tombs such as the Tomb of the Leopardi, in Tarquinia (from the fifth century BCE), were scenes of dancers, musicians, and gymnasts; depictions of hunting and fishing; and mythological/religious motifs. The aim behind these paintings, according to art historian Argan (2008), was to 'substitute [for] the spectacle of the world' (p. 112). Progressively entering the darkness and losing interest in earthly matters, the dead were assumed to be in need of something that could awaken their attention. Strong contrasts and colours, stark boundaries, and exaggerated gestures were attempts to penetrate death's obscurity. As Argan characterised the image in the context of Etruscan art, it 'has to substitute [for] a lost reality, or even better, this is the only reality capable of penetrating the dozed sensitivity of those who have passed the horizon of life' (p. 112). With time, the Etruscans lost sight of this purpose for the pictorial endeavour, and their painting blended with classical art, probably through the influence of Greek culture. Nevertheless, traces of the original intention to wrap the dead with images of life and hence close the gap between these two realms by means of painting remained visible for a considerable time.

The Etruscans were far from the only civilisation that has sought to wrap humans in images. Similar cases come to us from the Roman cities of Herculaneum and Pompeii. In the latter's House of Mysteries (or *Villa dei Misteri*), the surfaces of the walls are filled with a rich variety of scenes melding mythology and day-to-day life. The figures engage in dialogue with each other across the walls: they look and point at each other. Surrounded by such dialogue, passers-by cannot but feel involved in the exchanges and events portrayed, especially the Dionysian initiation ritual that constitutes a core element of this set of paintings. In a process of blurring 'the borders between visual and actual space' (Grau, 1999: p. 365), viewers become part of the painting and the world it portrays, and the image starts appearing as 'a portal through which in one direction the gods pass into the real world and in the other real people enter into the image' (p. 366).

Pompeii and Herculaneum represent unique artistic experiences, partly because they are the only extant sites from ancient Rome where paintings were directly made on walls; however, the underlying tendency to wrap the viewers in the images, and thereby problematise their perceptions of the separation between physical and pictorial space, informed much of Roman art. For instance, Roman artists applied several techniques for exploiting the space represented by the walls. In Rome's Altar of Augustan Peace (*Ara Pacis Augustae*), interior space is shaped through a merging of bas-relief (depicting scenes from mythology) and elements of nature (mainly leaves) impressed in and on the walls.

Argan suggests that the Romans experienced the wall not 'as a solid surface, but as a spatiality or imaginary depth' presenting a 'hypothetical space, a plane of projection' (2008: p. 147). For them, the wall was not a pictorial space. The use of stucco would later inject such spatial experiences into the context of painting too. It allowed for the creation of thick, modulated surfaces that permit viewers to explore a multiplicity of angles of observation of the image and that let in actual life (in the shape of light and shadows) to mix with the visual impressions generated by the objects as represented in the image.

This displacing effect was even grander in the Roman Catholic and Greek Orthodox churches designed under the influence of Byzantium. While often undecorated and square from the outside (consider, for instance, the Mausoleum of Galla Placidia from fifth-century Ravenna), these churches boasted interiors replete with visual detail that in a literary sense embraced, sucked up, and devoured the viewer. The use of mosaic in particular, with its variety of widely different materials capable of absorbing and diffracting light in varied ways, exerted a deceiving and displacing effect on the viewers. Similarly to the Roman stucco work, it distorted viewers' perceptions of the dimensions of the space in which they found themselves, thereby causing them to transcend physical space altogether (cf. Argan, 2008). As Greek Orthodox churches still attest today, worshippers get surrounded by glittering light generated by candles mirrored in the metal and the glass tiles composing the images seen, by the smell of incense, and by sounds of bells. This exposure to a full-spectrum sensory experience brings viewers, through their senses, in touch with the divine. Traces of this phenomenon are evident also in many Catholic churches, the above-mentioned Church of St Ignatius of Loyola at Campus Martius in Rome being one of them. Constructed in Baroque style from the first half of the seventeenth century (and already adopting Renaissance perspective at that relatively early stage), this church is characterised by a majestic *trompe l'oeil* nave. Painted by Jesuit monk Andrea Pozzo, the ceiling displays the welcoming of St Ignatius into Paradise by means of an illusionistic arrangement. Upon entering the church, viewers see a broad cupola opening up to a sky filled with figures that seem to be floating upward. Two markers on the floor identify specific observation points from which one can lose oneself in the image (today, a mirror in one of these spots enables viewers to obtain the full experience), hence also suggesting specific viewing points and practices that are needed if one is to 'get' the image. Indeed, the Baroque era in its entirety was guided by an intent to metaphorically wrap viewers in something more – a new political order (see Hauser, 1951/1999). Although we do not have the space to embark on discussion of this here, the general phenomenon is the material impetus for the ensuing historical developments and the next portion of the chapter.

Figure 2.6 The Bourbaki Panorama.

In the eighteenth and nineteenth centuries, attempts at allowing viewers to step into images became especially popular with panoramas, which were popular attractions depicting particularly important historical scenes. The Bourbaki Panorama in Lucerne, Switzerland (see Figure 2.6), provides a fine example. Still accessible to visitors today, it showcases the Swiss population hosting and caring for fleeing French soldiers tired and devastated in the face of the Franco-Prussian War of 1871. Painted by Edouard Castres in 1881, the panorama allows one to walk along a cascade of images, together cast as a unified whole surrounding the viewer, who moves in space to envision the misery, horrors, and care that those fleeing encountered. It remains a stark visual reminder of the horrors of war and of the importance of solidarity with people who seek refuge from them.

The history of European painting also bears its own witness to many attempts at either rejecting geometrical perspective or mixing it with other types of pictorial spatialisation. This is typical for the paintings of Paolo Uccello and Piero dell Francesca. Another example is found in the practice of ordering (i.e., the manner of 'arrangement of figures and of the source of light') that was subject to theorising by Charles Perrault in the seventeenth century, among others (see Mirzoeff, 1999: p. 46). Reverse perspective too found a foothold, affording inspiration from playful inversion of the position of vanishing points (Florensky, 2002: p. 201). Also, anamorphism survived over the ages.

In this system, the vanishing point is located not in front of the image but in the same plane as the picture, just to the right or left. A viewer who is not in the correct position sees just a misshapen-seeming triangular mass. In recent decades, anamorphic images have gained popularity as a mechanism for placement of televised advertisements during sporting events, where they allow adverts set flat on the ground to resemble upright signboards. They are a popular choice also among street artists. Finally, if we delve into the painting traditions that were born after the invention of the photographic camera (such as cubism, futurism, and Dada), many more examples of attempts to break free of the spell and authority of geometrical perspective reveal themselves.

Perspective allowed images to convey messages in what seemed to be a natural transposition from the outside world, although this 'outside' often referred to biblical stories and myths. Images thus became tools for narration, lending themselves also to use as tools of propaganda (see Argan's and Hauser's discussion). If we look back at Byzantine art, we find a different angle. In the same manner as Hindu icons, these images, especially those referring to the divine, do not focus on narration. They are objects of contemplation. Viewing a Byzantine icon is not an act of reading a particular meaning so much as an act of contemplation. It is a transformative experience that speaks of the agency and performativity of images.

2.2.2.6 The Politics of Perspective

As the previous section may have made obvious, central geometrical perspective is but one way through which a sense of depth can be reproduced in the world of images. Yet, this relativity notwithstanding, perspective gradually grew in influence from the sixteenth century onward, becoming recognised as a 'natural' model of vision. Of critical importance is the fact that geometrical perspective had a particular politics to it. As Figure 2.3 illustrates, that perspective expels the viewer from the image, even though the privileged viewer can exercise control over the field of vision to some extent. Far from articulating a natural fact, this principle seems imbued with a specific cultural view – and a rather arrogant one at that. According to Mirzoeff, the novelty to what we dub Western perspective 'was not its ability to represent space but the fact that it was held to do so from one particular viewpoint' (1999: p. 40). In other words, it represented for many power and control more than anything else.

Centring everything at the eye of the viewer – just the one eye, mind you – Cartesian perspectivalism (per Jay as cited by Foster, 1988: pp. 5–7) wrought something more profound. It marked the entry into the modern age, an epoch that Scott McQuire (1998), paraphrasing Martin Heidegger, has characterised as the 'conquest of the world as perspective' (p. 22). This epoch postulated a new relation between representation and subjectivity. Within the space carved out, the human being 'becomes that being upon which all that is, is grounded as regards to manner of its Being and its truth. Man becomes the relational centre of that which is as such', in the words of Heidegger (cited by McQuire, 1998: p. 128). In speaking to the Western desire to elevate the human to the level of God, perspective, according to Christian Metz (1982: p. 49), inscribes 'an empty emplacement for the spectator-subject, an all-powerful position which is that of God himself, or[,] more broadly, of some ultimate signified'. In 'pushing' viewers out of the image, perspective marked, in addition, a separation between the external world and the internal psyche. According to the dogma of perspective, there is no reciprocity in actuality. Lifted up to the position of a god or royalty, viewers feel entitled to exercise control of the image and no longer need to situate themselves in

Looking, Seeing, and Historical Notions of Vision and the Eye   41

relation to it. It is clear from these attributes that perspective embodied a very particular politics of visibility and rendered the act of looking synonymous with an act of ordering and of control. To make the specificity of this position clearer, let us again look sideways and remember how, for instance, Chinese scrolls or Mughal paintings liberate 'the viewer from his [sic!] seat to wander off within images' (Sheikh, 2013: p. 152).

Power constituted the heart of geometrical perspective, one could claim. Calling perspective 'one device by which artists sought to capture and represent visual power', Mirzoeff (1999: p. 41) has argued, further, that the most important thing was to convey visual power, not geometrical procession (consider the growing prominence of perspective in cinematic images). The lines of power reconnect with previous metaphors here, with the idea of the eye as a supreme judge or, as Alberti had it, as the 'prince' of rays. This usage was not purely metaphorical; it was very much incorporated into the design of such structures as theatres. In the age of King Louis XIV, the king was always seated at the exact spot where all lines meet. Figure 2.7 illustrates this. His perspective was perfect and, more than that, was the only perfect one. This approach supported the idea, or ideology, that the authority (the king, the prince, or some other sovereign entity) is also the one ideal viewer: both the one with assumed total vision and the one that all should see. Geometrical perspective was therefore employed to create a

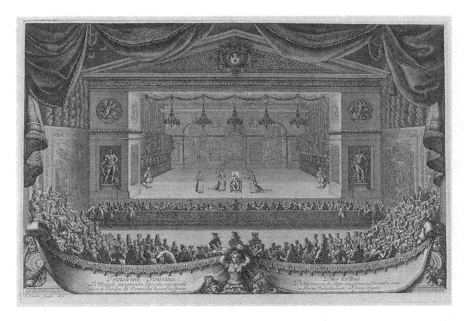

Figure 2.7 The theatre of Versaille during the performance of Moliere's 'Malade Imaginaire'. Paris, 1674.

space that was simultaneously aesthetic, analytical, and political. As Mirzoeff suggested, the regime employed a 'powerful formula for visual standardization: a mathematical vision which could be continually projected onto the real in a social context in which mathematics was increasingly offered as the universal measure of knowledge' (1999: p. 19).

Accordingly, one could say that this use of geometrical perspective paved the way for development of the Panopticon, which, as Foucault (1995) has shown, is an apt metaphor for a disciplinarian society. Jeremy Bentham's Panopticon indeed expressed yet another shift in relations between viewing and power. In Mirzoeff's portrayal:

> in order to be exercised this power had to be given the instrument of permanent, exhaustive, omnipresent surveillance, capable of making all visible as long as it could remain invisible. It had to be a faceless gaze that transformed the whole social body into a field of perception.
>
> (p. 50)

A true accomplishment born of the Cartesian separation of body from mind, perspective managed in no small measure to tame, domesticate, and control the visual media that were used to show images. It interposed itself in the lengthy struggle between text and image that had characterised mediaeval Europe, wherein religion (the Church) armed with a text (the Bible) waged war against icon-loving 'heathens', even if those icons were Orthodox or Catholic ones (see Flusser, 2006). Perspective contributed to rationalising the image, wresting assumed magical powers from it, and positioning it on terrain of representation that could become technical. Today, news imagery, social-media photographs, cinema, games, and many virtual-reality environments still benefit from the *longue durée* of central perspective, providing a means to order pictorial space in ways that can be reproduced, transmitted across time and space, and shown in multiple locations at once.

Clearly, theories of vision, understandings of pictorial space and its organisation (via such means as central perspective), and their embedding in broader political constellations provide us with a wealth of perspectives on understandings of visualities. We turn next to the question of what an image is, showing that images are by no means necessarily constrained by any one mode of perspective or grid.

Note

1 Some scholars have expressed doubts as to whether ancient Greek thought, which gave birth to some of those alternatives as well as to what they opposed, should be deemed a part of Western civilisation proper. Citing the works of Martin Bernal and Cheick Anta Diop, Ziauddin Sardar stated in his *Postmodernism and the Other* that the Greeks 'were hardly European' (1998: p. 206). In any case, their influence on Western thought is undeniable.

3 Tools for Analysing Images

Images and ways of seeing are so important that many of the concepts we use in the West for knowing bear etymological links to the ability to see. We could cite the notion of theory, which has particular importance in the social sciences and the humanities. Etymologically, this term refers to contemplation and vision in Middle French (*theorie*) and to a contemplative, speculative approach, in contrast to more practical undertakings, in post-classical Latin. In Ancient Greek, θεωρία was the action of viewing, sight, spectacle, and contemplation, through which our ability to see is tightly intertwined with how we conceive of our ability to know.[1] While seeing and knowing are thus interrelated, they are linked in many further, more complex ways too. Images, or ways of seeing, are by no means easily understood by all involved – even when there are no language barriers to take into account. They have to be assessed in light of the kinds of knowledge relations in which they are entangled.

If we take theory to mean a set of ideas – in essence, the act of viewing, contemplating, or seeing a set of ideas – it is useful to recall that in classical Latin 'idea' refers to an eternal archetype and in post-classical Latin it also denotes form, image, and likeness. According to the *Oxford English Dictionary* entry for 'idea', thirteenth-century British texts employ this word for 'images existing in the mind'; therefore, we might take theory to be the act of viewing and contemplating a set of images in the mind. And academic work puts forth a theory as a particular perspective on the phenomena to be studied.

Our aim for this section is to offer the reader concrete tools for analysing images. After laying some groundwork to map out the terrain – or explore the 'family' if we are to follow W.J.T. Mitchell – of images, we move, again aided by means of real-world examples, on to consider specific theoretical apparatuses – among them semiotics, social interactionism, and phenomenology. And again we will contrast Western hegemonic and modern views/practices against instances from other parts of the world and other epochs in our ongoing attempt at decolonising our approach to visual studies.

DOI: 10.4324/9781003084549-3

3.1 What Exactly an Image Is

'What is an image?' is a question (or perhaps 'the' question) that has preoccupied scholars interested in all things visual over the ages, whatever their location or theoretical framework. Starting in the mists of Antiquity, with traces to be found in the debates regarding the functioning of vision that we addressed in Section 2.2, this dialogue has been dominated overall by two clearly defined, opposing camps. On one side we have the 'materialists', who believe that perceived reality is some 'thing' out there that transcends the presence of an observer, something that exists even in the absence of perception. On the other side, there are the 'idealists', who look at the physical world as an emanation, genuinely a figment of the mind that is formed as it is perceived, i.e., a materialisation of the imagination that comes to us in the form of images via a photograph, a painting, a story, etc. Mary Jean Carruthers suggested that the phenomenal world is 'figmented' (per Ingold, 2010: p. 17), or filled with such elements as readily cross the boundary between apparently distinct media). While the former group, focused as they are on an objectivising perspective, seems to neglect the importance of experience, the latter appears too narrowly focused on the subjective level, hence slipping very close to risky invocations of solipsism. Dialogue between these two schools of thought occupies difficult ground. It may even seem impossible at first. Yet, with this book, that battlefield is exactly where we want to position ourselves. We want to enter this debate at the intersection of these two stances, offering peace with a third approach. Our endeavour's focus is on the meeting point between the observing subject and the observed object. Joining a host of scholars in related fields (among them Belting and Mitchell), we believe that an image is intrinsically formed 'in between', within and through the interactions between observing bodies and the world surrounding them. The visual media that are attended to in this exchange are crucial for grasping its nature. An image is formed via the look as a medium, essentially within a relation – between the internal and external, the personal and the collective, the world of ideas and the world of things. Anti-dualistic in nature, it takes shape when these supposedly opposed entities come together. The image emerges within the event of interaction, unfolding both spatially and temporally, at the intersection of seemingly opposite entities. Thus, it carries elements of both self and other, of the internal and external, as an intersection or in-betweenness that cannot be reduced to its constituent parts.

This quintessentially relational character of an image is what makes it so powerful in human life. If we agree that humans develop values, meanings, and skills in and through exchange with the world surrounding them, in actions and repeated practices, then images seem to be a natural companion to their journeys on this Earth. We live our lives in the company of images (cf. Favero, 2017). Images are there to help us order and contemplate, or to envision, cross boundaries, and create social cohesion, but they can also hurt, attack, and insult. This may explain why so many individuals over the ages and in many, many places have chosen to accompany (and be guided in) their lives with images, why they often demarcate the beginning and ending of a life with cascades of images while also leaving to images also the vital duty of keeping memories alive for future generations. We will explore this dimension by looking at the manifold ways in which images can be approached, analysed, and theorised upon.

3.1.1 The Image Emerging In Between

An image is a connection between us and the world beyond us. It provides humans with that layer of 'firstness', in the lexicon of Charles Sanders Peirce, that leads them to recognise the extent to which they are part of the world. We could compare it with a membrane. In biology, a membrane is a thin layer forming the border to a living cell. The membrane is a porous boundary and regulates the traffic of molecules and substances between the cell as a whole and the world surrounding it. Likewise, images (visual and not – see below) are a perceptive boundary that regulates the exchange between the world of human subjects within and the outside world right in front of them. As Belting has suggested (2011), images are a point of conjunction between mental activity and the material world 'out there'. They hence remind us of the extent to which whatever is internal (mental) does, in fact, originate somewhere and that everything we see out there is, to some extent at least, also a result of something internal, emanating from a particular point of view, or perspective. This idea echoes Berger's suggestion that 'the world as it is is more than pure objective fact, it includes consciousness' (1972: p. 11). This stance allows us also to suggest a constructive dialogue between theories of intramission and extramission, a focus on modes of attention and on ways of becoming visible.

Many theories of visual perception classically have focused on a perceiver who sees the light reflected or emanated. From this standpoint, the viewer either perceives (passively, in a sense) a mirrored image of the world or actively constructs it nearly *ex nihilo*. In our theory, however, viewing is part of humans' experience and a key aspect of our very being in the world. This cannot be detached from what we do while perceiving. Active and passive marry here. We perceive images in situated contexts. We perceive them in particular environments while being there and walking, listening, sitting, smelling, or engaging in whatever other kind of activity might occupy us. As Ingold has suggested, 'perception is not an "inside-the head" operation, performed upon the raw material of sensation, but takes place in circuits that cross-cut the boundaries between brain, body and world' (2000: p. 244).

As science advances, we are gaining deeper insight into how humans develop their visual skills (and sensory skills more broadly) through capacities for progressively deducing and anticipating happenings in the world out there. We do not simply mirror what is in front of us. People learn, to use a metaphor borrowed from Donald Hoffman (2019), to distinguish whether an orange and black fluffy-looking object amidst the leaves might be the tail of a tiger and hence constitute something risky that had better be avoided. In essence, Hoffman, Christoph Koch (2019), and other neuroscience-minded scholars suggest that humans develop skills in growing more and more able to move and act in their environments and are less bothered about what is ontologically there or not (except when engaged in the task of ruminating about ontology). This conclusion, often referenced via the shorthand 'fitness beats truth' (FBT), is rooted in neuroscientific study of human evolution (see, for example, Prakash et al., 2021)[2], yet its kernel – the idea that performance and action motivated by the environment are more important than 'truth' for human life – is echoed in other disciplines' traditions. They underpin Ingold's perspective, which, in turn, is based on the work of Gibson (1979), Merleau-Ponty (1962), and Zuckerkandl (1969). They appear also, although formulated on completely different theoretical terrain, in the views of sociologists Hockey and Collinson (2006), who make a similar argument in their analysis of the functioning of vision during long-distance running. Here too, the subjects may not be highly interested in analysing the truth of what their vision tells them; rather, they are more inclined to try avoiding any risky footfalls that might jeopardise the results of their running. They learn to avoid obstacles; to look out for rocks and ruts; and to anticipate the movement of cars, other people, dogs, etc. Taking a step sideways, we find that the same ideas appear in Buddhist philosophy, which historically has been preoccupied more with action in its ethics than with truth, epistemology, and ontology (cf. Batchelor, 2015).

Returning to the question of the image while carrying these thoughts with us, we may venture to suggest that an image is what allows us to connect to the external world and quickly conduct evaluations of what surrounds us. This is the case even in the absence of a fully formed representation of everything that is in front of us and of any sort of solid enquiry regarding its truthfulness.

Every image can be seen, then, as constantly forming part of a dialogue not just across space and time (bridging past, present, and future) but more generically between humans and the world surrounding them. And this relationality entails also some degree of reciprocation. Berger states this in *Ways of Seeing*: 'When we "see" a landscape, we situate ourselves in it' (1972: p. 11), and we might add that this situating is not static – we are there as if on the move. It is entirely true that our progressively greater exposure to being visually depicted has resulted not merely in heightened awareness of the implications of seeing but also in a growing awareness of what it means to be seen (and of the politics attached to this). We have already touched on this, and we will get back to it in discussion further along too. For now, let us dig further into what an image is and can be.

3.1.2 The Family of Images

Before we go any further in speculations regarding the nature of images, we'd best start unpacking terminology that will simplify explanation of our reasoning. The first distinction we need to make is that between 'picture' and 'image'. According to Mitchell (1984), a picture is always a material object, one that can be hung, touched, burned, torn apart. It is something that contains what we have called an aesthetic difference in a visual medium. A picture, we suggest, still is not quite what you directly perceive when you look at it, whatever scholars who follow the 'mirroring reality' approach to visual perception might contend. As for an image, in our use of the term it exists at a higher level of abstraction so is less concrete. We will let Mitchell elaborate: 'An image is what appears in a picture, and what survives its destruction – in memory, in narration, in copies and traces in other media'; in sum, 'you can hang a picture but you cannot hang an image' (2015: p. 16). In essence, an image is an 'immaterial entity, a ghostly, phantasmatic appearance that comes to light or comes to life in a material support' (p. 17), and it does so only as part of an interaction. Also, Ludwig Wittgenstein has stated that an image 'is not a picture, but a picture can correspond to it' (2009: p. 108). So, at base, pictures rest on some kind of support, a visual medium such as a canvas, an LED screen, or a marble statue. This physical aspect is not always self-evident, especially in a 'post-digital world' (cf. Favero, 2020), but a picture always is the container of an image stored in, on, and through a material medium. The image within a picture, in order to be perceived, needs to be activated by a set of interactions, which may be ordered by cultural conventions and restrictions (e.g., addressing what is deemed appropriate to look at), techniques of depiction (such as geometrical perspective and details of rendering), and choice of *topoi* (what is actually depicted and what might be evoked through not being depicted).

As we noted above, Belting pointed out that images emerge only in the interrelations between bodies and media. Interestingly, his theory of images implies that bodies and other media, as images, change as our visual experiences unfold. In his theory, this change affects the other elements involved also. Proceeding from this understanding, we find that our ways of seeing images have an impact on what we consider our bodies to be (and to be capable of), along with what we understand media to be and to afford us. Images, thus, are always tied to ways of being and ways of understanding the world. Pictures, on the other hand, as containers for images experienced in interaction, do not fully control the images we get to see – motivations, tasks, and cultural factors all play a role in what we end up seeing. While Yarbus's eye-tracking experiments discussed in Section 2.1, 'The Look As a Medium', demonstrated this decisively, in later sections of this book we approach this from a different angle, by means of examples gathered from visual practices in non-hegemonic and non-Western contexts.

We find utility in a typology that communication scholar Jan-Marie Peters (1961) has suggested for studying pictures. According to him, a picture conveyed by a visual medium can be analysed on three dimensions: its content or referent (in Dutch, its *voorstelling/inhoudelijke* aspect), its formal qualities (*vormgeving/vormelijke* aspect), and its substance or material dimension (*substantie/materiele* aspect). Following such a model helps us study the referent in the picture, such as a tree, a rendering of your grandmother, or oneself. This is the supposed 'window' to the historical moment that, for example, photographs have been posited to bring to the surface. And this is also, typically, what a photograph promises (but also fails to) deliver.[3]

The formal lines of dimensions enable readily addressing the extent to which choices of style may add meaning to the explicit content of an image (or remove it). In this project, we can benefit significantly from maintaining the distinction between denotation and connotation, for instance. In the conceptual framework of Roland Barthes, the former (the denotative dimension) refers to the *analogon* itself while the latter opens room for the various ways in which meaning can be added to an image by means of contextual and stylistic references. In his early analysis of press photographs (1977), Barthes suggests that every photographic image is a paradox characterised by the co-existence of a message with no code (the analogues) and one with a code (the treatment). It is a simple 'reduction' of reality carrying a perfect analogical correspondence with that reality, yet on the same level it simultaneously is a result of the interference of culture and ideology. More than simply 'denoting' images, therefore, it 'connotes' too. Connotation adds layers of meaning that are external to the *analogon*, to the 'thing out there' (the thing that gets inscribed in the photograph). This is the trick played by 'form'.

Finally, there is what Peters calls substance. In considering it, we focus on the materials supporting the image – i.e., what we have called the visual medium. Encompassing what produced it, its materialisation, and how it encourages or precludes/restrains the circulation of images, this is a fascinating area especially in 'post-digitality', one that is much discussed accordingly. What is the materiality of digital visualities? And what about those projected on a screen? While semiotics and iconology (explored later) are probably the theoretical apparatuses most suitable for analysing matters of visual form, the dimension of substance requires the support of other approaches – principally, we would suggest, of phenomenology and materialist approaches to media and mediation.

Phenomenology is a philosophical tradition and research method that focuses on the systematic study of the phenomena that appear in consciousness and, hence on actors' lived experiences. It has aided in exploring the manifold ways in which humans perceive and engage with the world of vision and images. Foregrounding the body and the materiality of vision and that of visible objects, phenomenology has proved especially fundamental to addressing non-hegemonic Western visual practices. One of the best examples is that of Elisabeth Edwards and her analysis of photographs' role among Australian Aboriginal communities. In her path-breaking essay 'Photographs and the

Sound of History' (2006), she suggests that photos in this context are 'relational objects'. Central in articulating histories that have been suppressed, photographs not only make up a part of the visual realm but constitute an element in a much broader performance. They are held, caressed, stroked, and sung to. They become sound, the sounds of multiple speaking voices, of songs, of memories verbalised as stories and as many renderings of an oral history giving material form to the relationships between specific individuals who engage with each other through such images. Under her approach, therefore, photographs are first and foremost 'things that matter' (p. 28), functioning also as an extension of the self toward a society. Phenomenology likewise is central to the image explorations promoted by Eck and Lawrence Babb in the context of Hindu practices (which we have already approached in this book) and equally to the work of Christopher Pinney (2001), who posited a need for 'corpothetics' rather than for aesthetics for understanding the meaning and function of images in such an Indian context.

From material-media studies we also can recognise valuable attention to the role of infrastructure and cultural techniques for understanding how images come about. For example, for Siegert (2015) cultural techniques allow for a 'cut' between the symbolic and the real, where pictures and the ways in which they may be handled are elemental for this task. In his understanding, before any meaning can emerge, a cut needs to be made that facilitates the emergence of this meaning (see also Kember & Zylinska, 2012). Specific embodied and material techniques are important for this, hence the importance of the veil in connection with painting, whereby the work points both to an absence and to the momentary imperceptibility of the veiled. This situation manifests itself even when a physical veil is present (for example, in some theatrical settings or in front of particular religious paintings). Taking a different angle, Parks (2020) has illuminated the vast infrastructural components that together permit satellites to orbit Earth and send sensor readings to ground stations on the Earth as the *sine qua non* of satellite images. The infrastructure of visual media is particularly important for understanding what kinds of images may eventually emerge.

We can now circle back to the distinction between images and pictures. Images are experienced as an unfolding event within interactions, and pictures (whether photographs or oil paintings), held via visual media, are only one source for their apprehension. So how should we understand the ways in which we 'see' images, and what sources might there be apart from pictures for doing this? Let us dig further into other possible distinctions and ponder the various forms that images may take. When penning his famous piece 'What Is an Image?', which we cited above, Mitchell (1984) suggested that the family of images can be divided into five main branches: graphic (pictures, statues, designs, etc.), optical (comprising images such as mirrors' and projections'), perceptual (involving sense data, 'species', and appearances), mental (dreams, memories, ideas, and phantasms), and verbal (metaphors, descriptions, and writing overall). Not all of these categories are self-evident. It is easy for us to grasp images that emerge in interactions with visual media such as graphic and optical media. Matters get more complicated when we address those images that emerge from interactions with verbal media. This is the terrain of *ekphrasis*, of images suggested by or created with verbal stimuli (cf. Ingold, 2010; Mitchell, 1994; Rancière, 2008). Not necessarily growing out of the interaction with pictures and other visual media, these images instead are evoked by written words, or by the sounds composing verbal descriptions of scenes. This is also the delicate area between that which can be said but not shown and *vice versa* (on *ekphrasis*, see Mitchell, 1994). Interestingly, and perhaps somewhat counterintuitively, eye-tracking experiments have shown that our eye movements follow similar patterns when we look at a drawing of scenery and when we listen to a verbal description of said surroundings. The activity of 'seeing' images is hence not tied to graphic and optical media alone.

This aspect is particularly evident when we address Mitchell's 'perceptual' and 'mental' images. The former category is populated by 'strange creatures that haunt the border between physical and psychological accounts of imagery' (1984: p. 505). This is the terrain of ghosts, shadows, and mirages of all those appearances that are not so easy to refer to. Shadows are a phenomenon especially worthy of attention (see Casati, 2004; Favero, 2020) as they defy many human assumptions about images (these are discussed further on in the book). As for mental images, the emergence might occur at times of day when we are not fully awake, not entirely conscious of our environment, or in an altered state of mind. But they emerge as well in heightened states of consciousness – for instance, during meditation sessions. Lucid dreams might flicker in front of us before we are entirely awake, an idea might emerge as a clear image during a shower after extended exercise, and a dream might provide life-changing guidance. In the Abrahamic religions (Judaism, Christianity, Islam, etc.), prophets often received guidance specifically via dreams and visions, sometimes drawing on these to direct their followers on arduous journeys that took many years. Carl Jung took this further by suggesting that dreams (a form of imagination) have a prospective function, steering the dreamer toward the act of making (new) conscious decisions during the day. And thought leaders in Silicon Valley are dubbed visionaries today, while corporate and state bodies alike devote time and energy to articulating 'missions' and 'visions' to guide organised actions in meaningful directions. While visions are increasingly crafted on the basis of empirically observable phenomena, individuals' serendipity, visions, and dreams certainly are still important for many at the helm of private businesses... and far beyond.

3.1.3 Images, Relations, and the Senses

The reflections above open space also for contemplating the multisensoriality of images. As we saw with the example of *ekphrasis*, images emerge also when we are reading or listening to verbal descriptions or are hearing acoustic sounds. Images and sounds are interrelated, and one can evoke the other (cf. Edwards, 2006). Among those stressing this aspect was Jean-Luc Nancy, who found that the image is never only visual; 'it is also musical, poetic, even tactile, olfactory or gustatory, kinaesthetic and so on' (2005: p. 4). Therefore, with *The Future of the Image* (2008), Jacques Rancière articulated a need for a new notion, which he termed 'imageness', capable of highlighting the visual strength of non-visual sensory stimuli.

These ideas give further momentum to Mitchell's idea that '[m]edia are always mixtures of sensory and semiotic elements [...] mixed or hybrid formations combining sound and sight, text and image' (2015: p. 14). With this in mind, we might honour Pinney's suggestion that the 'visual should be conceived of as a continuum ranging across different qualities[,] for which different paradigms are called' (2006a: p. 135).

Playing with multiple senses simultaneously, images hence end up interpellating the whole body. This is a relationship that can be tackled from several angles, and surely in both philosophical and neuroscientific terms. Following Belting (see above), we could say that in its delicate play across different media and the senses, an image highlights an interplay of body, memory and imagination too. Belting reminds us that images are not a mere matter of visibility. As we have noted, for him they consist of a point of conjunction, between 'mental frames' and the physical, material world out there (2011). It bears recalling that he found an image to be always both internal and external, personal and collective. Modern neuroscience accords with this stance – coordination of the senses through the faculties of the central nervous system is now taken as axiomatic. The discovery of the mirror neurons (or 'Gandhi neurons') marked a turning point, further blurring the boundary between self and other, between perception and action (Gallese, 2009; Ramachandran & Hirstein, 1999; Rizzolatti & Sinigaglia, 2006). Building on a series of studies conducted with monkeys, researchers showed that looking at someone doing something causes activation of specific areas of my brain, areas that get activated if I were doing it myself. As Mirzoeff put it, today's awareness forces us to acknowledge how 'our minds and bodies are continuously interacting, forming one system' (2015: p. 87).

Many other scholars have addressed specific angles to the multisensoriality of the image, giving special regard to its connection to tactility. In *Art and Visual Perception* (2004), Rudolf Arnheim states that 'in looking at an object we reach out for it. With an invisible finger we move through the space around us to go out to the distant places where things are found, touch them, catch them, scan their surfaces, trace their borders, explore their texture' (p. 13). Probing the same elements, Merleau-Ponty suggested that a corporal principle is at the very core of our engagement with images. In 'Eye and Mind' he states:

> 'A human body is present when, between the see-er and the visible, between touching and touched, between one eye and the other, between

hand and hand, a kind of cross-over occurs, when the spark of the sensing/sensible is lit, when the fire starts to burn that will not cease until some accident befalls the body'.

(1993: p. 125)[4]

Indeed, Florensky too touched on this idea, sometime earlier. His analysis of the icon offers what resembles an act in defence of the surface: 'Acute is the mind that resides in the fingers and the hand of the artist'; this 'acute mind understands, without the need of the intelligence of the head, the metaphysical essence of all those relations of strength of the surface of the representation, and penetrates these essences in depth'(1977: p. 111).

All of these – intrinsically distinct (and perhaps competing) – systems of knowledge spotlight that images do much more than merely portraying and documenting. They do things to us, interact with us, guide us, merge with us; they are literally part of our bodies and lifeworlds (see also Marks, 2000 and Jackson, 2012).

3.1.4 What Images Do

So far we have zeroed in mainly on the meaning of images. Yet, as may already have become evident from our reflections, an image is not only matter for showing or telling (it is not mere representation); it is also, as we implied when addressing, for instance, the work of Edwards, a thing that acts in the present and in the presence of specific situated viewers. Relying upon the faculty of imagination, an image is also importantly a statement of presence and existence. A 'force that draws the form of presence out of absence', it makes possible the co-existence of 'the presence of a world and presence to a world' (Nancy, 2005: p. 22). More than a 'sign', an image is also a 'force-sign' (p. 23), a 'symptom' (Didi-Huberman, 2015) that liberates both 'imitative' and 'contagious' qualities (see Frazer, 1890/2009). By approaching images exclusively on terrain of representation, rather than spaces also of action, we often miss this fundamental aspect. As Didi-Huberman (2003) concluded, 'we ask too little of images', in that, 'by immediately relegating them to the sphere of the document [...] we sever them from their phenomenology, from their specificity and from their very substance' (p. 33).

The capacity of images to be and to do (rather than simply mean) is an aspect of visual cultures that has piqued the curiosity of several scholars. Bakewell (1998), for example, discussed them as being created to act upon and within the world, rather than purely to represent it. A 'more-than-representational' approach of this sort, which you will have noticed that we ourselves advocate, can be found also in inversion of conventional relations of agency as explored by Mitchell in the 2006 book *What Do Pictures Want?: The Lives and Loves of Images*. Instead of focusing on the human subject, who seeks to fulfil wants and desires via images, whether for erotic fulfilment, powerful vistas, or exploration of the unconscious, Mitchell asks there what kinds of desires, demands, or needs the **images** might have as they traverse a range of media (graphic, optical, perceptual, mental, and verbal). And, as we have noted, Edwards took an anthropologist's stance when addressing the role of photographs among Aboriginal Australian communities. Her notion of relational objects highlights the centrality of photographs in articulating heretofore suppressed histories and thus contributing to materialisation of relations between humans and, thereby, to crafting of communities. On a much more mundane level, we would invite you to reflect on the extent to which specific images may, in fact, set off or spark situated behaviours. Think of a picture of Che Guevara, or one of the Buddha. Think about how they have for generations functioned as symbols of certain desirable human qualities (liberation of the oppressed, compassion, etc.), with these associations getting triggered in viewers by the images themselves. Our attention today cannot but shift to the portraits of Mahsa Amini that prompted thousands and thousands of women (with others alongside them) to take to the streets in defence of human rights.

If we bring together all the perspectives we have addressed so far, images appear to be quintessentially a matter of relations. They emerge and intervene in relations between people. They stitch together relations across media and the senses, also creating links in relations across presences and absences and across time, relations between action and reaction. Berger foregrounded the intrinsically relational nature of looking when he suggested that we 'never look at just one thing; we are always looking at the relation between things and ourselves. Our vision is continually active, continually moving, continually holding things in a circle around itself, constituting what is present to us as we are' (1972: p. 8). Images invite transcending these boundaries, thus literally putting people in motion and exposing them to an endless game of seeing and being seen. They draw the viewers into the image, thereby moulding them into a part of history.

A further domain of theory typically addressing images as performative objects is that designed for the intersection of art history, philosophy, and theology. The study of religious icons (especially Byzantine ones – see Argan, 2008; Evdomikov, 1970; Florensky, 1967; Lindsay Opie, 2014; Marci, 2014; Pencheva, 2013; Sendler, 1985) has expanded human knowledge of images as more-than-representational items. Neither illustration nor decoration, they are understood as a tool for communicating directly with the realm of the divine (of the invisible), as a 'proper' means for entering it. The parallel with Hindu icons is striking. Quite prominently, in the case of Byzantine icons too, the image apprehended is understood by believers to contain the essence of the divine, and it generates, via use of reflecting materials, manifold dialogues with its viewers, who interact with visual media in aims of experiencing divine images. All such images and pictures seem to require moving away from linguistic and semiotic models of analysis, to performative ones. They also put a question mark on the primacy of the linguistic models that have long dominated Western approaches to images. While this is one of the factors that have led scholars to ask how fully Greek civilisation can be considered Western (see the argument laid out by Sardar, 1998), the 'Western' is far from monolithic in any case. We will return to the nature of Byzantine icons, to explore the extent to which an understanding of visuality may hold an alternative path to considering contemporary visual technologies such as virtual, augmented, and expanded reality. We proceed in another direction now, paving a path for beginning to study images from a practice-theory angle.

3.1.5 How to Start Studying Images

When outlining how we have chosen to approach the study of visual cultures, we discussed the lens of the look as a medium. It enables us to focus on three things:

1) The look and how it becomes understandable via particular mediations. This entails several alternative approaches to understanding vision and to the role of specific mediations (e.g., Renaissance perspective) in ordering and organising what can be shown, what may be seen, and the kind of viewing arrangements promulgated and the choice of *topoi* in advancing a particular way of seeing. Understanding (and studying) well-known cases, such as the male gaze (Mulvey, 1975), Orientalist gaze (Said, 1978), and medical gaze (Foucault, 1960), as specific organised skilled practices of seeing assists in attending to and understanding phenomena related to visual culture among particular communities of practice. But we could also pay attention to the roles of mirrors, *camerae obscurae*, shadows, the blind person's stick, or specific models of the eye in our efforts to study how looking and the look have been and are understood.
2) Visual media and how they have been created to allow being looked at. Here, we could start by attending to the role of material mediations, without which no one can see images at all, and how these have been created and thought of. For example, many publications on digitisation of photography report on studies exploring the intrinsic meanings that switching from chemical-film-based visual practices to networked, software-based images have ushered in as photography has grown ubiquitous, pervasive, and fundamentally reliant on metadata and ease of retrieval from archives (Gunthert, 2008). The role of the carriers of images (their vehicles) is highly relevant for an understanding of visual cultures. From this perspective, the laying of underwater telecommunication cables for global interconnectivity (see Starosielski, 2015), the launching of various satellite-borne imaging systems (Parks & Schwoch, 2012), etc. prove crucial for deeper enquiry into what 'networked', 'ubiquitous', or 'pervasive' might actually mean. Similarly, the surface qualities of visual media deserve our attention if we hope to understand differences among screens, for example (see Flusser, 2006; Casetti 2015).

3) Images and the roles of ways of looking. This is central to understanding images in any way. While the other two modes of enquiry home in on the look, vision, or particular visual media in endeavours to explain phenomena involved in visual cultures, from this perspective we ask specifically what kinds of images people actually see when they attend to carriers of images (to specific visual media). We have discussed experiment-based research evidence that people might see very different kinds of images even if looking at the same visual media, in line with their motivations, desires, capabilities, etc. At exhibitions of visual media, one of the two authors tends to walk with his daughter and simply observe what is on display (usually artworks). Father and daughter discuss what attending to these from their specific viewpoints shows them. The abstract paintings, sculptures, and non-figurative art usually yield a range of images, seen by attending differently (and from differing standpoints), but even figurative art created with techniques familiar from Renaissance perspective affords seeing mutually distinct images from looking at the same visual media in very different ways. The other author of this book meanwhile has been exploring the world of images from an autoethnographic perspective, alternating observation of the visual culture of death with moments of introspection on what one sees while meditating and when engaging in long-distance running or climbing. In empirical research, perspectives of such sorts introduce us to the ways in which particular communities of practice make sense of what they see.

Having delineated these various points of entry to the study of images (and visual culture), we do not, however, recommend that a scholar choose one and stick to it. The benefit lies, rather, in being able to connect these approaches to each other, to combine and contrast them so as to achieve the most fine-grained understanding possible of what images are and can be about. For purposes of study, you might nevertheless find it useful to foreground one perspective, as many scholars tend to do.

We will now take a glimpse at further traditions of theory that have engaged with questions of these types, emphasising the role of images emerging within interactions that are always situated, embodied, affect-laden, and filled with significations / ways of ordering, all of which also influence how we understand politics and the political.

3.1.5.1 *The Study of Images as Signs*

The first territory we invite the reader to step into is the realm of semiotics (or semiology), which, as the discussion above hints, may be defined as 'the study of signs and symbols and their use or interpretation'[5]. Swiss linguist Ferdinand de Saussure, who introduced the term during his lectures published in 1916, defined semiotics as the 'science that studies the life of signs within society' (1974: p. 16). In his view, language was a set of rules operating within society. Made up of signs expressed by sounds, language could be examined via a rough distinction between what he called the *langue* and the *parole*. The first is the collectively owned system itself; the latter is the use that people make of it. Within his dualistic system, the sign has both a 'signifier' (the word, the sound, and the code expressing the idea) and a 'signified' (the thing out there, the *analogon*). For his system, which was based on the study of language, both written and spoken, Saussure tried to provide a general theory of how meaning is produced by means of language use. Saussure's theory sparked interest among scholars of visual cultures. Furthermore, several other researchers who compare the images we see to some kind of mirror images of an external world could be understood as following this approach.

Better aligned with our argument that images may be seen very differently in accordance with who is doing the looking, at what visual medium, with what kinds of motivations and desires, is Charles Sanders Peirce, who developed a pragmatist theory of signs under which all signs have a triadic structure and offer experiences contingent on who is experiencing them. While Peirce's final model of signs was highly complex and is worthy of study in its own right (Jappy, 2013), the three-dimension structure deserves particular note, for its influence on study of visual cultures. The icon, the index, and the symbol refer to distinct ways in which particular aspects of, for instance, a picture 'make claims' about what they depict. Iconicity's claims centre on the ways in which a thing is depicted and understood as such, as with the way in which a picture depicts smoke; the index ties in with the kind of referential claim that is made (e.g., with regard to smoke as an index of fire); and the symbol involves conventionalised understandings, in which, for instance, fire is understood to mean warmth, destruction, or purification, depending on the context. We will look at Peirce's system more closely in the following section so for now we will continue mapping the landscape, by turning to a thinker whose approach we touched upon earlier. The work done by Barthes with regard to images (in photography, advertisements, etc.) has had a major influence on scholars of visual cultures. He combined Saussure's and Peirce's ideas into a specific and eventually also poetic melange (in which he ultimately incorporated phenomenology too). Barthes found society to be made up of hidden systems of signification (1972). Existing at all layers of society; these, in his view, were the real glue holding societies together – 'any system of signs, whatever their substance and limits; images, gestures, musical sounds, objects, and the complex associations of all these, which form the content of ritual, convention, and public entertainment: these constitute, if not languages, at least systems of signification' (Barthes, 1967: p. 9). For his *Mythologies*, mirroring the attention paid to popular culture by Antonio Gramsci (1971), Barthes analysed various expressions of culture: wrestlers, films, books, detergents, the iconography of Abbè Pierre, Greta Garbo, the latest model of Citroen, French elections, cooking, wine, and milk, photo exhibitions, etc. To him, the semiotician's duty was no less than unveiling the logic of the hidden sign systems in which humans live. Taking Saussure's 'sign' a step further, Barthes sliced the signifier in half. Barthes saw the sign as, in reality, characterised by the dimensions of denotation and connotation. We introduced these above, but now we explore them in greater depth. While the former indicates the thing out there itself, the *analogon*, the latter speaks of the manner in which a society to a certain extent communicates what it thinks of the thing. Hence, it enters the field of ideology. A flag could denote a particular country for Barthes, yet it may also connote a particular set of values. The US flag, for instance, represents the land of freedom to some and for others a capitalist way of life that is harming the planet. In his detailing of the procedures of connotation in the arena of photography, Barthes addresses several qualities that we will unpack further when laying out Chapter 5's roadmap for analysing images. The main point of his analysis for the present discussion, however, is that photographs possess a double-layer character: they are at once a message with no code (the analogue) and one with a code (the treatment). This dualism of Barthes famously translated into another key distinction, one that has inspired scholars all over the world. From analysing photographs, he suggested that they comprise two dimensions, the *studium* and *punctum*. He regarded the former as 'a kind of general, enthusiastic commitment without special acuity' (1993: p. 26). He cast the *studium* as belonging to the order of 'liking[,] not loving' (p. 27), as aimed not at moving and impelling the viewer but, rather, at politely offering context and information. In his view, the *punctum* constitutes the most important, and most mysterious, aspect of photography. About this he wrote: 'I will not seek it out (as I invest the field of the *studium* with my sovereign consciousness) it is this element which rises from the scene, shoots out of it like an arrow and pierces me' (p. 26). In a sense, then, even though at times associated with a purely semiotic approach *á la* Saussure, with the *punctum* he came closer to Peirce's underscoring of interaction, identifying an affective, even magical quality in images. It is the latter aspect that will be more specifically addressed in the following section.

3.1.5.2 *Moving from Signs to Images as Experienced*

While semiotic approaches allow us to disentangle some of the ways in which images have a particular code that may affect us, Barthes's recommendation to focus on the *punctum* moves the focus toward the experience of images. This is the area that holds interest for phenomenological scholarship. Shifting attention away from signs and toward experience, phenomenology is conventionally conceived of, as we hinted at above, as the study of direct experience, of phenomena, of lifeworld or consciousness. Phenomenology owes its beginnings to Edmund Husserl (1859–1938) but for most readers, probably is associated more closely with works by Merleau-Ponty (1908–1961), Heidegger (1889–1976), and – especially importantly for the social sciences – Alfred Schütz (1973) (and his student Thomas Luckmann). Husserl saw phenomenology as the systematic study of the structures of consciousness and the phenomena that appear in it. Merleau-Ponty, in turn, always foregrounding a sense of intersubjectivity and relationality, suggested that phenomenology looks upon human beings as destined for the world (1945/ 2005: p. xii). Humans are interwoven with the world and hence with what they observe. Therefore, phenomenology is not interested in objectivity; rather, it rejects such a logic and focuses instead on the study of events that we might conventionally qualify as subjective, such as emotions and perceptions. Interested in the ways in which specific percepts evolve, phenomenology thus puts forth another vision of what science can be. In that endeavour, phenomenology strongly stresses the primacy of the body. In the corresponding vision, we perceive the world through our bodies; we are embodied subjects, involved in existence; and we perceive phenomena and only after that reflect on them via the medium of language or thought etc. In a way, the enquiry is a bit like continuing to act in the manner of children who learn by touching, listening, and looking before they start to speak and produce verbally rational reflections. This attitude marks an important point of contact between phenomenology and ethnography. Both highlight the presence of a sensing subject at the centre of the enquiry, stressing the importance of the body. Research rooted in participant observation and other types of qualitative approach are anchored in an interest in understanding different modes of being, and any such understanding is firmly embodied. Ethnography extends phenomenology's initial interest in self-reflection to an interest in the other (this was Schütz's main concern in expanding on Husserl's early work). The stance of phenomenology accords appropriate room for exploring materiality, tactility, multisensoriality, and also – especially – performativity and affectivity. Phenomenology, we claim, is of particular utility for addressing non-Western, non-hegemonic, and non-dualistic visual practices, not in a self-centred way but via foregrounding of solid awareness that humans perceive their environments in complex affective and embodied ways, which play out differently since they hinge on where one grew up etc. It is also a mode of being and is seen as useful for sensitising researchers to their own processes of forming understandings and meaning-making.

In work expressing this emphasis, Pinney's analysis of popular religious chromolithographs in rural India showed how visual practices, in a context of Indian popular culture, are a matter of the above-mentioned corpothetics rather than Western aesthetics (2001: p. 157). In his words, this is an 'embodied, corporeal aesthetics' standing in opposition to '"disinterested" representation, which over-cerebralizes and textualizes the image' (Pinney, 2004: p. 8). His research participants prioritised questions of efficacy rather than representation. The divine is, in this setting of popular Hindu imagery, understood to be literally present in the image. Here, as we already addressed in Chapter 2, the act of seeing, as Babb (1981) and Eck (1998) have shown, involves reciprocity. With divinity literally embedded in them, images become, in Hindu contexts, living things: 'For many centuries, most Hindus have taken it for granted that the religious images they place in temples and home shrines for purposes of worship are alive' (Davis, 1997: p. 6). In contexts such as these, the image transcends itself, foregrounding instead the act of seeing as the core of the spiritual activity. Here, images are 'things that matter' (Edwards, 2006: p. 28). They are to be touched, stroked, and worshipped. They should be honoured with milk, honey, water, colours, etc. One should play with them, mirror oneself in them. It is in adherence to this logic that Hindu icons, similarly to Byzantine paintings, are decorated with metals and a plethora of other playful elements. As the notion of *Darsan* (as discussed in Section 2.1) implies, the act of looking is also an act of being looked at here, one of ongoing inter-penetration leading to full immersion in the image. As Eck (1998) expresses these conditions, 'because the image is a form of the supreme lord, it is precisely the image that facilitates and enhances the close relationship of the worshipper and God and makes possible the deepest outpouring of emotions in worship' (p. 46).

In this understanding, one becomes 'what one sees' (Babb, 1981: p. 297) in an act that could probably be inserted within the logic of contagion of qualities and hence of magic. A 'liquid logic' (Dundes, 1980) seems characteristic of this particular way of gazing, which calls to mind the insight into relational objects that Edwards obtained from looking at the role of photographs among Aboriginal Australian people. Again, central in articulating histories that have been suppressed, photographs are not only part of the visual realm but constitute an element in a much broader performance. They are, as we saw, held and sung to. And in the course of the interaction they hold us and they transform into sound, of everything from individuals' voices to a vast tapestry of oral history expressing relations between specific individuals who interact with each other by means of the images.

Scholars and artists working at the juncture of art history and theology have likewise pointed out the kinds of relations with the sacred and the divine that images allow for, at least for those following relevant systems of belief. For example, Florensky expressed interest in regarding images such as sacred icons (1993) as a passage. He portrayed these images as portals allowing human beings to move across the border that separates the worlds of earthly and of celestial matters (Florensky, 1977). For him, the image grants access to a world 'ontologically reflexed', a world upside-down where truth can be perceived anew, with fresh eyes. Nancy too addressed this dimension of images. Regarding the part it plays in the improbable paradox of being 'a thing that is not the thing', he conceptualised an image as a particular kind of presence, material in exhibiting, bringing to light, 'setting forth' (2005: p. 22) – though always through a distance and articulating a distinction. The image is here, but it approaches the viewer from there, 'across a distance'. In other words, images do offer themselves but only **as images**. That is why Nancy considered images sacred. The sacredness resides in their capacity to be right there and yet be 'distinct'. Nancy's reminder that 'sacred' etymologically references separation, setting aside, being removed or cut off, or withdrawing stresses his point that what is sacred has to be at a distance. It is something that cannot be touched, as many scholars of rituals have pointed out (Evdomikov, 1970). An image, Nancy says, 'crosses the distance of the withdrawal even while maintaining it through its mark as an image' (2005: p. 4). In this framing, then, an image is simultaneously withdrawal and passage, albeit 'a passage that [...] does not pass' (p. 4).

3.1.5.3 Proceeding From Experience to Politics

A focus on the experience of images shows how conventional models of signification tend to fall short of coping with the role of the body, multiple ontologies, and varied forms of agency, especially as we try to grapple with different ways of understanding and living in the world. An image being the sacred, let alone the divine, is at odds with many Western assumptions underpinning how we understand ourselves as the active meaning-makers in our encounters with images. That said, the long history of approaching images as something to be desired while also something to be feared attests that they are not easily tamed. They dwell in our minds, bodies, environments, and systems of signification (Freedberg, 1989). As Belting (2011) has suggested, questions of images are often questions of faith, on both the historical and global stage.

The experiential side of images has been studied through the lens of iconology, which has, similarly to the study of signs, transited from heeding more rigid structures to foregrounding rich interplay between experience and specific visual forms. Iconology too has an important point of contact with ethnography. This has to do with how it features the notion of context. For an iconologist, a picture must be seen in relation to the context surrounding it. Its journey is important. Originating with Aby Warburg (1866–1929), who mentioned the term for the first time in 1912, iconology probably found its most well-known advocate in Panofsky, who after the Second World War embarked on an attempt to turn art history into an objective scientific endeavour of sorts. According to him, any image exists on three distinct levels: pre-iconographical description, iconographical analysis, and iconological interpretation. Encompassing different layers of information, these three when combined make up the terrain where an iconologist should move. Firstly, the pre-iconographical description focuses on how a specific picture is composed, with what kinds of materials; the focus is on forms, colours, and general atmosphere (Böhme, 2013). The iconographical analysis elaborates on the allegories, symbols, and narratives inherent in the image. But it is the third layer that is of particular importance for our discussion. At its best, it contextualises the image in question to some political terrain, asking why that particular image emerged and what kind of work it does in a far broader landscape of visual culture.

Later developments in the study of images and visual culture have brought calls for a new iconology, one that discusses the complexity of images sensibly without reducing the analysis to transposition to a rigid system of signification. For example, Mitchell coined the term 'critical iconology' to denote a 'self-theorizing visual culture' (1986), Belting recommended an anthropology of the image as a new iconology, and Horst Bredekamp (2015) and colleagues applied iconology to the terrain of scientific imagery in a manner that entered dialogue with Warburg and with science and technology studies.

Whatever specific approach you might choose, attending to iconological description facilitates discussing the power of images, not just in individual-level and collective experience but also as tools in power struggles, as carriers of political positioning and agendas. A true terrain of trade, of 'interdisciplinary indiscipline' (per Mitchell, 1995), visual culture therefore can be seen as a space in which the tools and analysis trajectories that we have 'met' thus far meet and merge with political and critical analysis. Images in this space both 'do' and 'mean', simultaneously. Against this backdrop, the single-lens camera, embodying the politics of Renaissance perspective, cast a long shadow as it became not only symbolic of an entire era of imperial expansion of Western powers but also a tool suited to enabling that expansion. An instrument for 'worlding the world' (Spivak, 1985), the photographic camera made it 'possible not only to think of the world as a single entity, but to traverse and administer it as one' (McQuire, 1997). Changing the way in which we saw things, the camera genuinely made it possible to think of the world, in Heidegger's phrasing, as a picture, a revolution receiving particular attention in relation to the first published photograph of Earth from outer space. This picture can be viewed, measured, and hence controlled, in considerable contrast against Earth itself, as Joanna Zylinska (2015) argued in her work on nonhuman photography.

In parallel with this, images have also been central to the activity of narrating for (and hence also cultivating attraction to) diversity. Here we inevitably stumble into the territory of a patronising Western attitude to Middle Eastern, Asian, and North African societies, which Edward Said labelled Orientalism (1978). A system of representation that creates an essentialised difference between 'the Orient' and 'the West', Orientalism increasingly produced images of other cultures as 'alienized and essentialized, [...] reduced to a timeless essence' (Carrier, 1995: p. 2). The images referred to above are both visual and literary within the schema we described in connection with optical and graphic media, as well as *ekphrasis*. We can find them in paintings, literature, and photography. Regarding the latter, postcolonialism scholar Ali Behdad has concluded that 'the Orientalist photograph thus "nurtured" the desire for the Orient, helping its development as a cultural phenomenon throughout the West' (2016: p. 19).

Orientalism cast Eastern cultures as the antithesis of the West or, rather, produced them as antithesis of the West. These images were alluring, staged, often eroticised, and always created in opposition to some image of the West: 'The Orient exists for the West, and is constructed by and in relation to the West. It is a mirror image of what is inferior and alien (Other) to the West' (Komalesha, 2008: p. 2). Let us unpick its highly pertinent entanglements with the image and politics a bit more.

In the logic of Orientalism, agents of a West that saw itself as developed, dynamic, rational, modern, etc. essentialised 'Oriental' societies accordingly as static and undeveloped. Dualism hence thrives at the very root of Orientalist depictions. These build on classical colonial dichotomies that, as Akhil Gupta explained, anchored 'the West' to progress, development, science, technology, rationality, order, and modernity and 'the Orient' to stasis, stagnation, underdevelopment, poverty, superstition, disorder, and (thereby) tradition (1998; see also Cohen, 1998; Spencer, 1995: p. 236). Serving interests of imperial power, Western imagination hence was allowed to see 'Eastern' cultures and people as both alluring and a threat to Western civilisation. Reflecting 'the wishes of the westerners, their ambitions, their obsessions and symptoms' (Faris, 2002: p. 78), Orientalism in some respects follows the logic that Adam Kuper pointed to many decades ago when describing essentialisations produced by anthropology – 'modern society was defined above all by the territorial state, the monogamous family and private property. Primitive society therefore must have been nomadic, ordered by blood ties, sexually promiscuous' (1988: p. 4).

Therefore, the scholar should regard Orientalism not merely as an ideological discourse (a power narrative etc.) or as a neutral concept safely wrapped in art history but, rather more, as a network of aesthetic, economic, and political relationships that were maintained and upheld by particular images. Through politics, then, images may become ideological in the true sense of the term. Namely, Antoine Destutt de Tracy, who coined the term 'ideology' in 1796, understood it as the science of ideas. Indeed, as Mitchell has argued (1986), the word idea's etymological connections to seeing and the relationship between form and the notion of the image indicate that iconological and ideological analyses have more in common that what we might see at first glance.

In addition, in its production of alterity, Orientalism went beyond consolidation and frequent production of ethnic and 'racial' identities by intervening also in arenas of neurotypicality, gender normativity, and sexual standards. In Said's account, the depiction of harems and odalisques was central to Orientalist imaginaries. For instance, in breaking the taboo of invisibility of the harem, Orientalist paintings and, later on, photography reproduced and strengthened the power imbalance between the looker and what is looked at. They favoured a gendered gaze that empowers the looker and disempowers the one gazed at, thus leaving the latter in the position of an object of the former's claim to a 'right to look' (cf. Mirzoeff, 2011).

Proceeding from a psychoanalytical understanding of the notion of the gaze, Laura Mulvey coined the term 'the male gaze' in the 1970s to elucidate the gendered nature of exchanges of looks in the context of cinema. Her analysis, published in 1975, laid bare how cinema conventions tend to reproduce patriarchal relations with the woman relegated to the role of an object of men's pleasure. Mulvey's reflections resonate with Berger's observation that in much of Western art history 'men act, women appear' (1972). This somewhat narrow view's dualistic reduction has since been challenged in a variety of fields, among them that of queer theory, importantly (see Mayne, 2000). Nevertheless, the power asymmetries in looking relations remain significant, and these continue to be gendered in many cases.

As this wading into gazes shows for varied terrain, in multiple environments, images are clearly a part of the project of producing what Foucault (2020) called docile bodies – i.e., those bodies that would fit the needs of a modern neoliberal state. From Orientalist imagery to depictions echoing the male gaze to manifold examples of today's institutional or scientific photography portraying colonised subjects, mental patients, prisoners, etc., images have been essential in the construction of a host of ideas of normality that we are finally starting to identify and attempting to overcome.

The perspectives described above – studying images as signs, moving from signs to experiences, and then turning one's attention from experiences to politics – offer you an array of possibilities for embarking on the terrain of image analysis. These are usefully thought of together with a focus on the look as a medium and on the materiality, affectivity, and performativity of visual media and of the image emerging within particular ways of looking. We invite you to look at these as elements that can be combined with each other and set off in mutual contrast too. They are anything but mutually exclusive paths. Each theoretical perspective addressed can be interlaced with another to help you explore the multifaceted nature of image worlds in the best way possible, although we also need to be aware of theory-to-theory discrepancies. Any theory-based approach foregrounding the role of practices can be – and, in fact, must be – an act of 'assemblage' (Latour, 2005), emerging as you follow the actors (be they humans, visual media, particular images, or a range of phenomena discussed as beyond-the-human). This brings us around again to Mitchell's words 'interdisciplinary indiscipline', and on the following pages several examples manifest how this assemblage can be put to use on the terrain we are exploring. You will find examples of how the theorising done so far can be applied to specific cases and territory. The next section of the chapter begins presenting these, by focusing on one of the main tensions in studying images that make claims to 'objectivity': that between the icon and the index.

3.2 The Tension Between the Icon and the Index

If images emerge during the interaction between a viewer and a picture, who or what do we see then when we look at an image? What characteristics describe the depicted, and how does the depicted show itself to us?

These are some of the oldest questions in portraiture, and those involved have generally taken a keen interest in directing how a portrait 'should be' viewed and understood. Is the purpose to ennoble what is depicted, or perhaps to vilify it? Or should the depicted appear as an example of a social group, and hence re-present (i.e. stand in for), more than a single person? Perhaps the idea is to focus on the singularity of a particular face instead? These questions have been recurrently tackled by means of many, very different depiction techniques, which range from various modes of self-display of a person being depicted to intricate ways in which the depiction is steered via guidelines (as is the case in passport photos) or machinic assemblages when images need to be processed by machines. While these techniques are intended to guide both the viewer and the producer of the image, in practice a 'correct' way of seeing is difficult to circumscribe precisely **because** the image that gets seen by a human being emerges only within an interaction, in the temporal unfolding of the event of seeing the image.

One tension that tends to remain in all depictions is the delicate balance between the 'icon' and the 'index'. At the fulcrum is the question of the relationship between what we see (colours, forms, outlines, edges, etc.) and what is supposed to lie outside the frame of the image (e.g., are there colours, forms, or outlines formed in order to depict a person, an angel, a miracle, or dust?). While broader iconographic and iconological analyses are useful for deciphering specific meanings of images – and the kinds of visual orders that they often contribute to – we begin our discussion here by going back to Peirce's distinction between the icon and the index (which we briefly introduced in the previous chapter). This seemingly simple distinction is particularly useful for contemplating the relationship between what we see and what we consider to be known in light of what we see.

3.2.1 *Peirce's Distinctions*

The semiological approach that Peirce developed in the late nineteenth century is one of the major sign theories still in use today. Care should be taken to distinguish it from more structuralist accounts, such as that of Saussure. In particular, Peirce's pragmatic, practice-theory-based approach grants greater contextual interpretive flexibility than other, more linguistically oriented approaches.

Of special importance for Peirce's theory is his keen awareness that all signs have iconic, indexical, and symbolic dimensions; that is, all signs are triadic. Any sign that could be thought of as purely iconic, indexical, or symbolic is largely a theoretical abstraction and not to be found empirically. In the discussion that follows, we will consider the icon, then the index, and finally the symbol.

In this triadic understanding of signs, an icon is 'a sign that refers to the Object it denotes merely by virtue of characters of its own which it possesses, just the same, whether any such Object exists or not' (Peirce, 1988: p. 291). Accordingly, an icon is a type of sign that is visible or decipherable because of particular surface markings on an image-carrier, be they made by subtraction (e.g., carving or denting) or by addition of surface materials (e.g., application of oil pigments, gluing on of paper or cloth, or weaving). In consequence, the iconicity of a sign is always medium-specific, meaning that specific qualities of iconicity are produced only by corresponding image-carriers.

What frequently remains confusing for many image analysts is the suggestion by Peirce that '[m]ost icons, if not all, are likenesses of their objects' (Peirce, 1988: p. 13). This seems to imply the existence of a relationship between the icon and the object depicted that is based on likeness. In day-to-day life we have clearly learnt to decipher a likeness between a portrait of a person and the embodied person standing in front of us (it might be an excellent likeness or not a very convincing one). For purposes of analysis, however, we recommend that the reader stick to the first definition of an icon presented above, under which an icon refers to an object denoted merely by virtue of its own properties or character. To capture the icon dimension, Peirce characterised a hypothetical purely iconic sign thus: 'A pure icon is independent of any purpose. It serves as sign solely and simply by exhibiting the quality it serves to signify' (1988: p. 306). Peirce provides as an example a geometrical diagram, which is of utmost value for studying the world, although it does not 'exist in the real world'. An icon of that nature conveys 'no positive or factual information; for it affords no assurance that there is any such thing in nature' (Peirce quoted in Jappy, 2013: loc. 3545). No such thing as a pure icon exists in the real world. It is an abstraction only; after all, Peirce's sign theory stresses the triadic structure of every sign (as icon, index, and symbol).

While some commentators exhibit a tendency to focus on signs as either wholly iconic or entirely indexical (or symbolic), we find the triadic understanding of signs useful for considering the multiple dimensions to any sign. To facilitate discussing the kind of likeness presented iconically and its relationship to the environment (e.g., being the likeness of a particular person), Peirce introduced the useful notion of the index, which has become a staple of image theory, particularly in the field of photography. For Peirce, the index is a sign that 'refers to its object not so much because of any similarity' but, rather, by association because of existing in dynamic (including spatial) connection both with the individual object, on one hand, and with 'the senses or the memory of the person for whom it serves as a sign, on the other' (Peirce, 1988: p. 305).

The index, hence, is a dimension of the sign that stands in dynamic connection with the object it indexes but also, and just as much, with the senses and mind of the person who is in relation to it. For Peirce, the index is a relational category, not an ontological statement about the world as such. This indexical interrelation among object, sign, and perceiving body greatly affords understanding the situatedness and contextuality of interpretations. Many scholars remain content to point out indexical interrelations between images and the objects depicted; however, if an image 'refers to the Object that it denotes by virtue of being really affected by that Object' (Peirce, 1988: p. 291), the importance of the perceiving body in this constellation cannot be overstated. This is particularly so since 'being really affected' may

66 *Visual Studies*

be understood in various ways. Its meaning changes if we move from a uniform ontology and worldview to the multiplicity of understandings of environments that exist globally, whether grounded in domains such as quantum physics, Hindu scriptures, Buddhist practices, animism, human–animal relationships, or any of various other ways in which we culturally learn to focus our attention (cf. Descola, 2013).

3.2.2 Photorealism

A crucial pillar for a triadic understanding of signs is awareness that the associated indexical character particular to a sign is lost if its object is removed (see Peirce, 1988: p. 304). This is especially true in the oft-discussed cases of iconic depictions that simulate indexicality – such as photorealistic computer-generated imagery. There, photorealistic iconicity serves to symbolise a particular kind of indexicality that the perceiving body has learnt to associate with indexicality, while the indexicality associated with being photographically present is not there anymore, once the visual medium for visual display has changed (see Figure 3.1.)

Computer-learning systems known as generative adversarial networks have been put to use for photorealistic depictions now employed in such settings as advertisements, social-media posts, and job sites. With this technology,

Figure 3.1 Picture created with the help of StyleGAN2 for the website Thispersondoesnotexist.com.

photorealistic iconicity evokes the idea of indexicality for a living observer even though the images depict people who do not exist. While these images do not index a living body depicted in the image, from the standpoint of the triadic understanding of signs it would not be correct to claim that these images do not index at all. But what do they index? These kinds of questions are particularly important today as artificial intelligence grows better and better at emulating audiovisual media that traditionally have been considered to be 'trustworthy'.

Interestingly, scholarship ever since the 1990s has held the indexicality of digital imagery to be unclear (cf. Mitchell, 1994; von Amelunxen et al., 1996). Digital images are used both in service of tracing and mapping real, lived environments (by such means as digital cameras, photogrammetry, satellite imaging, and lidar) and in order to simulate fictitious worlds (in animation, films, games, and various special effects). They are used both for measuring what is out there and to dream up what never has been and might never be. Accordingly, digital images may index outside environments that have been traced or, just as well, may not have any associative connections to them other than symbolic ones.

The index is of value also for considering the means with which pictures are made visible and hence the effect of the index on the iconic qualities of images. Choosing a particular sort of slide film and a specific set of optical lenses for impressing photographic images within a film camera might favour specific colours/textures or a particular atmosphere that may well be difficult, if not impossible, to produce by other means. This is a factor in why, while there are various digital technologies available, quite a few photographers and artists continue to use analogue cameras, develop film chemically, and print images in a darkroom. This example clarifies that all images index also the technical means by which images are made visible, along with the carrier media that are employed to exhibit the images in a specific environment (e.g., wooden statues, liquid-crystal displays, barite photographic paper, or a painter's canvas). This indexicality oftentimes functions as a diagnostic criterion in work to distinguish, for example, an optical-camera-origin photograph from a photorealistic computer-generated one, even though empirical research has shown that professional photo editors and photojournalists cannot make this distinction anymore by merely looking at images displayed on a screen (Lehmuskallio et al., 2019).

We tend to fall prey to category errors in associating iconic qualities of signs with indexical ones. While photorealism is a pervasive cultural form that carries this association, it behoves us to remember the particularity and specificity of photorealistic iconicity. Photorealism, in the ways in which it is usually rendered (e.g., in output from generative adversarial networks), relies on monoperspectivism in its division of the picture space, coupled with a restricted range of optics and focal planes in the rendering of the image. Partly in conjunction with the specific perspective it depends on, photorealism is a symbolic form (per Panofsky, 1991) that orders and arranges the ways in which we think of the image and its effects on the environment. This recognition leads us to ask what the symbolic means here.

Thus we arrive at the third dimension of signs that Peirce identified: the symbolic, which most of us are familiar with from everyday parlance. He defined a symbol to be 'a sign which refers to the Object that it denotes by virtue of a law, usually an association of general ideas, which operates to cause the Symbol to be interpreted as referring to that Object' (Peirce, 1988: p. 292). Here, 'law' refers to not a written codex signed into force by some parliament but a codified and widely enough understood association between a sign and its object. While many images, photographs especially, get discussed in indexical terms (because of the assumed trace-like relations between image and depicted object) and images become visible as images because of their specific iconicity, it is the symbolic dimension that provides them with particular currency in the realm of images. Consider photorealism again. It is societally relevant primarily because of the symbolic uses within which it is involved. It might function in legal proceedings, mourning the dead, or carrying images of loved ones in one's pocket. In legal settings, photorealistically depicting that which is to be remembered supports making one's case, in mourning the dead it reminds viewers of the earlier presence of a living being, and the renderings of loved ones carried with us function to activate affective pathways related to love.

But digital cameras allow for presenting the captured likenesses in visualisations very different from these also. One example is diagrammatic depiction of biometric information. Alternatively, the processing might produce human-readable textual metadata or output that only machine-vision systems can 'see' (non-representative images such as the 'operative images' we will discuss later). Therefore, digital cameras are usefully understood as sensors, because digital files afford merging with a vast spectrum of databases, for a range of visualisation options, as well as for transposing surface markings with light to different registers – such as those of text, sound, numbers, or equations (Lehmuskallio, 2016). Amidst these rich possibilities for variation, employing photorealism is an active cultural choice, based on 1) assumptions as to what it can achieve (e.g., eliciting a sense of trust, asserting authority, or conveying the feel of a certain era) and on 2) particular means of organising pictorial space, usually following Cartesian perspectivism (as we discussed on our journey through history). Just as Cartesian perspectivism is, also photorealism is a symbolic form (see also Hausken 2024).

Together, the icon, index, and symbol constitute a triad that we consider useful for distinguishing the dimensions of signs such that we can trace their specific ways of suggesting interpretations. In image analysis, there is particular merit to focusing on the interrelations between the icon and index. After all, particular forms of iconicity are taken to refer to indexical relationships even though this indexicality might be mainly in the eye of the beholder, not a factual relation between a sign and its object to be deciphered by others.

3.2.3 Analysing a Photograph

Take a look at the photograph depicted in Figure 3.2. Study it closely. What kinds of iconic qualities does it possess? Look at the colours, surface properties, sharp, and fuzzy edges, and modes of occlusion. How is the picture space ordered? Which areas are rich with detail, and which less so?

Pay attention at first to the iconic qualities, the 'how' of depiction, the visual form (this is the pre-iconographic description in an iconological analysis). Then take a look at who or what is depicted. What sort of cultural expertise renders you able to say who or what you see? List everything as specifically as you can, and then contemplate why you came to your conclusions. If you are seeing hair, what causes you to interpret iconic surface qualities of this sort as hair? Or, should you see a young woman here, how did you arrive at the conclusion that what is depicted is young, or to be categorised as a woman? Again, be as specific as possible.

Then, focus on indexical dimensions with the picture. If we are to be able to infer indexical qualities of images just by looking at them, we need to

Figure 3.2 Photograph of a framed print for museum display purposes.

Source: Maija Tammi: One of Them Is a Human #1, Erica. Archival pigment print, 60 × 65 cm, framed. Photograph by Miikka Pirinen.

have some mental model of how the image came about. Was it produced in a well-lit studio with a 6×6 film camera, then developed chemically and finally printed on barite paper? Or is it a snapshot from the latest mobile camera-phone, with in-built image-processing algorithms smoothing out surface structures? Might it perhaps be a computer-generated image based on a text prompt and created with a Generative Pre-trained Transformer 3 model using deep learning to render images?

Increasingly, with advances in digital images, we will not be able to tell the difference by looking at the images alone (see Lehmuskallio et al., 2019); we need contextual information, on how the images came to be. Figure 3.2 is an interesting example in that it was submitted to and shortlisted in the 2017 National Portrait Gallery Taylor Wessing Photographic Portrait Prize competition because of a tension that may arise in looking at it. While many viewers saw this depiction as a well-lit professionally shot photo of a young woman with Asian features, others experienced uncanniness when looking at the surface of the skin, although they were not able to point to a precise origin for this feeling. The uncanniness was heightened by the title of the series, 'One of Them Is a Human', which directly thematises the boundaries of being a human and spotlights frequently debated human–machine relations and the relations between humans and other living organisms.

For iconicity, successful pictorial rendering of skin is of special importance, since human skin often serves us as a specific criterion in identifying someone as human rather than an organism of another sort or a machine construct. Human skin is formed of layers: the epidermis, the dermis, and the subcutis. Each of these three layers of tissue has distinct functions in protecting us from the environment and for the reception of sensory stimuli. While photographic images such as that in Figure 3.2 are unable to reproduce skin as a physical medium, they do render a representation of skin on a digital display or when printed on paper. Interestingly, a plausible photographic representation of skin can be achieved by photographing other materials too, a phenomenon that photographer Maija Tammi took advantage of for this image (and, in another example, one that food photographers exploit when using acrylic or glass cubes to simulate ice cubes in a drink).

Tammi's photograph is of the android Erica, whose skin is made of silicone and whose face was carved by averaging facial images of 30 women whom Erica's creator, Hirohito Ishiguro, considered to be beautiful.[6] Therefore, the portrait photograph indexes an android created at the ATR Institute in Kyoto, Japan, whose face, in turn, indexes the average from the 30 photographs, which informed the design of the eyes, nose, and other facial features. A gendered gaze is applied to moulding silicone, while it is also questioned via the portrait photograph highlighting the feminine character of the android created. This chain of representations (cf. Latour, 1999), far from exceptional in its length, attests to how single photographs tend to index a wide range of pictorial practices, which get ordered in particular, culturally accepted (or contested) ways with the ambition of conveying iconically specific meanings. This image makes use of a neutral grey backdrop, which is a familiar staple of portrait photography more broadly (including that for passports and school yearbooks), and a conventionalised pose, with the upper body visible and tilted approximately 60 degrees to the right.

Tammi played with an age-old trick of consciousness, displaying a trickster figure that appears initially as one thing (a portrait of a young woman) but is later revealed to be something else (a portrait of an android). Ishiguro, on the other hand, as the creator of the android provides a further image-theoretically productive reading. He explained: 'I wanted to be an oil painter because I was so interested in the human itself, that I wanted to represent it'. His interest in the human narrowed to an interest in representation, with oil painting initially selected as the visual-media mechanism for pursuing this. When one considers the great portrait painters from Rembrandt to Velázquez, whose many masterworks were created with the medium of oils, one can readily understand why Ishiguro sought to be an oil painter in aims of representing humans. While his choice to create androids instead was not clearly explained in interviews (he might have moved on from oil painting for any of several reasons, from insufficient painting skills to the funding available for robotics), we can see that Ishiguro does not adhere to Western conceptions of animate and inanimate beings. He maintains that Erica the android is alive in particular ways. We can, hence, further refine our analysis.

In a film by Ilinca Calugareanu, who studied filmmaking at Manchester's Granada Centre for Visual Anthropology, Ishiguro continued his musings: 'In Japan, we never distinguish between people and the others. We basically think everything has a soul. So therefore we believe Erica has a soul, like us'.[7] The notion that Erica possesses a soul complicates the relations of agency in Figure 3.2, because from that perspective we might be left unsure of how much the photograph was produced by Tammi as photographer vs. the production process being the other way around, with Erica the photographee perhaps being the more active director of the situation. In this constellation, the relations of indexicality could be traced from an alternative direction – the photograph itself might be to a lesser extent an index of a rather passive Erica and might show rather more an active depictee who exercised agency over the choreography of the photographic act. Was it Erica's soul which made the image emerge in the first place, directing the photographer Tammi to the puzzle in the first place?

The clearest conclusion following from the preceding contemplation is that any analysis of Figure 3.2 remains partial if it is conducted only by focusing on looking at an image and deciphering its indexical relations through reference to an assumed act of depiction. Instead, the image should be understood as a part of social relationships, within which the image has its particular role to play. This is why we accentuate the role of practices within which images are embedded.

3.2.4 Awareness of Agency

This stance on images is related to one that Alfred Gell developed in his work on agent–patient relationships, suggesting that '*persons* or "social agents" are, in certain contexts, substituted for by art objects' (Gell, 1998: p. 5; emphasis in original). While the term 'art' raises particular expectations in many Western readers' minds, in this context an art object is understood to be any material artefact that plays a meaningful role in social relationships, whether considered to belong to the realm of the Western art world or not. Gell even suggests that, in some cases, human bodies can take the position of the 'art object', positing that 'an idol in a temple believed to be the body of the divinity, and a spirit-medium, who likewise provides the divinity with a temporary body, are treated as theoretically on par, despite the fact that the former is an artefact and the latter is a human being' (1998: p. 7). For Gell, art objects hence should be approached not only for their aesthetic and formal qualities. They are not merely signs, codes etc. Rather, they were intended as performative items, with the art object being endowed with a form of agency of its own. This gets mediated by indexes, motivates responses, and elicits interpretations and engaging reactions.

Gell's theory of agent–patient relationships is a theory of mediation, within which the parameters for the possible or permissible are not set in advance. It allows for serious consideration of the various and multifaceted ways in which images may participate in social relationships and at times gain agency in forms that more narrowly conceived semiotic theories of meaning cannot accommodate. This kind of work directs attention to what appear to be irrational mechanisms of performance and utterance, not in order to medicalise them but to inform understanding. Religious processions, fan cultures, pilgrimages to museums such as the Louvre, and various other seemingly irrational manifestations become decipherable by means of a focus on social relationships and the forms of mediation they entail.

For solid analytical examination of images' roles in relationships, Gell suggests focusing on the index, since it is often the keystone for explaining causal inferences of some kind. For instance, an indexical relation is evoked in the suggestion that a particular person was sitting in front of a camera so as to be iconically visible in a photographic image being viewed much later. The causal inference, which on occasion creates tensions (such as those examined above) between iconicity and indexicality, tends to rely on a cognitive operation that Peirce denoted as abduction.

Abduction is a form of reasoning that is employed to explain a particular circumstance, such as 'apparent irrationality', by supposing it to be covered by a more general rule. The operation is inductive in the sense that it functions to predict an otherwise seemingly irrational circumstance. Abduction does not necessarily yield valid conclusions; as an everyday form of reasoning, it is not sustained by strict methods of empirical science. The utility of abduction lies instead in restricting the set of possible explanations, and indeed it commonly is employed to that end.

It is in this sense that Ishiguro's assertion that Erica the android has a soul becomes understandable. Ishiguro outlined an abduction that he presented as commonplace in Japan: everything has a soul. Scientific experimentation cannot prove this claim to be true. How would one scientifically measure 'having a soul'? The conclusion is neither necessarily false nor necessarily true. It might be either. Hence, abduction is a suitable form of reasoning for a range of cultural and religious activities that may be delicate, elaborate, and complex. When applied to image analysis, this technique for rendering our environments predictable tends to proceed from diagnostic elements that are iconically visible in an image. The diagnostic criteria for limiting the range of explanations to be considered might centre on, for example, 'anomalies' in facial depictions. For instance, the lower-left portion of the face portrayed in Figure 3.2 could suggest indexing the image as not having been produced by optical media at all. Perhaps deep-learning algorithms generated it. Without further contextual knowledge, this posited indexical relation cannot be confirmed. Indeed, the conclusion often remains a matter of contextual knowledge and/or faith.

3.2.5 Studying Photographers

In an empirical study conducted before the widespread emergence of AI forms of photorealistic image rendering (cited above in passing), researchers asked professional photographers and photo editors in the news and journalism field to distinguish photorealistic computer-generated images from photos taken with a camera and optical media in real-world environments (Lehmuskallio et al., 2019). Interestingly, most participants thought themselves able to distinguish between the two even though major advances in photorealistic rendering had already begun making this difficult. Surprisingly for the participants, quantitative analysis of their responses proved them unable to do so. The researchers then turned the metaphorical lens on the professionals more directly.

The researchers iteratively analysed the *ekphrases*. Participants supplied reasons for their choices both in writing and in a focus-group discussion later. The authors characterised the professionals' rationale for the distinction between photographs and computer-generated images as involving 1) understandings of what photographs look like (i.e., the iconic quality of photographic images), 2) how photographic technologies (such as lenses, sensor size, and resolution) indexically influence the iconic quality of photographic images (e.g., via distortion, lens flare, blur, and bokeh), 3) what kinds of environments to be photographed even exist (i.e., which indexical relations between environments and photographic images can exist at all), and 4) how photographs differ from other kinds of images more broadly in a discourse on visual media – focusing hence on the symbolic dimension.

The quantitative analysis had demonstrated the participants' inability to make these distinctions correctly. This made it clear that their attempts at distinguishing stemmed from abductions that relied on probable answers and rules of thumb. What is especially interesting in the explanations given is that these appear quite convincing. Abductions do make sense in the moment of analysis. For example, one participant supposed a given image to be a photograph because of the '[a]ngle of view, distortion due to a wide-angle lens and the vanishing of the horizon', and another's identification of an image as a photograph was rooted in '[t]he amount of detail, the randomness and the "mistakes" within the world of the image, [such as] bad lighting in the foreground' (Lehmuskallio et al., 2019: p. 13, emphasis removed). These iconic qualities, which were abducted to be results of how photographs tend to look and from how photographic equipment affects photographic images are deciphered in line with tacit knowledge and (implicit and explicit) know-how, however incorrect the results might be.

While the relation between the icon and the index is often abducted on the basis of prior knowledge and skills, there are times when novel visual technologies and optical media complicate previously taken-for-granted understandings of image types and technologies. Photo theories return to these relations particularly often, not least because of the significant changes wrought in technical imaging in the last few decades. Today, even amateurs can access highly sophisticated image algorithms that predict what photographers or the public might want to see. These are available alongside deep-learning techniques that support creating images of situations that never arose and of non-existent environments. Still, abduction and the 'icon, index, symbol' framework remain useful analytical concepts as visual technology evolves. What changes in these, at least somewhat, is how images become iconically visible, what they actually index, and what kind of symbolic currency they might carry.

3.2.6 *Debating Indexicality*

Photo theorists tend to disagree on the question of indexicality itself. Does indexicality connect with an ontological understanding of the world, or are we dealing mainly with socially constructed relations of reference that may in themselves be complex and even 'apparently irrational' at first sight?

For analysis purposes, we follow a recommendation for 'examining the ways in which images are always enmeshed in networks of material infrastructure, technical operations, discursive attributions, and cultural practices from the outset' (Lehmuskallio & Meyer, 2022). To have any hope of understanding indexical relationships, with the attached claims to truth, and these images' social role and epistemic function, one has to detach the gaze from the individual image and begin to focus in on the role of situational assemblages, which we understand as 'situationally ordered heterogeneous entities used to make claims and decisions' (ibid.). Only then can we bring our analysis to bear to explicate the unruly relations that are claimed to exist between bodies and the technical inscriptions made of those bodies.

Tools for Analysing Images 75

In short, the 'icon, index, symbol' triad and forms of abduction become understandable only as parts of broader material and symbolic practices, which is why we turn next to the role of social interaction.

3.3 The Role of Social Interaction

Shared ways of seeing and knowing allow similarity of abductions across individuals, whereby all actors involved understand what is meant when someone suggests that, say, the android depicted has a soul (as addressed in the preceding section) or, for that matter, that a particular cow is beautiful (see Section 2.1, discussing Grasseni's work). From a practice-theory perspective, these shared ways of seeing and knowing are developed within communities of practice – i.e., within those kinds of interactions wherein that which is seen and known becomes meaningful for others too. The people involved in these communities of practice do not purely interpret the world (i.e., see and know it); they also mould and carve it, as they live out their lives. Hence, particular visualisations used in these communities of practice arrange and order what to attend to, alongside how to do the attending itself. This visual organisation work can be described as creating specific visual orders (see Seppänen, 2006), as patterns get reinforced via repetition in the image content and forms of visual media.

We introduced examination of asymmetrical visual orders, so-called scopic regimes, in connection with Chapter 2's Cartesian perspectivalism, the Orientalism addressed just above, and pointed towards other work that has addressed these as overarching regimes, but visual orders may be approached in other ways too. We can study them *in situ* and *in actu* as the specific ways in which communities of practice arrange their mutual work and other life practices. Some visual orders are surely constraining and steeped in power relations. They may, for instance, affect how young people think about themselves and the communities they belong to through the image flows produced within capitalist advertising machinery. A visual order hence might be asymmetrical, restrictive, and detrimentally power-laden but need not be *per se*. Visual orders can also be guided toward being communally beneficial and imaginative, as may be the case for groups having found ways of life that they deem nurturing and caring. Visual orders can just as much bear desirable attributes that may be considered socially beneficial.

Thinking about the potential of visual orders allows us to imagine alternative varieties of ways in which images and imagery may be used. The notion of skilled vision (per Grasseni) has been developed for studying the processes that individuals and groups alike undergo in aims of learning a new way of seeing – precisely as the professional photographers in the image-origin discrimination study had cultivated over the course of a news or journalism career. The benefit of approaching seeing as a learnt and acquired skill is that, rather than take our ways of seeing for granted, we thus home in on them as specific ways of cultivating attention. Cultivation of attention is, just as much as skilled vision, a culturally acquired feat that develops within and through social relationships. The photographers interviewed in the above-mentioned study shared, assessed, and cultivated their ways of seeing by discussing 'good' images in newsrooms or when facing a decision on whether a particular photograph is 'publishable' at all (see also Mäenpää, 2022; Zelizer, 2010). The equivalent is true for other forms of skilled vision, as data visualisations' heightened value for work with sensor data collected by rovers on Mars attests. In the latter case, the material cannot be merely subjected to automatic analysis. It demands regular discussion such that hypotheses about the importance of specific iconic content can take shape, whereby abductions can make sense (a few scholars have addressed this issue; see Goodwin & Goodwin, 1996; Vertesi, 2015; Lehmuskallio et al, 2019). One particularly vital feature of skilled vision is the insecurity inherent to its application, which leads to a felt need for discussing imagery or for consulting textbooks, image databases, or the like if one is to assess a particular image 'correctly'.

A focus on skilled vision hence affords pinpointing the ways in which visual orders are created and upheld, paying heed to the dynamic quality of seeing. This seeing is far from fixed; it constantly gets reassessed. While visual orders may become, at least partially, visible via such mechanisms as content analysis – e.g., examining sets of images published in specific journals and magazines over a particular span of time – skilled vision cannot be studied by looking at images alone. Rather, it calls for participant observation (and other participatory methods), interviews, visual and sensory techniques, and other qualitative methods for data collection, given that the social relationships intrinsic to seeing are not deducible from images alone.

Scholarly attention to visual orders, and to the skilled vision required for ordering the visual, involves examining precisely such patterns and regularities. These can be detected especially in the act of seeing and in the act of creating images. Social dynamics of seeing in specific environments attracted particular interest among social scientists in the 1950s and 1960s, most famously in the work behind Erving Goffman's *Gender Advertisements* (1978) and the writings by Edward T. Hall on social proxemics. We can take their work in order to think through some of the implications of this kind of research.

Both Goffman and Hall were influenced by ethologists' endeavours, and their modes of observing how humans behave borrowed methods and techniques accordingly from studies conducted on animal behaviour. While Goffman was particularly interested in the 'interaction order' – i.e., in observing and analysing how and in which order specific interactions unfold – Hall turned his attention to the spatial dynamics of these interactions: how specific communities of practice design and operate in physical environments.

What connects the work of these two scholars is their interest in the varied forms of social interaction, ranging from intimate personal encounters to public ones. They also had a common focus on ritualised ways of ordering these interactions that are culturally meaningful. Both used a wide range of visual techniques to advance their work. For instance, Goffman employed several observation-based techniques. He noted interactions he had personally witnessed, of various types, and these observations informed his understanding of the ways in which interactions are ordered and, most importantly for our purposes here, how visual orders are socially created and maintained over time.

One observation with special importance for visual analysis is that interacting with specific visual media is not the only route by which images become visible. They also are a part of how we present our bodies in social situations, while also being bundled up with how we come to understand those presentations themselves. This means that the information we provide may be embodied or disembodied, as well as made accessible in another kind of medium with its own specific characteristics. The difference between embodied and disembodied social interactions holds particular significance in respect of the reciprocity of interaction, because face-to-face interactions exhibit a specific mutuality: every act in another person's presence is at the same time a possible signal that is interpreted with the means that those doing the interpretation have at their disposal.

For social interactions in co-presence, those involved 'must sense that they are close enough to be perceived in whatever they are doing, including their experiencing of others, and close enough to be perceived in this sensing of being perceived' (Goffman, 1966: p. 17). This constraint to the interaction complicates face-to-face encounters such that sets of codes for proper behaviour must exist if interaction orders are to remain and may be followed. It is within the constraints that these patterns and entire visual orders in situations of co-presence emerge. Those orders may differ significantly from the various forms of disembodied visual interaction.

A mistake frequently made in visual analysis is strict differentiation between embodied and disembodied images, as if they share little, if anything, in common. Here, Belting's recommendation to consider images *in corpore* holds value, for stressing the role of the human body in perceiving and showing images, as well as for providing a way to consider the long history of image-making, image use, and operating with images as we study situated embodied interactions. Recall from Section 2.1 that images *in corpore* may be distinguished from those in effigy, images that become visible via other media than the human body. Although Belting never discussed Goffman's or Hall's work directly, his references to anthropologists from Marcel Mauss to Claude Lévi-Strauss and Victor Turner (see Bräunlein, 2004) testify to his sustained interest in situated social scientific studies of visual practices.

We argue that Goffman's and Hall's contributions provide systematic accounts that ground studying visual interactions in social settings, in that the work of both stressed the importance of observing and understanding human beings in situated environments. Goffman examined use of images *in corpore* under the 'body idiom', the manifestations of which 'comprise bodily appearance and personal acts: dress, bearing, movement, and position, sound level, physical gestures such as waving or saluting, facial decorations, and broad emotional expression' (1966: p. 33). Humans learn to employ this idiom in conventionalised ways, and in many social settings it is in following particular conventions in body idiom that one can most easily 'fit in' while revealing little about oneself except one's agreement to take up a particular role for a specific social occasion (such as that of a musician, waiter, guest, or host for a dinner at a restaurant with live music).

3.3.1 Involvement

Expression of the body idiom differs with the kind of social settings one faces, with whom, and in what sort of role. Accordingly, Goffman introduced the useful term 'involvement' to highlight 'the capacity of an individual to give (or withhold from giving) his concerted attention to some activity at hand – a solitary task, a conversation, a collaborative work effort' (1966: p. 43). Involvement, or the distribution of attention, is a culturally learnt form of behaviour, which differs both within societies (depending on class, age, gender, status, etc.) and between them. For visual analysts, the distribution of attention in social settings is of particular assistance in understanding the role of embodied images and body-related idioms, because attention is the scarcest of our resources and is used selectively.

Goffman distinguished between main and side involvements. The former is an involvement that 'absorbs the major part of an individual's attention and interest, visibly forming the principal current determinant of his actions' (1966: p. 43), while the latter can be carried out alongside a main involvement, as in the case of whistling while painting a wall in a joint effort with others. But more important for visual analysis with a practice-theory tack is another of his distinctions, between dominant and subordinate involvements. Choices in attending to these reflect one's interest in the social occasions in which the involvements are enacted.

Dominant involvements are the subset that social occasions require us to honour, which we do by means of body idioms considered proper for doing so. Subordinate involvements, on the other hand, are activities that one deems acceptable in the given situation even though they do not contribute to handling the dominant involvement. For instance, the dominant involvement of following certain turn-taking rules could be the main involvement in participating in a social occasion while one also engages in such subordinate involvements as scrolling through social-media feeds while waiting for one's turn or knitting while listening to a university lecture.

The lines by which interactions are ordered may be loose or rigid, and they may centre either on dominant or on subordinate involvements. Zen literature, for instance, offers several examples of joint meditation practice (based on concerted attention in which body posture and inhibition of subordinate movements are key) wherein the Zen master hits disciples if their contribution to joint attention during the dominant involvement wavers. In a similar vein, Goffman cited some conditions wherein 'rules may even govern "the conduct of the eyes" ': during meditation and prayers at some' convents, the act of casting one's gaze around the room 'may constitute an unacceptable subordinate involvement' (1966: pp. 48–49).

The study of body idiom and involvement is particularly useful to those interested in the ways in which situated interactions are visually ordered. Again, these embodied visual orders are a major means through which the images in effigy around us coalesce. Work on them requires focused, concerted attention. Furthermore, embodied motions, which demonstrate specific skills in using one's body, must be learnt before they can be employed, and this process of learning is highly contingent on culture.

3.3.2 Proxemics

Pointing to merits of studying situated interactions in specific physical environments, Hall took note of the importance of participants' physical distance for differentiation among expected forms of involvement. His work on proxemics distinguished among intimate, personal, social, and public involvements, all of which become visible in interaction not only because of forms of address, turn-taking, etc. in the mutual discourse but also in the physical space between people within the environment.

His work draws our attention to the crucial phenomenological observation that those engaged in situated interactions have a specific Origo, a certain 'I–here–now' from which they interact in particular environments (for discussion of the Origo, see Bühler, 1965). In all situated interactions, the Origo's particular directionality affects both the means of sensing and the communication. Hall was quite explicit in mapping out the perceptive qualities of our sensory systems, focusing on the roles of foveal and peripheral vision, smell, auditory cues, pressure on the skin, and the directionality of all these in space. They combine to inform awareness of our biological capabilities in context with multiple mechanisms of cultural moulding.

Having conducted empirical case studies especially in spaces occupied by the middle classes of North America, Hall posited that the distinctions implicit to our proxemic use of space might be related also to the functions of our sensory apparatus. On this basis, he modelled the varieties of use explicitly.

Hall considered public space to start as the actors come within a distance of approximately three metres, roughly the limit of the range at which our vision and audition can readily perceive individuals. At this distance, one is able to see the whole body of a speaker while nuances of facial expressions and voice prove hard to discern. This distance is targeted in many settings of lectures, political speeches, and mass events, and our understanding of what 'the public' looks, feels, and sounds like forms on its basis. For visual analysis, the learnt involvements in public space and ways of presenting and conducting oneself there has import for comprehending not just the needs of a given public (cf. Jürgen Habermas (1990) and his critics, e.g. Fraser (1990)) but also the atmosphere (per Böhme, 2013) and the associated social aesthetics (MacDougall, 1999).

Social space, in turn, is the realm of social conversation at cocktail parties or in office work, for which the ability to see and to hear is particularly important for involvement. Sensory engagement such as touching, smelling, and tasting each other is usually much more strictly regulated in these environments. Within the social domain, in concerted attention to one another, the face is clearly visible as a part of a broader context where facial expressions and acknowledgements such as nodding are clearly ritualised (i.e., socially codified), and the range of acceptable secondary involvements is less broad than in public space. Nevertheless, social space does leave room for disinvolvement. One may have one's back turned, direct one's gaze to one's mobile phone, or be reading a book or newspaper – presence in social space does not necessarily lead to mutual involvement. Again, situated activities in social space have a particular feel, depending on the communities of practice in question.

In personal space, ritualised touch is possible and permitted, in forms such as touching someone's hand or gently pushing someone away. The field of vision grows narrower and clearer, and details not visible from further away emerge. Talk is clearly audible, and differences in vocal tone are easily discerned, as are sighs and other such vocalisations. Within personal space range, it is difficult to smell another person clearly or to sense the other person's body heat, though, so this remains a domain reserved mainly for audiovisual interaction.

Finally, Hall identified intimate space as proximity of 0.5 m or less. Playful wrestling, the most intrusive of bullying, caressing, and love-making occur within this space. The field of vision narrows, and entire faces or whole limbs are hard to discern; rather, we see only portions of them. Voices change, with larger distances' clearly articulated talk giving way to whispers, moans, and growls. Body temperature, smells, and touch become important means of sensing and signalling, giving rein to modes of sensory involvement very different from those in social or public spaces.

Hall's proxemic distinctions are certainly somewhat dated in some of their specifics (the distances listed, forms of proper involvement cited, etc.) and tied to a very particular social context. Yet they still help us think about the kinds of social spaces in which situated interactions occur, coupled with the sensory involvements possible and reasonably expectable in each. Just as dominant and subordinate involvements are, sensory involvements in social spaces are strictly ordered. For instance, some forms of interaction that are permissible in intimate range or in particular physical spaces bring on fines or prison sentences if conducted in public space.

3.3.3 Focused and Unfocused Interactions

Goffman's work and publishing on forms of involvement, more or less simultaneous with Hall's on proxemics, provided an additional useful distinction, that between focused and unfocused interactions. Focused interactions have to do with people's mutual engagements, and unfocused interactions involve modes of sharing social space without actively being involved in interactions with one another.

Famously, he paid attention to modes of civil inattention: ways of sharing social space and acknowledging the other as being there without engaging in focused interactions with the other. Goffman explained:

> In performing this courtesy the eyes of the looker may pass over the eyes of the other, but no 'recognition' is typically allowed. Where the courtesy is performed between two persons passing on the street, civil inattention may take the special form of eyeing the other up to approximately eight feet, during which time sides of the street are apportioned by gesture, and then casting the eyes down as the other passes.
>
> (Goffman, 1966: p. 84)

This choreography of the eyes in providing the courtesy of civil inattention is of particular importance for visual studies, as it clearly demonstrates the embodied constraints we feel and enact as part of our body idiom. There is much less leeway for playing with one's eyes when in shared social space than individualistic accounts of behaviour might imply. Visual orders provide the means, with 'how we see, how we are [...] allowed, or made to see, and how we see this seeing or the unseen therein' (Foster, 1988: p. ix). And visual orders are, instead of being based mainly or entirely on pictures, optical media, or other sorts of visual technology, rooted first and foremost in our embodied ways of being, in the ways in which we are involved in a situation (or remain uninvolved), in how we share the biggest gift of them all – our concerted attention.

3.3.4 Staring

For visual analysts, maintaining sensitivity to social space, to forms of involvement, and to the specific social aesthetics of these is crucial because embodied interactions are increasingly accompanied by various forms of mediation, for which images in effigy play a vital role (see Figure 3.3.)

In 2022, the British Transport Police launched an advertising campaign targeted particularly at users of London Underground trains and tube stations. While the campaign focused on several embodied behaviours that could be understood as sexual harassment, it paid particular heed to staring. One of the posters, declaring that '[i]ntrusive staring of a sexual nature is sexual harassment and is not tolerated', recommends texting incident reports to a

82 *Visual Studies*

Figure 3.3 A poster from an advertising campaign against sexual harassment.
Source: Transport for London (TfL) and Rail Delivery Group (RDL).

specific number from one's mobile phone or ringing an anonymous hotline. The campaign's objective of stopping sexual harassment is certainly laudable and is pointed against a gendered asymmetry in believability identified in news reports and court cases on sexual violence (Banet-Weiser & Higgins, 2023). Using advertisements for asking to stop intrusive staring is intended to curb said behaviour, and hence provide a safe space for travel. But staring is also a culturally formed activity, and identifying a particular form of mutual interaction as staring and, further, the identification of a particular stare as being of a sexual nature prove more complex especially in novel cultural settings.

We can make sense of staring as a form of social interaction only through comparing it to other forms of mutual engagement, such as civil inattention in public space, or to forms of 'face engagement', in which two or more persons enter a mode of focused interaction. In these forms of engagement, prolonged looking at the other person is seldom permissible, and looking away, averting one's gaze, and making only quick glances are much more commonplace.

While the ad campaign explicitly associates staring with sexual harassment, staring fills a function also as a form of negative sanctioning, employed for the purpose of controlling public conduct – for example, when an authority figure glares at someone in efforts to influence behaviour without (yet) physically approaching or talking to the person in question. It finds application also in efforts to defend 'one's space' from possible aggressors, asserting one's claim with a cold stare. Staring hence can be characterised as a form of looking at another person so as to influence the imagination (as in a sexually motivated stare not backed by any intention of actual mutual face engagements), as embodied addressing of a situation (e.g., when an authority figure levels a stare at someone to influence behaviour), or to signal potential consequences (in cases such as that of a cold stare signalling not to approach the starer).

If one is to identify a stare as a stare, one must know the rules. What are the proper ways of using one's eyes in face-to-face encounters in this situation, this space, and this community of practice one is spending time with? Any encounter begins with initiation, and one person's mode of initiation may be unfamiliar to another person present. Opening moves typically are made 'by means of a special expression of the eyes but sometimes by a statement or a special tone of voice at the beginning of a statement' (Goffman, 1966: p. 91). Then, the initiation's success hinges on a reply, of one form or another, even if that consists just of lifting one's head, moving the torso, or making a perfunctory vocal response. This provides a clearance sign for being at the disposal of the other. Some forms of looking at someone that are intended as an opening move may get interpreted as a stare, and stares typically do not receive a clearance sign. The action may be seen as variously a sexual, authority-asserting, or protective stare on the basis of the situation and the recipient's background.

The stare is so important, and at times uncomfortable, because mutual glances are a particularly relevant mode for social interaction. The choreography of looking and being looked at is central to sociality, establishing acceptable forms of mutual engagement. A stare becomes a stare by breaking the mutuality of eye-to-eye interactions. It constitutes an attempt to force the other party into an encounter that said party wishes to avoid. Whereas mutual eye contact is a way to show openness to face engagements, looking away as a form of civil inattention provides means with which one tactfully abstains from supplying clearance signs for further engagements.

The advertising campaign in London, instead of just noting that intrusive staring of a sexual nature is not tolerated, itself acts as a mediated form of staring. Its capital letters articulate a stare that otherwise might emanate from an embodied authority figure's eyes. Staring, as a cascade of images *in corpore*, here is transferred to an image in effigy, which performs the task of visual ordering via the form of written text (which would be verbal media in Mitchell's classification of the main branches of the image family). Paradoxically, instead of inhibiting staring, the advertising campaign exploits – and thereby underscores – the role of the stare for visually ordering social interactions. This well-intentioned campaign, by calling attention to specific modes of looking at other people, at the same time orders how those looks 'should be' interpreted and directly recommends specific modes of action (i.e., texting and calling dedicated numbers). As Goffman noted, '[t]he more clearly individuals are obliged to refrain from staring directly at others, the more effectively will they be able to attach special significance to a stare, in this case, a request for an encounter' (1966: p. 95). The mediated stare, in written form, hence does not bring an end to staring *per se* but does offer a way of simplifying the set of possible interpretations of what a prolonged look might mean in contexts of using London's public transport. In this case a simplification of modes of interpretations serves the purpose of providing passengers safe spaces and modes of travel, it does so by employing in mediated form what it prohibits *in corpore*.

3.3.5 Mediated Staring: Surveillance Cameras

The British Transport Police use another mediated form of staring too, one that has grown ubiquitous in London (alongside many other cities): surveillance cameras. These do not avert their gaze or make only fleeting glances as humans do in social situations. The surveillance cameras typically record what they are pointed at – or, in the case of 360-degree cameras, surrounded by – registering what is happening in front of them and retaining the details over some extended time. Any human being on the London tube who acts in the manner of a surveillance camera would surely be identified as intrusively staring and might very well get reported and questioned intensely. The advertising campaign described above allows for attaching special significance to a stare, since particular forms of looking are situationally prohibited, but this particular significance is not extended to those authorities with the most extensive staring mechanisms, delegated to visual technologies.

This case creates an opening for talking about technical mediation of situated ways of looking, which has important implications for how we see, are allowed to see, and see this seeing or what goes unseen (see Chapter 1). Technical mediation of seeing is important for holistic reflection on situated interactions because we are seldom, if ever, in 'purely embodied' situations of engagement with each other. Our social interactions are intrinsically marked by a bifocality of vision (Peters, 1997); that is, our forms of vision touch the near and the far, with embodied presence and mediated distance.

Surveillance cameras grant authorities access to situations they would otherwise not have the time or means to access. This is marked by 'time axis manipulation' (Krämer, 2006): a sort of slice, or cut, from the embodied everyday. While some uses of surveillance cameras allow for a direct mediated stare, by someone sitting far afield in a control room and observing the goings-on elsewhere via a screen, in quite a few settings this observation is delegated either to algorithms designed for automatically recognising certain phenomena (such as deviance in embodied movements) or to *post factum* observation conducted if seemingly warranted by some event (e.g., a robbery or terrorist attack) (see Meyer, 2019).

Just as efforts to identify the intentions behind an embodied stare are fraught with problems, it is not always clear just from noting a surveillance camera's presence what the implications of setting up and using that camera are. Is the device a 'dummy', not an operational unit but a box mounted in aims of unsettling and scaring off those who might commit crimes? Is it instead mediating an image stream to another location, effectively functioning as the robot eyes of a human being, who might be sitting hundreds of kilometres away to monitor an environment that would be hard to inspect by standing on location for hours or days at a time? Or is the camera recording while unattended, and, if so, is it recording 24/7 or only at particular times of day? Might it be one tiny part of a vast assemblage comprising hundreds or even thousands of surveillance cameras feeding a database that gets automatically analysed second by second?

The difficulty of answering these questions without further knowledge highlights the great importance of a contextual understanding of the kinds of social relations present in any setting one hopes to analyse. But it also points to the range of occasions on which humans strive to explain a specific incident by seeking a more general rule (as considered in Section 3.2's discussion of abduction), because humans simply do not have the time to consider all possible hypothetical explanations and must pick one so that we can 'get on with life'. Abduction is not a form of reasoning applied by analysts alone but, as Peirce noted, a tool commonly employed every day as we make assumptions about such matters as the indexicality between a visual trace (an aesthetic difference in a visual medium) and its causation.

The notion of bifocal vision grapples with how we deal with the limitations of local, embodied ways of knowing and with concerted representations of broader events, which we tend to receive in mediated form. This mediation should not be conceived of 'only as television, cinema, radio, newspapers, and magazines', nor as 'the even more various apparatuses of information and entertainment'; rather, it encompasses 'all practices of social envisioning, reporting and documentation, including statistics, accounting, insurance, census-taking, polling, the work of social services and of the social sciences' (Peters, 1997: p. 79). In day-to-day life, we deal with an embodied presence and a host of condensed synthetic situations that use scopic media (Knorr-Cetina, 2014) to represent broad-based events in compressed form. Visualisations of data, statistical tables, and diagrams explaining workflows all exemplify these synthetic images that are so central for bifocal vision.

The role of bifocal vision in our social interactions triggers further reflection on surveillance cameras' role in inhibiting specific face engagements. The surveillance apparatus as a specific device seen, for instance, in a tube station could be argued to foster a panoptic society. Under its watchful eye, individuals internalise a societal gaze and form docile bodies accordingly (cf. Foucault, 1988, 2020). They do so as they follow an assumption that some authority might be looking at them via the surveillance camera and punish them if they do not punish themselves in advance by adhering to internalised codes of conduct through walking with a clear sense of direction and without raising suspicion. While this is a perfectly plausible abduction from seeing such a device in such a physical environment, it is a troubling one: the suggestion narrows *ab initio* what human engagements may entail. As Peters remarks in his discussion of bifocal vision, '[t]he irony is that the general becomes clear through representation, while the immediate is subject to the fragmenting effects of our limited experience' (1997: p. 79). The task at hand, therefore, is to remain open to other ways of seeing and understanding visual technologies. Regarding the case of surveillance cameras, we might approach them as audiences for which we can act out a play, in the manner of troupes of 'surveillance camera players', who have reframed surveillance cameras as television or as Web cameras for which theatrical plays are performed. This flexibility in interpretation allows for the emergence of critique that does not rely on technological determinism (e.g., on concluding that surveillance cameras necessarily lead to a panoptic society). It guides us rather more toward questioning and re-evaluating the contexts within which visual technologies get employed. If embodied face-to-face engagements are complex in their own right, our mediated everyday makes them even more so, especially since our ability to see is not always closely woven in with an ability to understand how specific devices tie in with an ability to act from a distance.

The notion of bifocal vision assists us in orienting ourselves toward both embodied and technically mediated forms of interaction, not focusing purely on one of these (whether face-to-face behaviour or social-media posts) but seeing them as entwined forms of knowing, understanding, and living out our doings, which we take turns in attending to. The concept of bifocal vision gains further layers of complication to peel back if we consider the proliferation of mobile phones and social media, in conjunction with the various social-interaction-embedding networks where new ways of expressing the desire to 'picture the world' are both made possible and actually stimulated.

3.3.6 Screens

Bifocality is lived out in the real world via relying on practices of social envisioning, reporting, and documentation that we receive in mediated form, be they printed on paper, written on parchment, or painted on linen canvases. With burgeoning digitisation of communication technologies, digital screens in various forms have clearly become ubiquitous in a wide range of settings. The SARS-CoV-2 pandemic further normalised the use of screens for human-to-human interactions: it reshaped various types of face-to-face meetings into face-to-camera and screen-to-face ones, thus also influencing social interactions' evolution from those evident in the settings analysed in the 1960s by Goffman and Hall. Screens' dual nature as providers of both protection and connection grew particularly clear during the pandemic: face-to-face meetings unfolded via screens, for the participants' protection against a virus that is passed on only through close bodily proximity. At the same time, countless screens, connected to cameras, microphones, keyboards, and communication networks, allow people in ever-rising numbers to spend time together and discuss life, even if the participants live on opposite sides of the planet. Empirical research conducted pre-COVID-19 attests to the felt importance of distant closeness as achieved via networked camera technologies. Scholars have offered a plethora of examples (see Niemelä-Nyrhinen & Seppänen, 2020; Prieto-Blanco, 2016; Venema & Lobinger, 2017).

For a practice-theory understanding of screen use, authors in several fields have started pointing more often at the various ways in which screens get embedded in human practices. Their projects encompass studying the ways in which people behave – ideally and in actuality – within such confined settings as the cinema, time spent in front of television sets, and visits to museums and galleries, but the studies venture outside just as often, examining public space. For example, Erkki Huhtamo (2016) has identified four kinds of human–screen relations, which he terms 'screen', 'peep', 'touch', and 'mobile'. The focus here is very much on the sorts of relations that individuals adopt with specific screen surfaces and on how these surfaces themselves are constructed and provisioned for human interaction. Tristan Thielmann (2018), in turn, examines the creation of particular screens, such as the radar screen, as a temporary result of specific kinds of work practices within which the screen initially had to fit and be useful. From other work, looking at urban mobile screens, Nanna Verhoeff (2012) showed how a screen may be approached and afford multiple ways of interacting and interfacing, which depend on the ways in which it is constructed and set up but just as much on how it gets used in the first place. Accordingly, Luisa Feiersinger, along with Kathrin Friedrich and Moritz Queisner (2018), have recommended analysing 1) the technological basis of screens, which from the very start affects the ensuing possibilities for action; 2) the interface design, which orients users in specific kinds of screen-based spaces; and 3) the perceptual level of human interaction with screens. What this and other, related work show most clearly is that screens differ considerably from each other, in size, portability, their interaction potential, and the interconnections they permit and encourage.

Screens such as those of mobile phones and tablet computers have already become part and parcel of a whole host of activities. Screens are used not just by people sitting or standing in front of them but also during walking, cycling, driving a car, and flying a plane (Feiersinger et al., 2018; Huhtamo, 2016; Verhoeff, 2012).

Social media applications interacted with on screens permeate day-to-day activities, at times generating instances of anxiety along the way. Scholars have adopted various lenses to examine these. For instance, Sherry Turkle (2011) applied the term 'continuous connection' to address pressures for users to be 'always online' and constantly present to/via devices. Meanwhile, Wendy Chun (2008, 2016) looked at the intersection of the body with the back side of the screen, the platforms, arguing that the proliferation of algorithm-driven social media has culminated in profit-based promotion of continuous connection.

We suggest that screen use is very much intertwined with the felt social proximity of those with whom we interact. We utilise screens not just for connecting to others but also as a tool of maintaining distance, of acting from afar. The study of culturally moulded distance, considered above in terms of Hall's proxemics, was introduced in the 1960s as a tool to 'increase self-knowledge and decrease alienation. In sum, to help introduce people to themselves' (Hall, 1969: p. x). Though television was in widespread use when Hall coined this term (and radio, newspapers, and letters were even more so), he focused primarily on means of keeping a distance in co-location scenarios, transposing findings from Heini Hediger's ethological work to the human realm. His scale of social distances discussed above – all the way from the intimate through to the public, each with its close and far 'phases' – was informed by his measurements of distances among middle-class white research subjects in the US. Hence, he assigned a very specific value to each of his four ranges, with the intimate being 0–1.5 feet, the personal 1.5–4, the social-consultive 4–10, and the public 10 to 30 or above. Within each distance band, as Hall's application of James Jerome Gibson's theory of perception suggests, we are able to feel and sense other human beings in a very distinct manner, as discussed at length above, and the differences become visible also in how we relate to images, hinging on the kind of social proximity that the images employed suggest.

The significance of proxemics for understanding video-mediated communication lies in its focus on human beings as organisms living in and related to particular environments and as creatures that have found ways of using space as a particular elaboration of culture. Maintaining distance is the prime means with which we organise our social relations, not least since letting someone or something get too close can be life-threatening. One need only recall what made distance so vital as the pandemic raged.

Since Hall did not devote great attention to television sets, electronic displays, etc., his use of the words 'screen' and 'display' demonstrably coheres around this constant regulation of felt spatial needs. As he applied it, the word 'screen' refers to blocking out. He explained that in Japanese homes one might find paper walls for visually screening out what lies beyond while the happenings behind the screen remain audible, whereas Central Europe often boasts thick walls that screen out sound too. This example alone illustrates amply that screens affect our perception of space alongside our ability to connect to others within it. They do not influence only vision, a central claim that we make for regarding all other visual technologies too.

3.3.7 Screen-Based Interactions

Decisions taken amid the pandemic regularly ruled out social proximity on account of risks entailed by excessive physical closeness between people. Instead of talking directly to others in face-to-face situations, we have found a wide range of our social encounters mediated via screens more generally, but screens serving us from a distance during pandemic-related lockdown promised protection against direct encounters that could have turned fatal. In an echo of its original sense (from the late thirteenth century) as an object of protection, a panel protecting against extreme heat and sparks from a fireplace, the screen became emblematic of social relations during the pandemic. Those who still had to work alongside other humans on-site started wearing face shields, and many clerks serving customers began doing so from behind a counter now protected with Plexiglas. This allowed nearly unhindered visual interaction though significantly muting the voices of interaction participants. Screens facilitated both protection and interaction here. In the course of fulfilling these functions, screens also reorient our perceptional and interactional resources. They favour or block vision, inhibit other perceptional modes (e.g., making it more difficult to hear the person on the opposite side talking), and rule out some aspects of perception entirely (sensing smells, feeling physical warmth, or touching the other).

In mid-pandemic connections from a distance – for example, linking with others via a computer screen, camera, and microphone from one's home – the screen continued to serve a protective function (it already afforded caution between two people meeting online before a physical date, for instance) while typically still letting participants see each other's facial expressions, perhaps even better than in face-to-face situations involving face masks. In this development, the screen grew even more fully invested with the set of meanings it has carried since the nineteenth century as a surface on which images are displayed (for a brief historical overview, see Casetti, 2013; Chateau & Moure, 2016).

While computer screens can be used for showing a wide range of imagery, the near-real-time interactions on that surface are of particular interest for our discussion.

Video-mediated communication has afforded connecting to others and played a major role in substituting for various modes of face-to-face interaction utilised previously. Instead of gaining access to people largely through a fixed camera pointed at others, as is usual in settings of camera-based surveillance, the people communicating mutually from a distance in these video-mediated settings can, if all participants are using cameras, microphones, and screens, obtain a physical presence in the others' household or workplace, not just as a representation of a person from afar but as an actual moving and interacting figure on a screen. These interactive figures shown on screens are, first and foremost, 'here' as images that can be interacted with in a specific location. What Sarah Pink has posited for photography more generally is particularly pertinent for video-mediated communication: 'Images [...] are inevitably and unavoidably in places: they are produced by moving through and not over or on environments, and they are not stopping points so much as outcomes of and in movement' (2011: p. 9). The images seen in video-mediated communication are thus always seen 'here', although the 'here' might be thousands of kilometres from the embodied communication partner. Screens, in Francesco Casetti's reasoning, 'have become transit hubs for the images that circulate in our social space. [...] [S]creens function as the junction of a complex circuit, characterized both by a continuous flow and by localized processes of configuration or reconfiguration of the circulation of the circulating images' (Casetti, 2013). Screens and images coincide at times, but the images we see on these screens are not principally representations of something outside the here and now. They are specifically here, now.

Hence, from a practice-theory perspective, what the increasing emergence of screens brings forth is a change in the ecologies of interaction. As curfews and lockdowns proliferated in aims of curbing the spread of the virus, screen use became ubiquitous for a wide range of practices that had relied on other communication media. With the access that participants gained to each other's locations via the cameras, mikes, and screens, a wider range of people could enter domestic settings as figures on a screen, settings that social rules for maintaining a distance would have kept closed to them.

Social interaction relies on negotiation of shared situational expectations, in which the participants draw on their stock of knowledge for assessing appropriate frames for interaction. Especially in the early days of such uses of video-mediated communication, shared situational expectations were difficult to manage. The unfolding social interactions often ended up violating some expectations of some participants. As individuals learn about and disseminate the meanings of specific spaces, partitions within them, props and their use, and the types of clothing suited to use within them, 'the less energy they will expend in establishing mutual expectations, in sanctioning, in meeting transactional needs, in normatizing, in role making, role taking, and role verifying, and in assessing status' (Turner, 2002). In contrast, the less they share understandings of how to interact mutually within specific spatial settings, the more energy they need to invest in ensuring the ability to interact in emotionally satisfying ways. Employing screens in video-mediated communication as interactive surfaces, using spatial props, etc. form an aspect of this: they all must be negotiated within the web of social relations in which participants engage. The extent of the social proximity felt plays a key role, influencing how rich or lean the device-borne communication has to be. And it is in the negotiation of how to use video mediation for communication that opportunities for intervention lie and, hence, for social and political change.

While face-to-face interactions bring participants together in a single co-located setting, video-mediated interactions, thanks to the use of screens, allow the emergence of what Peters called 'meanwhile structures', which entail 'techniques of shuttling between two points in space at the same time that are too far apart for the unaided human senses' (2020: p. 30). Although the interaction in video-mediated communication always occurs 'here' on account of the processual nature of the encounter and the possibility of turn-taking in discussions, the communication partners may be – and indeed often are – involved in these meanwhile structures. Peters borrowed the 'meanwhile' notion from the classic work *Imagined Communities*, in which Benedict Anderson claims that the opportunity of this shuttling between spaces in the same time emerged only with modernity. More specifically, the novel, the newspaper, the census, the map, and the museum ushered it in (Anderson, 1991). These media afford moving between scenes without the passage of time. They depict or explain particular events from one location, then move to another one to relate events taking place at the same time. For example, someone might read a newspaper story about an event in the Philippines and right after that an item about occurrences in Germany, both printed on the same page, a page that reports in parallel on events unfolding at nearly, or at times even exactly, the same time. While Anderson's thesis of historical rupture is not watertight, he and Peters have served visual studies well in pointing to the important interrelations between specific media technologies and ways of narrating.

In video-mediated communications, these meanwhile structures are apparent not merely in word-oriented narrative forms. They manifest themselves specifically in image use. In contrast to co-located face-to-face settings, the interaction partners in video-mediated communication meet human bodies connected via a complex and extensive web of information infrastructure while far apart. Just as we find with most photography, also in video-mediated communication those taking part prove unable in many cases to frame the encounter without bringing into play everything else that is present/occurring where they are situated in front of the camera and screen. Likewise, when talking to another participant in the encounter, they cannot help but notice if a family member or pet pops up in the camera's view, and they see the interiors of households that in many cases would remain behind closed doors were the meeting a face-to-face one. Two parties in video-mediated communication both are located 'here', interacting with images made visible on surfaces of on-location screens. On these screens, they see 'here' what meanwhile is happening 'there'.

With this novel manner of merging social relations and access to each other's spatially bounded settings has arisen a need to negotiate degrees of social proximity anew. Though most people entering video-mediated interaction know each other in advance, they find themselves coming together differently therein. As family members living separately, friends, work colleagues, and others who form part of the social web identified by Robin Dunbar (2010) engage regularly in video-mediated communication, previously distant fibres of the web get pulled together. Where additional people are to take part in the gatherings, their inclusion often demands intermediaries: entities of the parties' prior acquaintance who are deemed good enough filters. Among these intermediaries are specialist e-mail lists, networks of friends, and registries that include one's pertinent details. The mediation conditions the possibilities for the meetings, especially with regard to interacting with someone new and entering deep engagement with anyone whose modes of being differ significantly from one's own. Chance encounters grow more difficult. In some respects, then, these conditions have reduced the richness and density of our web of social relations. Some people felt this profoundly as the measures taken for creating the distance to curb the pandemic impinged on publicly accessible gatherings that 'stir the pot'.

For those who take diversity as necessary for a good life, the increasing use of screens for social interactions appears all the more problematic, not just (or even mainly) because video-mediated communication differs in nature from face-to-face interactions. In settings such as the wake of a pandemic, it introduces a kind of social sorting that complicates our time spent with strangers. Screens, while serving important functions for social interaction, also protect us from much of the happenstance inherent to public life that traditionally lubricates meeting and speaking with people who do not share our worldviews and ways of doing.

3.4 Immersive Viewing, From Byzantine Icons to Virtual Reality

With this chapter we attempt to apply the reflections ushered in so far by stepping now onto new terrain, that of immersive viewing. We will do so by suggesting what may at first come across as a bizarre dialogue bridging space, time, and philosophical approaches. Offering a concrete example of Mitchell's 'interdisciplinary indiscipline', we will journey backwards in time and sideways in space to bring contemporary immersive digital practices (specifically, virtual, augmented, and expanded reality) into dialogue with the visual ordering and the aesthetic principles that underpin Orthodox religious icons (and, to some extent, also the Hindu ones that you have already met in this book). Informing this dialogue will be references to phenomenology and, especially importantly, to Buddhist philosophy, with focus mainly on its non-dualistic principles. The latter attention also encourages taking a route toward decolonisation of our assumptions regarding the world of images. True to the spirit of this book, we address immersive viewing from a position centred on the dialogue between the situated practices of looking that are made possible (and encouraged) by the specific affordances of particular visual media and the images that are seen. In keeping with the overall approach we have chosen, we take care while doing so not to cut off digital images and visuality from other forms and aspects of – contemporary or earlier-rooted – visual cultures. To this end, we position the immersive viewing experiences in question at neither end of the analogue–digital continuum alluded to earlier in our discussion. Similarly, we situate them some way between the extremes of embodied forms of seeing and technically mediated ones. Starting with a brief introduction to contemporary forms of immersive viewing, this chapter paints a brief portrait of the contemporary worlds of digital images. We will then proceed to offer two examples from what we consider to be revealing expanded-reality experiences and use them to address some theoretical challenges that such examples pose. From there we will start the journey in time and space, before ultimately extending it across epistemological landscapes and proceeding to analyse the visuality that characterises religious icons and, finally, reflect upon the dialogues across these different visualities. Our hope is that the passages may help us look at contemporary, digitally produced, emerging arts and documentary visual practices with new eyes.

3.4.1 *Immersive Desires*

Owing not least to their popularity and diversification, forms of reality somewhere between the most seemingly prosaic and the 'purely' virtual call for attention at this juncture. Visualisations wherein physical and digital objects coexist and interact in real-time may be situated anywhere along a vast continuum extending from the 'real' to the 'virtual' yet conventionally get lumped together under the term 'mixed reality' (MR), which bears connotations of a highly granular mix. To accommodate the many nuances that come into play as the phenomenon grows in importance, we apply a different overarching term: we refer to expanded reality (XR) and augmented reality (AR) for the sake of convenience. The notion of expanded reality seems better suited to addressing 360-degree life-logging, plenoptic image practices, and other augmented forms arising around us – in fields ranging from gaming, cinema, and tourism to health and, regrettably, military applications. Extensively integrated also with artificial intelligence, the associated viewing practices seem, at first sight, to invite viewers to 'enter' an image rather than to observe it from a supposed outside. Addressing the space in between the 'actual' and the 'virtual' (Milgram et al., 1994), they foreground an act of immersion and unity instead of detachment. This is the practice-theory observation that provides us with our path onto this terrain. We address the immersive media as expressions of an attempt at entering the image, at crossing the divide between 'self' and 'other', 'self' and 'world'. We claim, however, that the desire manifested in this is not just an outcome of these media themselves. The same yearning for unity runs as a thread throughout the history of art across time and place, and today's immersive XR images are, more than anything ever was, an expression of this. We find also that today's immersive viewing technologies can be looked upon as expressing a broader shift heralded by the realm of digital images. Now, more than at any time before, images seem to have abandoned the prevailing duty to exclusively portray and represent. Rather, they claim a place on the terrain of 'presencing' and empathy, of contemplation and transformation. The shift to digital visuality seems to show us that images today can be the stuff of co-presencing. They are more 'present' (Favero, 2018) in our lives than ever before. In musings about photography, McQuire (2013) has suggested that today '[p]hotography is becoming less about capturing "memories" (as Kodak famously phrased it in the 20th century) than about commenting on present events as they are taking place' (p. 226). In line with what Wassily Kandinsky (1989) stated more than a century earlier with reference to the duty of art, images seem to be less interested in mirroring the world than in functioning as a prophecy, or providing us with a beacon for a different way of visualising and approaching the worlds in which we live.

Proceeding from the assumptions set forth above, we devote this chapter to critically addressing this potential shift and the conceptual continuity that stitches in the world of immersive viewing. Exemplifying our analysis by means of a focus on the world of XR art and documentary practices, we aim to offer insight unveiling the possible exchanges (conscious and not) that make up their present existence, functioning, and meaning. Through an approach that may contribute to decolonising knowledge at the same time, the chapter juxtaposes hyper-modern, 'avant-garde' late-capitalist image-making practices with an ancient, pre-modern visuality, that of the painted Byzantine icon with parallels also to contemporary Hindu icons. With debate on the decolonisation of film canons and visual culture having achieved prominence in the social sciences and humanities, we conclude that it is especially important to push this approach beyond the mere analysis and observation of 'other', supposedly non-Western ways of entering the visual field (which often is set within the analytical space of Western hegemonic visuality). In addition, we will strive for an integrative analysis by incorporating the Western, late-capitalist visual practices in connection with epistemological assumptions that underpin alternative visualities. Following this logic, our endeavour coheres around exploring the extent to which the insight gathered from analysis of the visuality of Byzantium's (and also Hindu) icons can help us carry out grounded rethinking of the assumptions that guide hegemonic (Western) approaches to the world of images, with special regard to emerging digital visual worlds. The reflections on Buddhist epistemology that we will embark upon take our response to this challenge further through an attempt at showing the extent to which the introduction of different epistemologies can provide us with a new language for analysing and describing this emerging terrain. A further pillar for our analysis is awareness of continuity in ambition within the field of immersive viewing. Though by means of different techniques, virtual reality (VR), XR, AR, and MR express a desire for immersion that resembles the one characteristic of some very ancient visual regimes indeed. As a consequence, the images that circulate in contemporary digitalised habitats can, rather more than take us into futuristic unknown territory, help us to, by means of the digital, 're-centralise' ways of engaging with visual representations that can be found elsewhere and 'elsewhen'. We would stress again that this chapter, being consistent with the rest in focusing on the level of mediation, delves into the techniques and practices that favour immersive ways of looking, rather than regarding the images in themselves as immersive.

3.4.2 *Some Reflections on Digital Images*

A quick foray into the broader contemporary world of digital image-making, image-viewing, and image-sharing practices reveals that images are becoming far more than material representation and narration. From social media to dedicated photo- and video-sharing sites, from 3D printing to VR, MR, XR, and AR, images seem to do much more than 'illustrate', 'reflect', or 'capture' a world somewhere out there. They take part in its very crafting. The images travelling in contemporary digital habitats create relations and materialities. They are increasingly multisensory and participative, hence weaving users into a tapestry with each other and further into the world that surrounds them. One banal example is the images that circulate on social media sites such as Facebook. Loaded with metadata indicating when and where and with whom they were taken, then accompanied by a large amount of written and visual dialogue, such images materialise communities and life trajectories. If we once upon a time addressed the act of making pictures – or of 'taking' photographs – as an act of killing, as Barthes would have it, or of preserving the past for posterity (as in the idea of photographs exhibiting an obsession with a 'mummy complex'; see Bazin, 1967), images today seem to cling more than ever to the present moment. As Mizuko Ito (2005) anticipated long ago in her path-breaking essay on Multimedia Messaging Service (MMS) content, images in our presence now call for 'visual co-presence'. They are increasingly made to share the present of the image-maker with that of a viewer located elsewhere.

However, upon their introduction and in their early movements, digital images were looked upon with some degree of bafflement and scepticism. For many people, they entailed a revolution that was bound to alter the world of human-made images fundamentally. Mitchell spoke of this as introducing a 'new model of vision' (1992, p. 223). 'New images' were, for him, 'a new kind of token, made to yield new forms of understanding [...] to disturb and disorientate by blurring comfortable boundaries and encouraging transgression of rules on which we have come to rely' (p. 223). He held that digital technologies contribute to 'relentlessly destabilising the old photographic orthodoxy, denaturing the established rules of graphic communication, and disrupting the familiar practices of image production and exchange' (p. 223). Pushing the argument still further, Crary suggested that the birth of digital imagery constituted 'a transformation in the nature of visuality probably more profound than the break that separates medieval imagery from Renaissance perspective' (1990: p. 1). Mounting fears that the 'new model of vision' brought by digital technologies would eventually kill photography (Ritchin, 1990) echoed painters' words of panic upon the invention of photography in earlier ages (starting in the first half of the nineteenth century). Yet we know that this technology for mechanical reproduction never managed to extinguish painters' art. In a sense, it breathed new life into it, liberating it from the duty of producing realist accounts of the world. Similarly, the arrival of digital technology prompted rethinking the mission and possibilities of photography. It has opened a new avenue of approach to photography and image-making – stimulating novel ways of getting images to travel especially. What it has **not** done is make images less important in and for human life. Perhaps the digital has even made images more 'present' (see Favero, 2018) and interstitial than ever in our lives. They reach us in our most intimate moments as well as the most public ones, interpellating our bodies, brains, and minds simultaneously. This aspect is crucial when it comes to the world of XR. Before we connect back to XR, however, let us stay a little longer with the difference between analogue and digital images. A manifestation of computer-driven decomposition and recomposition of discontinuous chunks of information (the pixel values), digital images appear at first to be significantly different from analogue images with their dots populating a continuous and indefinite landscape of visible information. And the principle behind the creation of a digital image most certainly differs significantly from that characterising analogue images. Digital images function through a process called filtering, which builds on assigning a value (a number denoting tone and colour) to a pixel at the level of the raster grid (via the processor). Because every unit (here, every pixel) always contains a predefined amount of information, it is limited in spatial and tonal resolution accordingly. A complete image, then, is nothing less (or more) than the result of this numerical act of giving a value to each individual pixel. This processuality is the reason digital images are conventionally addressed through notions of performance.

The procedure of creating a digital image, centred as it is on the presence of what Marshall McLuhan in the 1960s called 'electric circuitry' (McLuhan & Fiore, 1967), constitutes quite a significant break from the chemical procedure that characterises analogue photography. For many lovers of analogue photography, it has wrested away a feeling of certainty over the image's adherence to the referent, which the analogue seemed to provide. It also led to seemingly ubiquitous associations between the digital and immateriality. Recent developments in artificial intelligence take this into yet another dimension (you might cast your mind back to the discussion of photorealism in Section 3.2). The positions of those who assert an essential, radical difference between digital and analogue images, however, display what we would consider an overly narrow focus on the level of production – that is, on an opposition drawn between processor and chemical reaction. And no doubt, at this level, the rupture is significant. Nevertheless, we cannot help but find fascination in the sense some photographers express of a distance the digital has imposed relative to the real world. Digital photography is often accused of having at its core automated procedures that escape our comprehension capacity, yet how many of us really know how darkroom chemicals function deep down? As Zylinska (2015) has pointed out, photography has always been characterised by automation to some degree. Its development involved layering continuous integration of set, automated procedures at the levels of chemistry and mechanics early on (think of the winding of the film forward in the camera, automatic shutter-speed settings, flash cubes etc.), then electronics later, in combination with a number of automatic or instinctive reactions to the world surrounding the photographer. Photography has from its very inception been simultaneously human and nonhuman – 'it is precisely through focusing on its nonhuman aspect that we can find life in photography' (Zylinska, 2015: p. 132).

In this scenario it is worth wondering about the extent to which the digital truly has changed our way of experiencing and relating to images. McQuire wrote that, irrespective of the way in which it is produced and distributed, a picture 'remains much the same for viewers' (2013: p. 225). We believe that there is indeed continuity to be found here. However, there are significant differences too. We are faced with novel tools that allow images to form on mass scale, rich variety in visualisation practices, pervasiveness, etc. And the novel means always allow and, indeed, encourage new forms of engagement. We find ourselves involved with images dynamically, saving them, editing them, sharing them, enlarging them with a gesture of our fingers. Digital images wrap us in their own multi-sense act. On top of that, images come to us in new ways: their journey, travel, and distribution indeed bear new modalities and possibilities within their essence. To follow their travels, we had best engage with images along a multifaceted continuum, between the analogue and the digital, the 'actual' and the 'virtual', the manually and mechanically produced, the still and the moving. An integrative understanding lets us factor in other dimensions too – facets of the visible, the acoustic, the verbal that are part of a dialectic giving birth to artefacts, practices, and tokens that are, at once, new and old. They compel us to acknowledge the new and coexisting forms of 'imageness' (Rancière, 2008).

With digital technologies' arrival on the scene, images have therefore become more paradoxical than ever. They are objects invested with a duty of doing many (at times contradictory) things at once: of representing and presenting, of presencing, of crafting and connecting. This ambition, we would like to suggest, is far from unique to our epoch, though. Images have fulfilled this function in many cultural contexts (of the past as well as of the present, here as well as in faraway places). In Antiquity and in many religious contexts today, images often have operated as portals, two-way gates allowing an exchange between human beings and the world surrounding them. For instance, in relation to Byzantine-inspired imagery, Florensky wrote, from the standpoint of a monk, art historian, and theologian in the early nineteenth century, that an image is 'not only a window through which the visages depicted in them appear, but also a gate from which these enter the sensible world' (1977: p. 69). The work Edwards did in the context of Aboriginal Australia resonates with this understanding in terms of photographs functioning as relational objects. Photographs constitute an element in a much broader performance (for her informants, central to the act of articulating histories that have been suppressed), a performance that materialises the relationships between specific individuals who engage each other through such images. There is a similarity here to how representations of the gods are considered to be direct emanations/manifestations of those gods in the context of the Hindu devotional practices mentioned in the first part of the book. This is, as we saw, implied in the notion of *Darsan*: the act of looking is, in this setting, an act of being looked at, an ongoing interpenetration leading to complete immersion in the image (as mentioned in Section 3.1). These ways of looking are guided by the logic of what Pinney called corpothetics, which you will recall is an 'embodied, corporeal aesthetics' that stands in opposition to 'disinterested' representation trapping the image in an overly intellectualised and text-based form. Their logic foregrounds efficacy and presence rather than realistic representation, and it connects the act of seeing to that of touching. Babb's description of seeing in this context is telling – it is an 'outward-reaching process' (1981: p. 393) that directly engages the object seen. Seeing is a material exchange between the viewer and the viewed, one involving not just the eyes but the whole body. One truly does become what one sees.

We want to claim that these parallel ways of conceiving and engaging with images have been sidelined, especially in the West, by certain hegemonic narratives of realist representation (described near the beginning of this book) and by linguistic reductions. Proceeding from the latter, Barbara Maria Stafford (for awareness of whose work we are indebted to Pinney) in her writings on surfaces attacks the 'totemization of language as a godlike agency' (1996: p. 5) that seems to permeate Western culture. She suggests that Saussure's schema 'emptied the mind of its body' by reducing images to 'encrypted messages requiring decipherment' (p. 6). Starting with reflection on the fear of surfaces that in her view characterises Western scholarship,

Stafford's insightful scholarship directs our attention to thinkers' intrinsic desire to move beyond the surface of things, always chasing deeper layers of meaning (a Platonic legacy perhaps). Language constitutes one avenue for this, providing the viewer with the possibility of 'reducing' an image to the linguistic code it may be carrying. Pinney (paraphrasing Elkins, 1999) stated that 'the code is what matters, for this is the mechanism that allows pictures to be "read" (2006: p. 135). Pinney also highlighted Walter Benjamin's famous intuition related to it in the 1930s, about which the latter wrote that the future will see 'the caption [become] the most important part of the shot' (p. 133). And, with regard to the former, realist representation relies, as we saw earlier on, upon the conventions that were established by Renaissance central geometrical perspective. Grounded in the West's growing obsession with rationality, lines, and mathematics, and mirroring the articulation of hierarchies for relations between the senses and the intellect, central geometrical perspective came to constitute a scopic regime (i.e., a dominant theory of vision, in Jay's model). Let us remind the reader of a crucial point at this juncture: conventionally, that geometrical perspective was cast in metaphor with the aid of a window allowing measurement of a particular view. This portrayal, however, encourages a sense of separation between the observer and the observed, the self and the world. Inviting viewers to position themselves outside the image, it made reciprocity impossible. Instead of letting them situate themselves within the image, it offered to grant them a sense of control over the image. While central geometrical perspective does not represent the full spectrum of images produced by Western artists (even in the wake of the Renaissance, as we saw), it nevertheless constitutes a kind of hegemony that has progressively marginalised other kinds of approach to the world of images.

Let us now start exploring the extent to which we can regard XR as a challenge to these conventional assumptions. We give centre stage to both new and old contemporary ways of understanding the image that transcend prefabricated cultural assumptions. We begin this reflection by offering a couple of examples from the world of today's immersive art and documentary forms.

3.4.3 VR/MR Art and Documentary Forms

Draw Me Close is a 2017 MR 'experience', as the official presentation of the performance described it. Using a combination of hand-trackers and VR goggles, this play is a one-on-one work authored by award-winning playwright and filmmaker Jordan Tannahill.[8]

One at a time, the viewers are exposed to an intimate encounter in VR. In a small room, they encounter the director's mother, who died of cancer when he was a young boy. The performance stages his distant memories through an actress wearing sensors. In a live setting, she makes movements and gestures that the viewers receive in the shape of black-and-white drawings displayed by the VR goggles. While we have not yet had a chance to experience the live performance ourselves, we have interacted profoundly with viewers' testimonials after we viewed it online. This was more than enough for impressing on us the 'short circuit' that this experience frequently generates. As they enter a VR space filled with animated drawings, viewers are suddenly asked to abandon the realm of 'real-life' experience and enter one of simulation-based storytelling. This movement becomes tangible when the viewers are asked to draw on a canvas. Watching their own drawings become colourful traces within a simulated environment, they start closing the gap between the virtual and the actual. The full-fledged short circuit arrives at a later moment, however: when the mother (embodied by the actress) eventually requests permission to hug them. A disruptive moment, this brings the virtual further into direct contact with the actual, physically mediated experience of the viewers' own bodies.

We experienced a similar short-circuiting when viewing *6X9*, a VR experience produced by the British newspaper *The Guardian* and directed by Francesca Pennetta.[9] Simulating an experience of solitary confinement, *6X9* inserts viewers into a tiny greyish room as soon as they enter the VR space. One of the authors of this book, upon entering this experience, found himself seated on the bed in one corner of the room. The room was in semi-darkness, but he could detect a few objects within the space. Opposite the viewer was a door with a tiny window secured by metal bars. The author recalls that, at a certain point, he noticed the book and the magazine lying on a shelf next to him and that he heard voices filtering in from outside. As time passed, being in the room became progressively more disturbing. At one point, the room shook; the lights went off and came on again. The voices from outside the door grew louder and more pervasive. Warnings of a possible moment of panic started rising in him: suffering from claustrophobia, this viewer was feeling too warm and had started to sweat. However, he inadvertently interrupted that swell by touching the table in front of him in the room hosting the VR experience. 'Visible' only to his real-world hands, this table brought him into a kind of split consciousness: his hands and his eyes anchored him in two separate, though perhaps parallel, bifocal worlds. His mind-body complex was suddenly torn. Where was he? Rather more, who and what was he? Where was his body now that the sweat seemed to belong more to the virtual space and his hands to the actual one? Was he the person wearing goggles or the convict in the cell? Or maybe both? Should he trust his eyes or trust his hands?

Both experiences clearly direct our attention to the space in between self and other, perhaps better conceived of as between 'self' and 'not-self'. Through the multiple short circuits described above, we are interrogated. We also are called to question these boundaries and led to reflect further on our perception (mediated by the images) of the relations between body and mind. In consequence, we may end up reflecting on our awareness of the relativity of the self.

Let us briefly follow a side path here. We believe that, to grasp such insight fully, we ought to abandon the terrain of dualistic epistemologies. We might, in fact, be well served by contemplating the perception-related insight that characterises, for instance, what we have been referring to as Buddhist philosophy (we apply this gloss in full awareness that neither it nor 'Buddhism' is apt for describing the corpus of knowledge constituting the teachings conventionally attributed to the figure of the Buddha, but we would warn the reader about the epistemological traps often carried on the wings of customary terminology). While it is not within the scope of this chapter to wade deeply into this debate, we ought to point out that the principle of non-duality or of double negation, which is one of the pillars of Buddhist thought (Shaw, 1978), can enrich our understanding of this in-between space, this being neither self nor not-self. Avoiding reductions to binary oppositions, Buddhist philosophy suggests that between such poles we may contemplate the possibility of being simultaneously both self and not-self and also neither self nor non-self. Such resistance to dichotomies is key to the Buddhist (agnostic) way of addressing the world. Looking upon the subject as an impermanent, fleeting object in constant becoming, Buddhism engages with the world through a constant act of 'confrontation' (Batchelor, 1998: p. 18) rather than through a search for solid, stable answers. Grounded in contingency and ambiguity, it builds on recognition of transcendence and of the impossibility of fully knowing (see also Tucci, 1992; von Glasenapp, 1967). The logic of double negation takes a place on this terrain, one where human perceptions of the world may be neither fully true nor wholly false. Within this (circular) space, 'I' can be simultaneously self and not-self and, again, also neither self nor non-self. 'I' can be simultaneously here and not-here. An equivalent conclusion is valid for the terrain of images, which in Buddhism are simultaneously appearance, form (and hence illusion), and also not less true than objective reality (see Crosby, 2020; Divino, 2024). We suggest that the application of these (consciously unstable) epistemological principles can help us grasp what happens in VR/XR/MR. It can aid us in addressing the various shifts in identification that contribute to many viewers' perceptions. In such environments, viewers are simultaneously neither self nor not-self, neither presence nor absence, neither 'body' nor 'not-body'. They engage in a processual (performative) confrontation that eventually leads them to discover the fragmented nature of the self, the multisensory nature of human perceptions, and the continuum where the body-mind complex resides. This way of operating, which constitutes an attempt at decolonising our knowledge, can yield new insight into that possibly 'uncanny' territory. As we enact this effort by inserting elements borrowed from other epistemologies, we discover experiences that, in Freud's (1919) definition of the term, are 'strangely familiar' and hence both known and not-known.

The act of entering such image spaces entails abandoning ourselves to a curved, ephemeral, dynamic, and shifting frame that differs significantly from the square frame that is standard for flat/2D images. Rather than an act of pure seeing, of grasping, and perhaps also of controlling a totality (as a perspectival image would allow us to do), such image environments imply an act of acceptance of this totality, of becoming one with it, of abandoning any desire to dominate or even to understand. Viewers have to renounce the safeties of the window and accept being inside the image. Let us unpack this issue further.

3.4.4 Reframing Viewing

Hence, XR experiences pose several further challenges to conventional ways of approaching the world of images. For starters, these images are interactive – they are personal (hence marking a step away from 'mass' media) and multi-sense (appealing via vision, sound, movement, and tactility). Acknowledging this core element of their nature entails rethinking various terms in the course of our enquiry, terms foundational to the models conventionally applied for analysing images. For instance, how should we address the frame in a setting where it has morphed from a protective square that (as in Dürer's famous illustration of a perspectival frame in *The Painter's Manual*, from 1525) separated the viewer from the world and become instead an embracing environment within which the viewer can move? We must wrestle with how to speak of 'frames' when viewers are not external to (and hence are no longer in control of) the visual field. And how can we approach the various ways in which images come to us in the absence of the 'beamer', that politically dense apparatus that, with its fixed point of emanation of light, reproduces the principles that informed Renaissance perspective? Fruit of a long process of evolution from the *camera obscura*, the magic lantern, the silhouette, and the cathode ray tube, projection is, in fact, far from neutral.

Let us give some pointers to how these questions may be addressed. We can start with the notion of the frame. A key notion that, as we saw above, has intimately shaped the history of mechanically produced images (see, among many, Flusser, 2006; Van Lier, 1983/2007), the frame, which extends the window, seems to be what many image-makers have, across times and spaces, attempted to transcend. Strides in this direction, toward immersive viewing, present scholars too with a challenge, to which they have responded by coining new terms. For instance, the context of VR has brought us cave (Buczek, 2014), womb (Sloterdijk, 2011), and other metaphors for exploring the terrain. The need for transcending the frame is not purely an intellectual preoccupation: it is evident also to those who have engaged with this arena's novel cameras from a practical point of view. That said, a frame, albeit not a square and fixed one, is still present in such environments. One of our key challenges, then, is to find a suitable language for conveying its nature. Scholars in the field of VR have grappled with this question in hopes of highlighting the sense of totality that such spaces are designed to generate. For instance, Grau suggested that the essence of VR is that it 'fulfils the concept of total perspective' (1999: p. 365), and Hansen spoke about the quest for a 'fully mobile frameless vision, an "absolute frame" of the visible field' (2004: p. 170). Perhaps, speaking of a quest for totality is less helpful, though, than speaking of the entry into these spaces as immersion in a different kind of environment. This is a curved and dynamic space, shaping up in accordance with multiple modes of engagement that differ between viewers. Therefore, it requires, if we may borrow from Hansen again, a different kind of 'bodily spacing' (p. 163). As we mentioned above, the greatest realisation in producing and viewing immersive images with contemporary 360-degree cameras is that the viewers are constantly asked to reflect upon their position in relation to such images. In a stark difference from geometrical perspective, our place within this image is internal to the image itself, so we have difficulty in exiting and, hence, controlling it. Things happen behind the back of the image-maker just as much as beyond the viewer's sight, things that are outside the (narrative) control of both.

Simultaneously, the curved character of such spaces blurs conventional distinctions of before and after, front and back. When image-makers construct a sequence of events in immersive images, they cannot be sure that the viewers will actually see exactly what they want them to see. They must concentrate instead on giving the viewer an opportunity to be in the environment they have constructed. This is not a place for guiding anyone into seeing something in particular. It is a space of contemplation rather than of narration and representation. And the alteration seen here parallels developments such as the changing mission of the documentary filmmaker. In an April 2013 interview with Favero, documentary filmmaker and Delhi-based Raqs Media Collective member Shuddha Sengupta explained that 'the scope of the image-maker, documentarist, or artist today is no longer that of showing what was previously unseen given that today this, with the present spread of new imaging technologies, can be done by anyone. Rather her duty is to create a space in which viewers can share their own experiences and reflections around topics characterizing their everyday life'.

Employing one of the metaphors mentioned above, P. Sloterdijk (2011) spoke about immersion in 360-degree images as a descent into a womb. Spinning further thread onto this metaphor lets us regard it as a descent into (or a return from) the world. New immersive images offer us a chance for closing the gap between the observer and the observed (and between the self and the world), a gulf produced by Renaissance perspective and bulwarked by its modern children: the flat cinema screen and photographic image. While geometrical perspective expresses a modernist desire to 'picture' (and control) the world (per Heidegger, 1977), contemporary immersive images bring back to our attention Saint Augustine's depiction of human beings as being caught between the solid and aerial elements that according to him composed the Earth. In his discussion of the shape of the Earth, Ingold (2011) brought Saint Augustine's vision in contact with Immanuel Kant's. For the latter, the Earth was a space on which to stand rather than one for being immersed in. That idea cemented itself over the years in mainstream theories regarding perception. Ingold argued that Kant's vision held sway until it was contested by scholars such as Gibson and Heidegger, who, as Saint Augustine had, stressed the idea that 'people are of the earth, they do not just live on it' (p. 112). Contemporary immersive images seem to be bringing this idea to prominence again (see also Dolezal, 2009). When entering immersive image spaces, we are contained within the frame of the image – a curved, ephemeral, and shifting frame but a frame nonetheless. Rather than an act of seeing, grasping, and perhaps also controlling a totality, being in such spaces turns into an act of acceptance of this totality, of becoming one with it as we abandon any desire to dominate and understand it. Such a stance draws our attention back to Husserl's (1952/1989) idea of the body as that which 'feels', 'can' (and hence 'does'), and 'perceives', and hence as what constitutes the centre of all our experiences. It also brings to our attention Merleau-Ponty's (1962) attempts at closing the gap between the self and the world. Merleau-Ponty mused that 'when I begin to reflect my reflection bears upon an unreflective experience' (p. x) and that 'there is no inner man, man is in the world, and only in the world does he know himself' (p. xi). Later on in the same text he sums up his view:

> I am neither here nor there, neither Paul nor Peter; I am in no way distinguishable from an 'other' consciousness, since we are immediately in touch with the world and since the world is, by definition, unique, being the system in which all truths cohere.
>
> (p. xi)

If we are to follow this approach, the act of entering a space (no matter whether virtual or actual) is an act of acceptance that foregrounds a form of pre-reflexive observation and description rather than some rational explanation and analysis. Truth emerges here as an experience that is strictly dependent upon the observer, not on the thing out there: 'We are in the realm of truth and it is "the experience of truth" which is self-evident' (Merleau-Ponty, 1962: p. xvi).

Such a reading breaks down the barrier between the 'I' and the world that was sustained by rationalism. We can now transition toward that sense of oneness between the human and the world that makes up the fundament not only of Saint Augustine's intuition but also of many other knowledge systems, such as Buddhist, Hindu, and various animist ones (see Knott, 1999; Tucci, 1992; von Glasenapp, 1967). Suspending the distinction between the observer and the observed and between self and world, when combined with a sense of detached observation and acceptance of the world surrounding us, brings us toward the origin's co-ordinates in practices of meditation (see Easwaran, 1978). And it is with little surprise that we notice the extent to which VR and 360-degree images serve teaching of meditation techniques and working through extraordinary traumatic events. In the context of medical care, VR is interestingly used in two distinct directions. Firstly, experimentation engages with it as an extension of exposure treatment, employed to address a fear of flying, irrational fears of wild animals, and other types of phobia. It is widely used also in therapy for post-traumatic stress disorder. The second avenue, increasingly travelled, is that of VR environments' application to train medical personnel in better understanding the symptoms or reactions of mental-health patients – for example, for handling and preparing for cases of panic attacks. In VR, the therapist is exposed to a simulation of a panic attack with the intent of improved relations to patients. Here too, VR serves a bridging and barrier-breaching function. Before moving on, we should mention the growing popularity of VR as a tool for training surgeons and for conducting surgeries remotely, spurred on in part by the pandemic and work with medics in war zones.

3.4.5 Immersive Longings

The desire for immersion that these new images respond to and elicit is far from unique to them and also far from novel. This is a longing that has persisted throughout the history of visual art and of image-making techniques and technologies. We may regard it as a desire, ambition, or yearning that human beings, across vast stretches of space and time, have expressed in relation to the world of images – a longing to close the gap, through the image, between the human self and the world. Expressions of this yearning can be found in some of the examples we discussed in the first part of this book. But let us offer some more examples also, in order to showcase the diverse modes through which immersive viewing was reached in ages past.

At Pompeii's Villa dei Misteri (House of Mysteries), in the Italy of the second century BCE, the surfaces of the walls are filled with a rich variety of scenes blending mythology and day-to-day life. Painted figures converse with each other from opposite walls as they look and point at one another. A sense of involvement strikes visitors as they find themselves quite literally surrounded by the exchanges and by the events that are portrayed on these walls, with the Dionysian initiation ritual (a core element of this set of paintings) probably being the most evocative of the exchanges. The gazes that the painted characters extend across the room are among the main tools through which a sense of immersion is generated in the viewers. In an continual fading of 'the borders between visual and actual space' (Grau, 1999: p. 365), viewers become part of the painting and the world that it portrays, while the image starts appearing as 'a portal through which in one direction the gods pass into the real world and in the other real people enter into the image' (p. 366).

In Rome, in turn, the Ara Paci Augustae altar, dated to around 13 BCE, cultivates a sense of immersion by means of a game of materiality and shadows. As discussed to some extent above, the internal space of this altar to Pax (the Roman goddess of peace) is shaped through a merging of bas-relief, depicting scenes from mythology, and elements of nature (mainly leaves) that extend from and into the walls. While Pompeii (and Herculaneum) offer unique examples of the Roman use of painting on internal walls, these bas-relief and sculptural components display techniques that ancient Roman artists and architects more typically used for exploiting the space represented by the walls. Using the wall as a 'hypothetical space, a plane of projection' (Argan, 2008: p. 147), they found the wall to be not a boundary but a juncture, a portal between physical natural space and pictorial space. Later on, the use of stucco added such spatial experiences to the context of painting. It allowed for the creation of thick, modulated surfaces presenting views from multiple angles of observation. In doing so, it permitted actual life (in the shape of light and shadows) to mix with the visual impressions generated by the objects represented in the image.

Roman Catholic and Greek Orthodox church structures designed under the influence of Byzantium offer insight into yet another immersive technique, this one based upon a blend of materiality and composition. The mausoleum Galla Placidia, in Ravenna (from the fifth century AD), also discussed earlier on, embraces the viewer with visual details that are placed all over the walls. The use of mosaic in particular, with its extensive variety of materials capable of absorbing and diffracting light, has a deceiving and displacing effect on the people present here. Similarly to Roman stuccoes, it plays tricks on viewers' perceptions of the dimensions of the space in which they find themselves, hence leading to their transcendence of physical space altogether (see Argan, 2008). As Greek Orthodox churches still make evident today, worshippers are also surrounded by a broader set of sensory experiences, by the glittering and flickering light generated by candles mirrored on the metal and the glass tiles composing the image, by the smell of incense, and by the sound of bells. This exposure to a full sensorial experience brings viewers, through their senses, in touch with the divine.

We could continue by citing more examples from Antiquity, but our main goal was to show how immersive viewing gets supported by means of several techniques: portrayed gazes and the spatial disposition of pictorial elements (in the context of Pompeii), shadows and bas-relief (in the Ara Pacis case), and light and its manipulation (in the Galla Placidia example). For the next stop on our journey, let us fast-forward to modernity and observe how a quest for immersivity is also characteristic of many modern practices.

Stereoscopic images were created at the very dawn of photographic history. Along with panoramic formats, these expressed a concrete attempt at moving as far as possible away from the limitations imposed by the narrow square or rectangular frame accompanying the first cameras. These functioned to awaken physical reactions to a landscape or evoke arousal with regard to erotic or even pornographic imagery (Gilardi, 2002). Cinema responded to the same craving for immersion (and for a dynamic environment in which to move), with 3D movies. Supposedly born in response to the possibilities offered by sound for surrounding the viewer (see Elsaesser, 2013), 3D cinema speaks to a desire for, according to Akira Mizuta Lippit (1999), overcoming the limitations to perception imposed by screens and frames. In the words of Thomas Elsaesser, this is an attempt to 'self-abolish' the 'apparatic scaffolding and peculiar geometry of representation' (2013: p. 229). Both 3D cinema and formats following in its wake (IMAX etc.) can, therefore, be seen as direct precursors of VR, introducing 'the malleability, scalability, fluidity, or curvature of digital images into audiovisual space' (p. 235). The list of examples could go on with experiences wrought by cubism, Dada, and futurism, all of which manifested an attempt at bringing onto a single canvas multiple angles or moments of observation. Our journey could also take us further into the world of video installations, such as work by Ken Jacobs and Bill Viola, or of the 3D laser-mapping installations of Danny Rose or Miguel Chevalier. We argue that all these works, irrespective of the diversity of techniques deployed, are united by the desire to overcome the separation between the observer and the observed, the 'I' and the world typical of flat images. Instead of delving into these, we pursue more detail-level insight as to this yearning by taking yet another leap back in time, into exploring the principles that underpin Byzantine-art-inspired icons.

3.4.5.1 Transformative Viewing: A Dialogue Across Religious Icons and VR/XR/MR

Emerging in the ninth century as 'the privileged image' (Pencheva, 2010), icons have as one of their key characteristics a resistance against complying with any single type of mathematical reduction – whether geometrical perspective or others. They are constituted by a combination of techniques of composition as well as of material production, all of which contribute to offering each viewer multiple (sense-driven) points of entry. Supported by a specific spiritual vision, the pictures are dynamic, allowing viewers to observe them literally as well as metaphorically from a variety of perspectives (see Figure 3.4.)

The first thing to notice when diving into the visuality of icons is that these are neither fully bi- nor fully tri-dimensional images (Lindsay Opie, 2014). Icons are conventionally characterised by what is commonly referred to as 'reverse perspective', with the vanishing point often cast as behind the viewer (Argan, 2008; Florensky, 1967; Marci, 2014; Pencheva, 2010). Rather than being unaware of the principles of geometrical viewing, Byzantine painters seem to have developed a different (perhaps 'parallel') spatialisation of the relationship between the image and the viewer. In terms of design techniques, these images are divided into two main layers. The front layer, the one where the face of the divine or holy is portrayed, traditionally gets positioned on a flat surface, facing the viewer front-on. The rest of the image (from the head and the hair to the aura and the background) is typified, in contrast, by a rounded shape that is designed in accordance with the above-mentioned principle of reverse perspective (see Sendler, 1985).

108 *Visual Studies*

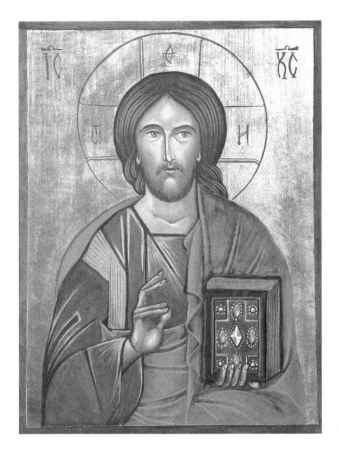

Figure 3.4 Sacred icon representing Jesus.

Source: Painter: Suor Maria Silvia Favero.

The explanation above seems cut and dried, yet debate has raged among icon-painters and art historians alike as to whether the vanishing point is situated behind the viewers vs. at the height of their eyes. What is clear is that, through this composition of foreground and background, viewers are simultaneously front-on with the face of the holy and also wrapped into it. As art historian Bissera Pencheva has suggested, the 'picture space' of an icon 'opens up in front of the image rather than behind it' (2010: p. 6).

There is more to the icon, however, which adds to its magnificent complexity. Were we to look even further into the visuality of the icon, we could state that, in its overlap of foreground and background, it offers a visuality explainable only within the logic of Buddhist double negation: neither inside nor outside, yet simultaneously in both positions. Meanwhile, the viewer stands before the icon. By way of their colours but also their use of metals, icons shine, often causing one's self to be mirrored in them. In fact, their golden background offers no actual representational context. The divine entity seldom appears surrounded by objects or landscapes. Instead, it invites viewers to mirror themselves and their own context of viewing in the picture. In this sense, icons are truly reflexive images. The thin golden foil that makes up their background is meant to bring the viewer in direct touch with the divine figure portrayed – 'instead of the light reflected from the outside world we find uniform gold, thanks to which the image itself becomes an independent source of light' (Lindsay Opie, 2014: p. 146). Symbolising 'pure divine light' (Sendler, 1985), the golden foil is to be understood within the spiritual framework that sustains icons. It is also informed by a visuality defined by a theory of extramission – 'the eye was active, sending off rays that touched the surfaces of objects' (Pencheva, 2010: p. 5). The foil is, hence, neither illustration nor decoration but a tool for communicating directly with the realm of the divine (of the invisible) and for entering it. There is no subjectivity involved on the painter's part here. The creator is just a conduit toward 'true participation at the world of divine archetypes' (Lindsay Opie, 2014: p. 146). As a form of 'sustained dream' (Florensky, 1977: p. 34), icons, like works of spiritual art in general, grant what Florensky called access to a 'world upside-down' (1977: p. 31). They raise the soul above earthly matters, bringing it in touch with another dimension (the 'celestial' one). Florensky suggested that this world (with its 'curvatures' – that is, its spiritual essence) manifests itself only through the interaction with the viewer, behaving, in his metaphor, like 'a magnetic field on top of a surface that gets visible only by pouring metal dust' (p. 52). Quite unlike paintings following geometrical perspective, icons are 'the cliff of celestial figures […]. Icons materially sign these penetrating and immemorial gazes, these super-sensual ideas, making inaccessible visions almost public' (p. 64). The strength of icons, Egon Sendler suggested, lies in their capacity to be 'images of the invisible' (1985). Other types of icon take exploration of the use of materiality even further. In the past in particular, they have been produced in relief or constructed with the assistance of materials whose texture can provide the viewer with a sense of direct tactile engagement. Pencheva stated that the icon is a site of 'tactile visuality' (2010: pp. 6–7), that is sensorially experienced.

Notwithstanding their figurative centre (an image of Christ, of the Virgin Mary, etc.), icons evidently have as their primary mission not that of representing but one of taking the worshippers elsewhere, to transform them through the act of viewing. Via artefacts such as icons, art provides human beings with a connection between the visible and the invisible world. Similarly to Hindu devotional images, therefore, such images are not a mere representation of something out there but a portal to another experiential dimension. Objects of 'visual ascesis' (Lindsay Opie, 2014) they speak of presence, contemplation, and transformation rather than narration. In a movement that perhaps carries things in a direction opposite that of Renaissance perspective, these techniques position viewers in the co-presence of possible parallel worlds. We could spotlight the evident parallel with Buddhist non-duality, alongside various other ties.

We could go even further on this exploration of the visuality of icons from Byzantium and its environs; however, what has been said so far may have served our purpose sufficiently well, by opening room for seeing parallels with the world of XR.

In the context of VR, the body gains centrality. It is interpellated by a series of acts that simultaneously connect and disconnect the viewer relative to the image and its content. The body is foregrounded not as a mere 'appendage to the self' (Dolezal, 2009: p. 209) but as the core tool through which engagement with the world – of whatever form – becomes possible. These acts seem to crystallise Merleau-Ponty's conclusion that humans can only be (and know themselves) 'in the world'. Such images also accentuate some extent of interactivity, asking viewers to actively engage with and move within the space depicted. With their multiple short circuits of mind and body, VR images provoke instances of dissociation, hence transforming viewers and reinserting them in their actuality in a new way – often at least temporarily in a new position. It is of little surprise, then, that VR experiences are being explored in medical settings for such profound applications as immersive surgery training and coming to terms with post-traumatic stress, eating disorders, and panic attacks.

The dialogues between the worlds of XR and those of icons may not be explicit. Even if 'only' possible, they surely speak of the manifold ways in which humans have striven to use images for more fully entering the world in which they live and for transforming themselves. Also, it is not beyond the realm of imagination that the visuality characteristic of the world of icons directly inspired several contemporary artists. That visuality is, after all, part of the cultural heritage of our world. Whatever interpretation we want to give to this dialogue, the parallels between these different regimes of visuality are many. They both address matters of interactivity and multisensoriality. Both also shift from a pure 'representational duty' and toward contemplation coupled with a transformative act of presencing. Taking us away from narration and realistic representation, they move toward that sense of oneness between the human and the world that makes up the fundament of many knowledge systems, as noted above. Hence, such visualities seem to flow against the hegemonic trends of Western visual culture that we have discussed. Disrupting the geometrical-political conventions that permeate conventional understandings of camera-produced images, they threaten the assumptions that we have inherited from Renaissance perspective and that have been consolidated by photography and film. A step into the elsewhen and the elsewhere can, accordingly, greatly assist us in grasping such contemporary digital visual practices found on new terrain. We hope also that it contributes to decolonising our overall understanding of visual culture.

Notes

1 See Oxford English Dictionary entry for 'theory'.
2 See Prakash C, Stephens KD, Hoffman DD, Singh M, Fields C. Fitness Beats Truth in the Evolution of Perception. *Acta Biotheor*. 2021 Sep;69(3):319–341. doi: 10.1007/s10441-020-09400-0.
3 A photograph, some scholars have suggested, can only provide us with a kind of 'generalisation' of the events that it is intended to portray. Entrapped in a single moment (the present crystallised there), it does not contain these events but only offers a kind of summary of them. It provides a 'pointer' (Chaudhary, 2012: p. 68) in that direction, an 'index' in the sense of an index finger and rather less an index as a guarantee of holding some 'truth' as several positivistic photography scholars would have it.
4 Recall that Merleau-Ponty regarded vision as attached to movement through the presence of the body. A part of the visible world, the body is at one with vision: 'I only have to see something to know how to reach it and deal with it' he wrote (1964: p. 120). Body and vision are inextricably connected through a series of reciprocal exchanges; one 'simultaneously sees and is seen' (p. 120).
5 See Oxford English Dictionary entry for 'semiotics'.
6 See Justin McCurry: Erica, the 'most beautiful and intelligent' android, leads Japan's robot revolution, *The Guardian*, 31.12.2015. https://theguardian.com/technology/2015/dec/31/erica-the-most-beautiful-and-intelligent-android-ever-leads-japans-robot-revolution.
7 There is further discussion in the video 'Meet Erica, the world's most autonomous android' at https://theguardian.com/technology/ng-interactive/2017/apr/07/meet-erica-the-worlds-most-autonomous-android-video.
8 *Draw Mm Close* is a joint production of the National Theatre's Immersive Storytelling Studio and the National Film Board of Canada, in collaboration with All Seeing Eye. The trailer can be seen at https://youtube.com/watch?v=4zokAxgRNYs, and further analysis is available in video form at https://youtube.com/watch?v=XrpUvRSb2E0.
9 For details, see video '6x9: a virtual experience of solitary confinement' at https://youtube.com/watch?v=odcsxUbVyZA&t=13s.

4 Applications of Visual Studies

A central tenet of our method of approach is that we need to understand the look as a medium and, hence, focus on the various ways in which images are mediated, whatever the means might be – the skin of one's body, dreams or hallucinations, framed photographs hung on a wall, or posts on Instagram. Without mediation, we claim, images do not exist, as they always rely on modes of interaction in order to become perceivable at all. This chapter examines a few telling examples of how the theorising conducted so far can be applied with regard to specific themes and topics. We will move from faces to cameras and then address the role of images in relation to death. Finally, we enter the realms of X-ray imagery and of shadows. Our hope is that contemplating such examples stimulates the reader's imagination and supplies inspiration for finding new, interesting areas of human life to analyse from a visual perspective. As you will see, our approach is not based on applying one method, but rather, to take our curiosities toward images seriously and start to ponder: how do they partake in our ways of living life?

4.1 The Significance of Faces

Image theorists, pondering on the earliest images created, tend to stress the human experience of death as one of the principal reasons for image use. In the absence of life, the body remaining starts to decay, and after some time only the skeleton remains. Decorated skulls found on grave sites suggest that the human head and specifically the face have played a key role in remembering a deceased person while possibly also articulating a connection to an afterlife lived elsewhere (cf. Belting, 2011). From this perspective, the skull acts as a visual medium allowing an image to emerge (with the aid of the decoration applied to afford doing so), whereas the face by its absence becomes an image *par excellence*, in that the image has to be activated and animated in the act of looking at said skull. In such situations, the image emerges only in the looking by the beholder, who is able to connect the decorated visual medium with specific ways of looking. At the end of the 19th century, in

DOI: 10.4324/9781003084549-4

Figure 4.1 Painted skulls in an ossuary in Hallstatt Beinhaus Salzkammergut, Austria.
Credit: Mihnea Stanciu, cc-by-2.0.

a small cemetery in Hallstatt, Austria, room was made for new burials by exhuming bones and decorating skulls of deceased citizens with elaborate ornamentation (see Figure 4.1). The skull became an image of the person to be remembered.

This way of seeing a face reminds us of the possibilities for crafting images on other faces too, especially on those that are alive. Our faces have numerous tiny muscles that are important for perception, eating, and breathing but also for forming facial expressions. The expressions worn on our faces serve explicitly communicative purposes, relying to a large extent on visual cues in as they symbolically communicate with others. The cascades of images that are created with the aid of infinitely variable facial expressions allow for rich, nuanced, and complex forms of communication. There is still ongoing debate as to whether some facial expressions might be anthropologically universal, not moulded by particular cultures. Do cultural differences ultimately prevail, or is there a universal way of codifying some basal expressions? Expressions of fear and laughter especially have been considered universals, whereas less 'basal' expressions get regarded as more culturally dependent. Whatever the precise answer to this question may be, it is clear from visiting people across a range of locales from India, Syria, Japan, Brazil, California, and Finland that the visual repertoire of facial expressions varies considerably across cultures. The kinds of images that we create with the assistance of our faces, then, follow suit.

Facial expressions tend to be socially codified, and hence the cascades of images that we show with our faces are much more restricted than we might initially think is the case. Consider the grimaces that children in a range of cultures are allowed to show, and then transpose them to the face of a middle-aged man. The endearing and/or annoying grimace of a child becomes threatening if sported by an adult. The threat portrayed by that grimace on the face of an adult is a threat to social order. A grimacing adult has stepped out of line and is not displaying decorum. Showing signs of uncontrollability, a grimacing adult shows failure to act in accordance with social rules for approved behaviour. The grimace hence becomes a symbol of being wicked, mentally deranged, or a threat to the physical wellbeing of those around the grimacer.

Interestingly, several of the visual cultures that one may encounter on social-media platforms encourage grimaces at times, through filters applying facial-recognition technology. For example, Snapchat, an image-sharing platform that is popular among teenagers and young adults, specifically invites its users to 'step out of line' by grimacing. Here, grimacing is introduced not as a threat but as an affectively liberating form of image creation and use, one that allows users to free themselves for a moment from the strictly regulated repertoire of facial expressions suited to 'offline' settings. This affective engagement with otherwise forbidden modes of image use carries excitement – and hence emotional energy (Collins, 2005) that can be directed to phatic connections (see Niemelä-Nyrhinen & Seppänen, 2020; Prieto-Blanco, 2016) among those grimacing together. The grimacing face, in being presented via an additionally mediated visual medium, gets transmogrified from a threat into a healthily exciting feature. The key here is that the strict codification of visual facial expressions is loosened because of an invitation, by the layered-in platform, to do so.[1] Family, friends, colleagues, and social media acquaintances reacting with surprise to these mediated grimaces affirms the excitement that the grimace entails (see Figure 4.2.)

While the grimace is a dangerous image in itself, questioning and at times threatening codified social orders, its danger lies also in the excitement it creates by shaking up the formal arrangements of interaction orders, the established scopic regimes encountered earlier on our journey. Intriguingly, the excitement feels so thrilling that people in numerous spheres have become captivated by social media platforms of these sorts, seeking them out to create grimaces for sharing with others. Audiences, aesthetics, and affordances on social media become entwined via affective engagements (cf. Schreiber 2017).

The visual media used for changing the role and meaning of the grimace work by collecting databases of 'masks' of social-media users, which rely on the same facial recognition technologies serving practices of surveillance, embedded in many of the surveillance cameras discussed in Section 3.3. The

Applications of Visual Studies 115

Figure 4.2 Snapchat filter used by author as part of social interaction with child.

mask used for identifying individuals is derived from a face template created by delineating and referring to specific points on a face. While several distinct techniques exist (for a history, see Lehmuskallio & Meyer, 2022), the face mask, informed by the landmarks particular to a specific face, always involves an individuating grid that can function for identification purposes. We could regard the grimace as a destabilising image even in the safe-seeming domain of these platforms – not because it challenges socially approved interaction orders but because it populates databases of templates used for biometric identification, a contentious action.

People's joy and excitement about capturing images of faces when they are grimacing facilitates capturing databases similar to those used in various instances for surveillance purposes. While social media platforms do not necessarily take part in any surveillance activities beyond the purpose of providing templates for matching selfie filters to faces, they do participate in recontextualising and, hence, normalising the use of biometric technologies initially implemented for surveillance purposes. This banalisation of surveillance casts specific technologically mediated looking relations as favourable. There is a parallel with the relations discussed in connection with castigating embodied staring while accepting the 'surveillance camera stare'.

In these relations, repeated and layered mediations of the facial image serve not only in translating specific images of faces to novel media (e.g., from the skull to the mobile camera-phone screen) but also in transforming their significance. If, as we argue, a grimace on the face of an older adult in an embodied face-to-face situation is socially considered to be rude, threatening, a sign of not abiding by norms, etc., the excitement brought by a threat becomes pleasant excitement in the context of technical mediation visible on a screen via filters from social-media platforms such as Snapchat. One is allowed to grimace in front of others, given that the specific situated visual cultures of the social-media platform involved seem to suggest it to be acceptable. In order to be technically able to do so, the mediation includes creation and collection of face templates, thereby contributing to acceptance of surveillance practices followed in other social situations – at public parks, at border crossings, or in entering any of a wide range of buildings.

The mediations of the face, we suggest, are extremely significant not only because they allow us to focus on what gets shown where and with which kind of visual media but also because each mediation **transducts** what is mediated, transforming what gets phenomenally experienced. Transduction provides a phenomenologically different mode of perception that relies specifically on the kinds of mediations that render it possible in the first place. A person grimacing in front of a camera carries an image in *corpore*. That image displayed with the aid of the body then gets transducted into another mediated form by being sensed and reproduced with the aid of a camera phone. In the example discussed here, transduction into a representational form is possible only by means of additional facial recognition technology, creating a face template and matching this with the sensed face in order to merge it with a filter developed for grimacing in social-media settings. The filter, being part of the image displayed on the screen, further transforms the image in *corpore* into an image in effigy, one that needs to be perceived quite differently in comparison with the image displayed on one's body through the play of facial muscles. Clearly, the image in effigy is not the same as the bodily image produced for depiction and then sensed: it has been transduced explicitly to be experienced as a phenomenon differently from the image in *corpore*. When seeing the image in *corpore*, one might be able to detect the smell of the morning coffee of the person posing for an image, of unwashed hair, or of a new light fragrance, and one might feel warmth or coolness from the person's body. In effigy, all of these additional cues available for sensing are not directly accessible anymore; in contrast, the image in effigy might be seen only on a small screen and through spectacles smeared with perspiration from a stressful meeting attended earlier. The multisensoriality in effigy is of a different kind, allowing alternative kinds of associations and percepts to form. These again might impact how the body itself is understood, as has been discussed in relation to selfies and the re-making of the body (Tiidenberg & Gómez Cruz, 2015).

As discussed by Stefan Helmreich (2007), transduction provides a way of thinking as a logical operation, which is on par with but different from induction, deduction, or the abduction we dealt with in Section 3.2. Thinking transductively 'is to pay attention to impedance and resistance in cyborg circuits, to the work that needs to be done so that signals can link machines and people together, at a range of scales, from the private to the public. To think transductively is to think from inside the infrastructure that supports the transmission of information across media', according to Adrian Mackenzie (cited by Helmreich, 2007: p. 633).

What this means for mediation of the face is that images do not just appear through very different kinds of media. How they appear and whether they may be perceived at all depends to a large extent also on the mediations that they are part of. As the wide range of smells, sounds, and haptic relations bundled with our seeing attests, transduction operations decisively reorganise what we get to see and how.

4.1.1 Structured and Unstructured Faces

If the grimace provides us with a way of thinking about the importance of social attributes, constraints, and visual orders in the realm of facial images, it points us also toward the relative structuration of faces. The face templates for modelling faces for those social-media filters structure the faces with the aid of fairly small nodes and lines, on the basis of previously identified landmarks and the relations between them. If presented on a screen, this structure offers relatively little visual information for a human observer. It does not assist a human being in identification work, as the face template is not created for purposes of human perception. Rather, it is a model for the face that is useful as an **operative image**, an image that is part of a specific practice, an operation, and does not necessarily represent an object in a directly recognisable way. The artist and scholar Harun Farocki has explained how important the work presented by Roland Barthes in *Mythologies* proved for this conception, as Barthes strove to operate through meta-language for maintaining his own practice. Farocki himself started to focus on '[f]ilms or photos that were taken in order to monitor a process that, as a rule, cannot be observed by the human eye. Images that are so inconsequential that they are not stored – the tapes are erased and used again. Generally, the images are stored and archived only in exceptional cases, but exceptional cases one is sure to encounter' (2004: p. 18). This operativity becomes feasible only when the work with images is structured in line with specific, usually predefined, processes. Structuration provides for consistency and, hence, stability, supporting mediation and phenomenological transduction into another form without loss of essential characteristics of the image that are important for carrying out specific operations. The image becomes informationally poor in the sense that it does not feature the full range of traces it once did, but on the other hand, it is powerful in effect, for it can be mediated across a wide range of technical infrastructural elements and locales. Structuration supplies ways of preserving meaning across transduction processes.

Immutable Mobiles

Mediation of faces into operative images is practical only once optical consistency is achieved (Siegert, 2015) – i.e., if the variations in faces and facial expressions are codified so as to follow a system whereby they can be reproduced relatively easily. This technical process of mediation into a legible form has been rightly criticised by Deleuze and Guattari (2004), who suggested that the operativity of the face is always tied to asymmetrical frameworks of power, within which any deviation becomes futile. The technical means have been most incisively described under the term 'immutable mobile', which Latour (1986) introduced in order to point to the means of simplifying any complex account into one that can be copied, carried, and mediated without loss of any significant characteristics. The grid and the map give us two of the immutable mobiles that in the history of facial recognition techniques have become elemental for turning faces into some form that may be taken up in a broad range of contexts, for a wide variety of purposes, from surveillance operations to creation of affective expressions of joy on Snapchat to unlocking one's home or phone primarily by showing it one's face.

This section has shown us how forms of social interaction, inclusive of its ethics and morality (e.g., in terms of who is allowed to grimace and who is not), may change significantly in encounters with novel forms of visual mediation. Transduction is a useful term for explaining these phenomenological changes, as it points to mediation's transformational effects on interaction. In digitally mediated environments, transductions allow for operativity and the formation of immutable mobiles, which over the history of colonisation and domination have become so important that at times the role of images *in corpore* gets lost. These transductions, nevertheless, are not unidirectional. Our capacity to imagine, open up worlds, and interact with images in a myriad ways provides us with tools and techniques for mindful attention – ones that are direly needed in environments geared toward asymmetrical forms of control.

4.2 Cameras, Environments, and 'Good' Images

Most social scientific work on photographs and the use of cameras focuses on particular kinds of pictures taken with photographic cameras. In contrast, in this section of the chapter we suggest a relational understanding of cameras, attending to their uses in the human quest to form novel kinds of epistemological relations with the environment. From this perspective, the use of cameras is tied less closely to specific representations (photographs etc.) than to ways of being, moving, and dwelling within the world. Such an understanding emphasises gestural and sentient forms of photography (cf. Altaratz & Frosh, 2021; Frosh, 2015; Hjorth & Pink, 2014), which become understandable through them embedded within specific situated assemblages. Particular camera constellations allow for solidifying specific relations with environments, whereby these relations may be taken up again and again. Images, instead of replicating, duplicating, or copying the world, are created to act upon and within it.

This is our point of departure for thinking through cameras. And this approach spurs us to understand cameras as more than photographic devices. Rather, if we follow the etymology of the term 'camera', these devices appear as rooms for decision-making (Lehmuskallio, 2020). As a cultural technique, the camera therefore is suited to study as a setting that allows us to make informed decisions as we live in and carve out our environments.

Cameras, from this perspective, are used to bring together various material mediations, techniques of the body, and symbolisation processes that are needed for purposes of being in the world. While cameras encompass a range of actors, both human and nonhuman, some intelligible to us and some less so, it is only the possibility of repetition that makes them useful extensions of our sociality. Repetition enables ordering the relations between the visible and invisible in ways that permit socially shareable knowledge to emerge. The historical singularity of particular events is disturbed by the enactment of repetition for which cameras are built.

Once these means of repetition are established, we can talk about camera constellations, which serve ordering of connections between what is seen and known. These constellations, somewhat similar to the constellations of stars, make only sense within broader models of how that which is depicted with cameras relates to what may be known about them, and how that which is known with the help of cameras may be put to further use. These constellations order how bodies, images, and camera technologies 'ought to' relate to each other once photographic devices are in use.

Each camera constellation provides a particular vantage point for discussing 'good images', in that images are qualified as good or less good by the kind of work they are able to do within a specific constellation. For instance, a journalistic photograph is a good photograph not so much because of some external qualities (such as the lighting, use of colour, or expressiveness of its subjects), but more so because it fits the requirements of particular camera constellations for news work, one aspect of which is the quest for speed, scalability, and reproducibility.

The good image in this sense is of particular interest for scholars of visual studies since 1) the importance of the good image for purposes of decision-making tends to emerge in discussions with a wide range of image professionals, who might not have a clear vocabulary for what actually characterises a good image, and 2) visual-studies scholars and image-making professionals alike frequently seek to work towards 'good images' themselves, criticising and acting against images and imagery that is considered to be 'not good' (e.g. socially, politically, aesthetically).

4.2.1 Good Images

So what does a good image do? It exhibits two main qualities: meshing with the sociotechnical arrangements within which the image is supposed to do its work (e.g., it fits particular data formats; fulfils a profession's standards; and can be sent, rendered, stored, and archived in specific ways), and it exemplifies the ethics and moral values defining what 'good' means for a particular community of practice (cf. Mäenpää, 2022).

The first of these dimensions may be studied by focusing on technical scripts, how-to guides, and particular infrastructural arrangements within which images are produced and circulated (for discussion of facial recognition in this regard, see Lehmuskallio & Meyer, 2022; for passports, Lehmuskallio & Haara, 2023; for how-to guides on sensors, Gabrys, 2019). For the second dimension, we turn to how the social good is understood and imagined. A good image in advertising or product sales fosters and engages with sorts of relations between individuals in society that are very different from those linked to a good image in phototherapy, in which the depicted works with representations in order to build a new sense of self.

Although the good image is a topic of study in its own right, it also ties in with a third sense of the good – i.e., the meaningfulness of one's own research and practice. Both scholars and practitioners should repeatedly consider the common good to which their work contributes. They must decide whether they intend to further mainly academic aims (theory development, methodological work, thick description of particular phenomena, etc.), or if they are also keen on changing the social relations and environments within which the work is conducted (e.g., by informing policy decisions, education, and funding decisions). The good image in this third sense carries with it deliberations about ethics, morality, and the good life, topics that affect research agendas, even if only implicitly sometimes.

4.2.2 Operative Images

Automated operative imagery has become so pivotal for ever more social situations using cameras that we may move through urban environments today without necessarily noticing the wide range of decision-making procedures within which we are embedded as we move along. Clearly operative imagery is considered by a range of social actors to work well, to consist of 'good images'. Today's photographic cameras increasingly function as sensors in projects of continually monitoring who and what moves within predefined environments. They resemble active radar devices pinging their environments rather than passive *camerae obscurae* waiting for light to fill dark chambers (cf. Rettberg, 2023; Toister, 2024). Such changes in prevalent uses of photographic devices call for a more-than-representation-aligned approach, since operative images in particular are seldom visualised for human eyes at all.

But what are operative images? Farocki, who coined the term, suggested that operative images are 'images that do not represent an object, but rather are part of an operation' (2004: p. 17). This use of the term indicates the importance of attending to the kinds of actions that images allow for, instead of confining our focus to surface properties of individual pictures. A turn toward the operative, then, is a turn toward the work images do in society, and the kinds of actions that unfold because of them.

The etymology of 'operative' is related to efficiency, and the word saw historical use for pointing to phenomena that 1) operate or work within a specified whole, 2) are essential to it, and 3) are effective. Operative images, therefore, are images used in order to effect a change in an environment, producing changes *de facto* as opposed to merely representing that environment.

Operative images are discussed most often in relation to automated computing systems that rely in part on optical technologies, such as automatic licence-plate readers, facial-recognition technologies, and missiles guidance that uses computer vision and pattern recognition to find a target in a hostile environment. In all these cases, the operativity of images is tied to processes of automated decision-making, within which optical information plays an essential, and hence operative, role.

Charlotte Klonk and Jens Eder have recommended a broader understanding of operativity in their treatment of image operations, or particular kinds of image-related events that 'cannot fully be understood either by reconstructing the intentions of the producers or by considering single moments of its reception' (2016: p. 1). These operations 'augment, and create significant events' (p. 3). In this understanding, operativity is not tied merely to automated forms of digital decision-making; it dovetails with study of the kind of imagery that is particularly important for grasping the unfolding of specific events. Within these events, 'images themselves also act. They have a dynamic of their own, suggest certain operations and crucially shape them' (p. 6). Image operations are part of specific constellations.

A more-than-representation approach to visual studies expresses an interest, accordingly, in the actions and agencies in which images are embedded. In this understanding, operativity is not just an additional dimension to image analysis but integral to understanding why and how images get used socially. That the operative does not need to be tied to automation, nor to forms of digital computation, underlies our approach to the term.

4.2.3 Cameras and Their Environments

While much of work in visual studies focuses on pictures and representations, our main suggestion here is to pay closer attention to the conditions of how these are made to emerge. Studying cameras and their environments allows us to shift the centre of enquiry from a representational orientation toward sensitivity to the fact that representations, while at times of significant importance, are not always so. There is much more.

A study of cameras as sites for decision-making, active in taking up particular relations to environments and often moulding these in turn, is particularly useful for more-than-representation-oriented visual studies. This approach stresses life-changing ways in which cameras function not as fixed photographic devices but as particular constellations allowing temporary fixing of relations among the environment, the observer, and analysis of the observational data collected. Instead of portraying the general historical development of image use through various phases as a pattern of increasing automation, we find value in considering separate stages in the emergence, stabilisation, and consolidation of specific camera constellations. These phases consist of:

1) Specification of a model for the coming observation.
2) Preparation for observation.
3) The act of observation itself.
4) Recording of observational data.
5) Analysis of the data.
6) Comparison in light of the model identified at the start.
7) Representation of the results.

This kind of work is more-than-representational in that, although it attends to representation (in stage 6), it explicitly encompasses a range of other elements that are important for understanding the work that a good image or a representation within a particular constellation seemingly should do. While various parts of the process (such as recording, analysis, or representation) may be automated, this is not necessary for studying particular kinds of images as operative – i.e., as efficient in their own right.

4.2.3.1 The Example of Observing Faces Within Their Environments

In 1840, John William Draper took one of the most famous portrait photographs of the nineteenth century, a daguerreotype image of his sister on a rooftop in New York (see Figure 4.3).[2] In numerous accounts of the history of photography, this image is mistakenly cited as the first portrait photograph ever taken. Even though it most assuredly was not the first 'portrait

Figure 4.3 Advertisement depicting an early portrait photograph from 1840.

Source: Duke University, Rubenstein Library.

from the life' (Draper, 1840: p. 217) produced by photographic methods, it was among the first and subject to a host of secondary uses. The fascination with Draper's daguerreotype had to do particularly with the novelty of the technology, which Draper as a chemist had studied meticulously by means of a series of experiments to progressively resolve technical constraints.[3] Draper joined forces with a fellow university professor in New York, Samuel F.B.

Morse, both to study the process of portrait photography and to provide it to interested citizens as a service (Gillespie, 2012).

In a contrast against today's speed and efficiency in taking portrait photographs, Draper and Morse needed careful study of the most fitting methods for doing so. Whereas Morse, a portrait painter and inventor, was more interested in particular iconographic decisions for daguerreotypy and used the images also as models for his paintings, Draper was a scientist at heart, and he carefully probed and refined the technical suggestions offered by Louis Daguerre, Sir John Herschel, and other early scholars working with this technology. The successful photographic act relied on a broad range of suitable elements being correctly assembled together, at the right time, in sequential order, and this knowledge was so much sought after that Draper's observations were welcomed with enthusiasm by the scientific journals of his time. He measured the angle for photography that best prevented shadows from obfuscating facial features; recommended the use of blue-tinted lenses, specific kinds of garments, and particular backdrops; and discussed corrections to assumptions about the amounts of time for which correctly prepared plates for daguerreotypy would remain light-sensitive for portrait purposes. These procedures attest that the photographer had to become quite literally attached to photographic materials, in a correctly ordered manner, such that the idea of photography could be translated into an actual picture. Importantly, scholars working with daguerreotypy at the time (e.g., Herschel and Draper) disagreed about some specifics, such as the need for achromatic lenses. At this early stage, it was clear already that the specific acts of assembling cameras, the chemistry, materials, circumstances, and the people involved were informed by more than constraints to the materials and people available. They were chosen to suit the respective understandings of photography.

In probing and tinkering with photographic materials, Draper and Morse had to begin by identifying means that would let them start observing photographically in the first place. They tried to gain an understanding of how lenses, chemicals, light, the depicted subject, paper, the camera device, and the environment all contribute to how an image may be transferred by means of photography from the depicted to another medium. This work was aimed at identifying models for their observation (stage 1) – pinpointing what is needed for rendering one able to observe faces photographically at all. To prepare for observation (i.e., for stage 2), Draper needed to collect and prepare the necessary chemicals, assemble the photographic device at an appropriate distance from the depicted, set up a backdrop to provide a suitable background for the image, and wait for the correct time of day in hopes of the weather being good enough to permit any photography whatsoever. The environment, then, was not just a backdrop for photography; it played a particularly important role for enabling photography. Sunlight, clouds, humidity, the angle of the sun, and ambient temperature all affected how the experimenters' chemicals reacted to photography, so much, in fact, that environmental conditions severely restricted how and when Draper could take photos. The stage of preparation prepared the photographer for dealing with the physicality and *kairos* of a particular environment, the propitious moment for commencing stage 3, the act of observation itself.

Creating the trace of that observation (stage 4), the event of the photographic act called for a well-prepared assemblage at that opportune moment, in order to call a new state into being. To be depicted, the depictee (Draper's sister) needed to stand still for six minutes within an environment that needed to stay similarly lit throughout the photographic act. In addition, she'd had to chalk her face white beforehand; otherwise, the light-sensitive emulsion could not have rendered her facial characteristics clearly enough (that particular facet of technical affordance would remain problematic until the late twentieth century for chemical emulsions; see Roth, 2009, and transducted later to digital environments too, cf. Buolamwini & Gebru, 2018; Mulvin, 2021). The recording of observations, in this case the moment of photographic capture, is most definitely reliant on a set of calculations, involving rules of thumb, happenstance, and precise operations, all of which affect whether and how images come into being. It is this unfolding event that is of special importance for understanding the image uses that would follow.

After the photograph had been taken and chemically developed, it required analysis (in stage 5) for judging whether the result was consistent with the knowledge behind the model identified at the outset (in stage 1), evaluating the preparations for this specific observation (from stage 2) and illuminating any possible refinements to the general procedure, assessing stage 3's act of observation itself, and checking the recording of the observational data (from stage 4). Any errors found in the recording had to be assessed in relation to the photographer's knowledge of the previous stages, gathered personally or shared by others. Extensive discussion in the scientific papers of the day addressed all of these stages, thereby assisting comparison with the various models regarding what photography was thought to be (stage 6). Much of this work from compiled knowledge relied on various forms of representing results (stage 7).

Even in the very first days of photography, a 'good image' was one that met both social and moral expectations related to what is 'good' and 'proper', but it had to fit just as much into the observational models that were created in order to do photography. Environmental conditions played a crucial role for what kind of photography could be done at all, and as a range of scholars have started to address, these photographic acts have ever since had huge impacts on the environment itself (Levin et al., 2022).

This portion of the chapter unpacked how cameras always co-depend on the environments within which they are used. They are used within specific contexts and need to be tuned to the conditions in which they are engaged with. Whether for passport photos or auto-detecting the presence of a pedestrian, observational models need to be constructed such that one may prepare for observation, record the actual event, analyse the data, and compare the outcome with what the models available/chosen suggest and possibly change these as necessary. While this is obviously true for the observation of environmental 'big data' such as weather or astronomy details, we have shown that it applies also for relatively simple forms of imaging, such as carrying out portrait photography. In fact, examining what makes for a good image becomes especially pertinent in the latter scenario, given faces' significance for reflecting social standards and moral values. We hope this treatment helps the readers reflect on so-called good images and the corresponding assessment criteria. Whose 'good' are we talking about, and in which specific case do these definitions hold?

4.3 The Visual Culture of Death

4.3.1 Images and Death – a Background Examination

Modern lives begin with a photograph. And they often end with one as well. Since the advent of photography, we have been learning to celebrate the second of these moments in particular with the aid of a mechanically produced image, impressing the image of the deceased on a surface (a metal plate, a piece of paper, a screen, or some other material) with the assistance of light for, we hope, eternity. An act of redemption, as Berger termed it, photographs are a way of saving something or someone from being abandoned and forgotten – 'what is remembered has been saved from nothingness. What is forgotten has been abandoned' (2013: p. 54).

Without doubt, death has served as a key metaphor for how we have learnt to approach photography. Look at these iconic quotes:

> To take a photograph is to participate in another person (or thing's) mortality, vulnerability, mutability. Precisely by slicing this moment and freezing it, all photographs testify to time's relentless melt.
> (Sontag, 1977: p. 15)

> [P]eople are so wonderful that a photographer has only to wait for that breathless moment to capture what he wants on film (...) and when that split second of time is gone, it's dead and can never be brought back.
> (Wegee as quoted by Mirzoeff, 1999: p. 78)

Common to these quotes is phraseology that portrays the act of 'making' a photograph – we prefer this term's conceptual cadences over those of more conventional ones such as 'shooting' and 'capturing' – as an act of termination, of ending supported by a degree of violence, of aggression, removal, negation. 'Slicing', 'freezing', 'taking', 'relentless', 'breathless', and 'capture' all feature in the extracts above. Such terms are far from alien; they sit as natural-seeming companions to conventional words such as 'shooting' and 'framing', which themselves are imbued with a strong connotation of belligerence.

We can regard the connection between photography and death as simple empirical fact. Early photographers approached the new medium with their eyes on death, as the daguerreotype offered the nineteenth century a valuable substitute for the cumbersome and expensive production of death masks. Attention to death was evident also in famous photographer Nadar's historical portrayals of the catacombs and cemeteries of Paris and perhaps also, albeit at a more metaphorical level, with Eugene Atget's portrayal of empty cities devoid of human life. The early years of photography bore witness also to a growing interest in using the camera as a tool to prove the existence of ghosts (a practice that has gone largely unstudied; see Chalfen, 2008; Clanton, 2016). On a related front, photography moved to the battlefield early on. Roger Fenton brought the Crimean War to viewers, showing them the aftermath of battles that cost several hundred human lives. Felice Beato famously did the same in India, documenting the consequences of the revolt of the sepoys, the Indian soldiers at the service of the British Empire (see Chaudhary, 2012; Favero, 2021). Because of the cumbersome apparatus that photography relied upon at the time, there was only a before and an after, no 'during the battle' – none of the co-presencing we have grown accustomed to as wars continue to rage before the eyes of various kinds of cameras, from documentary crews' to drone and satellite imagery. With the invention of more and more lightweight cameras in the early and middle parts of the twentieth century (the Leica 35 mm among others), photography stepped into the heat of battle, showing us not only the consequences of war but its actual unfolding. Among the most well-known are Robert Capa's photographs marking the extent to which the act of 'taking of a photograph ceased to be a ritual and became a "reflex"' as Susan Sontag argued (as cited by Berger, 2013: p. 50), although Capa's iconic work has been analysed as a performative ritual too.

From the mid-'30s, photographs of wars, killings, famine, mass migration, and other such critical events started filling the pages of newspapers to such an extent that, in Sontag's eyes, 'being a spectator of calamities taking place in another country' became 'a quintessential modern experience' (2003: p. 19). This connection has persisted to the present day. Indeed, we have become so accustomed to seeing images of these kinds that we might no longer react with shock to their content. Sontag anticipated this long ago when concluding that suffering in relation to such images 'flares up, is shared by many people, and fades from view' (Sontag, 2003: p. 20). Images of this type tend to portray a distant world (the world of the Other). They seldom show our own, especially if 'our own' is synonymous with 'the 'West'. We seem to get moved easily by members of our communities dying, so we reserve space for them by keeping them out of the pages of the newspapers, covering them with blankets before display on television, etc. Nevertheless, images of this nature have started appearing for shock value especially in relation to symbolically significant terrorist attacks (Zelizer, 2010). If people die elsewhere or differ in key respects from the 'kind' more typical of mainstream Western news media workers, the death pictures – exhibiting the Other – may be displayed more readily. As we place the finishing touches on this book, we encounter examples of migrants reaching the shores of Europe, satellite images of civilians' corpses in Ukraine, and videos of children dying in Gaza (it is worth bearing in mind that other locales present very different situations: for instance, as a matter of course, India's news media show images of people found dead in public places or being killed in road accidents). To gain better understanding of this phenomenon, we should probably take a step back and widen the scope of our reflections, taking into consideration the situated meaning of death in the West.

4.3.2 A Brief Cultural History of Death

With modernity and the accompanying establishment of bourgeois society and modern science, death has been progressively pushed out of public view in the West and in those parts of the world touched by Western modernity (see Hertz 1960; Despret, 2021). Modernity, Benjamin said, made it 'possible for people to avoid the sight of the dying' (1999: p. 93) and transformed the dead person into a non-value. Before that, death was a phenomenon that all people related to directly and via prominent mediation. And it is still so in many other parts of the world (small town or rural Southern Europe being an example close to us), as well as among some groups embedded in societies who have already rationalised death (e.g., members of the Orthodox Church in Finland). India is another good contemporary example of openness toward the dead: photographs of corpses are conventionally displayed for purposes of identification in all major newspapers. Corpses are also commonly displayed in public as they are taken to crematories or cemeteries. Smething similar used to happen also in Europe from Antiquity until the mid-1800s. Death could not be readily hidden from view as its hand reached also young people much more often than today. When the risk of dying young remained very high, death was a prominent part of the life of every citizen and also of the public life of a city. Mediaeval portraits depicting the deathbed as a throne testify to this. But it might be useful to remind ourselves also that until not so long ago Western societies hosted a number of rituals making death much more visible than it is today. In the very heart of Europe, displaying the body of the deceased at home and carrying the coffin in procession from the church to the cemetery made up a significant aspect of the rituals of mourning. Before delving into some of the various histories and traditions involved, we have another path to follow, though.

We may benefit from taking a moment here to reflect on how death has recently managed to return to public view, in a development prompted by recent events. Think of the images that emerged from Bergamo, Italy, at the height of the SARS-CoV-2 pandemic, which showed us coffins piled up in churches and school gyms; consider the improvised cremation grounds established in New Delhi's car parks at that time; and direct your thoughts to the photos of the corpses of civilians in Gaza and Bucha and of the bodies of lifeless migrants washing up on the shores of Italy. Death has found its way back into the visual realm with force, opening up a new chapter in image relations that we are summoned to tackle. And this chapter's pages sometimes include images representing not a perceived Other but us too.

Figure 4.4 represents for instance the funeral of the great-grandmother of one of the authors of this book, a lady by the name of Anna Maria Favero (dating from the late 1930s). The figure's images are part of two albums ordered by this family as a memorial to the respective lives. Elegantly bound in leather, with thin glassine paper separating the pages from each other, such albums constituted a luxury in which some families indulged to commemorate their loved ones. In some quarters, this tradition stood side by side with a custom of preparing a mortuary chamber in the house of the deceased. Arriving to offer a last farewell, friends and relatives were met with sweets and drinks, and the act of mourning transformed slowly into a ritual suited to renewal of the social order. As Benjamin pointed out, before modernity 'there was hardly a room in which someone had not died' (1999: p. 93). Over the decades and with the consolidation wrought by capitalism and rationality, death, and the act of dying have since been removed from day-to-day life. Hidden from public view ('abstract and invisible' in the words of Durkin, 2003: p. 43), death has progressively become a kind of negation, a loss, a missed opportunity. Alongside ageing, it is a hindrance to the natural productive cycle of life rather than fundamental to that cycle.

Figure 4.4 The funeral of Anna Maria Favero. Northern Italy, 1930s. Unknown photographer.

That said, traces of older approaches to death and dying can still be found, particularly at what we could call the margins of the modern. One of the authors regards the small town where he was raised in Northern Italy as exemplifying this scenario. It is still commonplace there for people (men in particular) to stand at the end of the church talking amongst themselves during the funeral. This includes relation-strengthening introductions between distant relatives who, as is common in diasporic families such as his, have not seen each other for many years. The other author has witnessed the importance of displaying the corpse of the deceased for those who are grieving in a setting in Finland, where the act of photographing the dead body carries special sacredness. While these practices are the province of specific communities, numerous examples could be found in other settings if we were to dig further. Funerals are moments of community-making, wherein the living, with the help of the deceased, renew the bonds that unite them. The visual is highly prominent in such events, and we could argue that its role is changing with the proliferation of cameras.

In the northern Italian town discussed above, deaths are announced via a specific form of printed notice known as *tilets* (from the Piedmontese dialect). This necrological formalism announces someone's death and funeral. Every day, inhabitants of the town, the elderly in particular, stop by these posters. They cluster in small groups, enquiring into who has died and why. Gossip spreads, filling the inevitable gaps in knowledge. The visual (and the tactile) is prominent also during the church ritual, where colourful flowers adorn the altar, the coffin, and the car carrying it. Friends and relatives approach the coffin at the end of the ritual. They leave a flower and touch the wood of the coffin, which functions in that moment as an emanation from, and union with, the dead. Until only a few years ago, people there were allowed to walk to the cemetery behind the car carrying the coffin. A silently weeping serpentine formation of people could be seen winding slowly through the streets of the village and heading toward the cemetery. This visual display, accompanied by the sound of feet against the pavement of the road, was a concrete public tribute to the dead and a reminder of death's omnipresence. Today the procession takes place by car but still manages to generate quite extensive attention – especially in the case of a locally well-known person's death. It is customary also that cards portraying the deceased are distributed to the family and friends both before and after the ritual. On documents 'officially' sanctioning the deceased's entrance to the realm of present absence, these photos can be a matter of protracted negotiations. Just as the photograph adorning the tomb is, the image for the cards is chosen after long and careful deliberation. Families tend to believe that it must convey a truthful impression of the character of the deceased; it will, after all, constitute a life-long (nearly eternal) memory. In many cases, the deceased has selected the relevant images before dying, and the set chosen might well be indicative of the person's interests, lifestyle, values, etc. Separately from the cards' context, these photos are often reprinted and distributed among the people attending the funeral (or family members and friends in general), thereby creating a circle of visual materials that surrounds the dead person. Such photos, we suggest, can offer a methodological focal point for interviewing family members, etc., yet their meanings go much deeper than that could take us.

If we were to look at these practices from the point of view of Turner's (1974) analysis of ritual, we could say that funerary rituals belong to that 'liminal' (see also van Gennep, 1960) moment in which 'structure' and 'anti-structure' come in contact with each other. One social order is interrupted and another is being constructed in its place, leading to the creation of what Turner defined as a *communitas*: a temporary community of individuals. The unifying force of that transient entity is probably the corpse of the deceased itself and the rituals that compose the funerary traditions: the visit to the mortuary chamber; the production of photographs, announcements, and posters; the Mass at the church; the sepulture; the dinner after that burial; and, one month after the death, and the *trigesima* Mass (which, according to tradition, sanctions the passage of the soul to the world beyond). Through the doings of this *communitas*, the deceased is progressively expelled from the society of the living only to be simultaneously reintroduced to it in the shape of visions and stories, of photographs producing sounds (stories) and stories producing images (imaginings). A circle is designed around the dead, and the gap between them and the living gets filled by images and stories. Just as photographs manage to generate 'open stories', characterised in Flusser's conceptualisation by circularity, by the possibility of always going back to where the act of scanning began (2005), so too stories produce visions, images that can get stuck to the retina of those listening. Photographs, as stories or even rumours do, 'anchor conscious and unconscious feelings' (Chaudhary, 2012: p. 60), bringing them into dialogue with each other and thus suspending their role as carriers of truth.

In our view, the experiences and practices that we have just described speak to some coexistence of multiple (at times contradictory) narratives of death in many modern societies. The visual helps us identify these practices and narratives – it directs our attention to what we might otherwise overlook.

We can dig into these matters even further. The sharing of photographs seems to position these images as more than mere visual representations in a manner similar to what Elizabeth Edwards described finding among Australian Aboriginal communities (we have encountered Edwards' work earlier in this book). These visual objects too are 'things that matter'. The photographs make a community visible, and by drawing a circle around it they tighten its internal bonds as the circle tightens. Here we encounter another opportunity for decolonising our assumptions, in this case with regard to photographic images. By importing a way of understanding images from a non-Western context, we obtain fresher understanding of images' role in connection with death and mourning in European contexts. The circulation of images of the dead, if interpreted in the manner of Edwards as a matter of relationality, tactility, storytelling, etc., points to the limits of a supposed rational (Western) way of approaching images. These are not simply depictions of the dead or of death as the end of a life (or as interruption to a cycle of production). We are faced here with an example of performativity wherein images function as agents catalysing humans' reluctance to abandon the dead to their destiny. Photographs' tales, along with several other types of stories, seem to keep the dead alive and present in the world of the living, to create a link between these two dimensions of life that Friedrich Nietzsche's thinking and many world philosophies have looked upon as part of a whole, a continuum, a circle. They are a way for us to confront what Heidegger (1962) called our 'being towards death'.

Next, we look further into this, challenging the reader to consider the extent to which photographs of the dead can be looked upon as passages through which we grant deceased beings entrance to the world of the living. Such reflections may force us to reconsider even more profoundly the linear narration of life and death that underpins conventional Western narrations. For this, come join us in a cemetery in Northern Italy.

4.3.3 Photographs of the Dead

On a sunny but chilly November day in 2017, Paolo decided to attend the Mass that the priest responsible for a small cemetery near his father's town celebrates every year on the occasion of All Saints' Day. Hosting the tomb of his ancestors on the Italian side of his family, this cemetery is intimately connected to the family's history. This year's Mass was a particularly poignant one, on account of the recent death of his father and of his father's cousin (whom Paolo would call an uncle). He therefore found himself sharing the space of the family chapel with two of his cousins and their young children as they all sought some protection from an early winter wind. As Mass ended, the daughter of one of those cousins, a 12-year-old girl named Alessandra, grabbed his hand, telling him that she had to show him something: 'I have to show you a really scary picture, Paolo. Please come!' He followed her and found himself facing the tomb of a young boy by the name of Mario who had died in 1952 at the age of three months. 'Look at this boy', Alessandra said: 'He gives me the creeps'. At first, Paolo found Alessandra's comment quite banal and unremarkable, yet as we stood in front of the stone interrogating ourselves about who that boy was, why he died, etc., she said something that caught my attention: 'He looks at me in a strange way'.

Alessandra had intuitively detected something fundamental about this photograph. This was the only picture in the whole cemetery that portrayed a dead human being. While cemetery portraits conventionally display pictures of human beings at the peak of their health, power, and beauty who gaze at the passer-by with pride, photos such as this one, of premature deaths, represent dead creatures unable to direct their gaze.

As these photographs generally attest, this absence of life can be noticed from the fact that the gaze is not active, that the posture is that of a stiff body often held up in a semi-erect pose before the camera. Also, the background has been retouched in some cases, probably for removing elements that reveal the construction of the image.

Alessandra had interpreted these differences in a very particular manner. Differently from all the other portraits, this one photo in the cemetery, of the boy, did not look at her. Rather than address the photo exclusively as a depiction of someone who had been out there at some point in time, a document of a past moment, Alessandra addressed it as a living thing, something capable of looking at her and wanting to exchange gazes yet failing miserably in this, hence the ambiguous look, and hence her discomfort in front of it. Alessandra therefore had cultivated a sense of reciprocal looking, of an act of give-and-take as takes place with most other photographs.

After Alessandra's comments, Paolo could not help but notice the images staring at him every time he walked into a cemetery or faced the wall in his parents' lounge where images of deceased family members hang. As part of a specific visual subculture, cemetery or commemorative photographs seem to constitute a kind of living jury judging our way of looking at them. Do they evaluate our own ways of moving in the world?

Inversion between the subject and object of the gaze, as experienced and suggested by Alessandra, is far from uncommon. This becomes quite evident if we allow ourselves to look sideways in space and time, returning to the context of the Hindu devotional practices discussed earlier in the book. Here too, images appear to express reciprocity. Let us remind the reader that, as implied by the notion of *Darsan* (see Babb, 1981; Eck, 1998; Pinney, 1997, 2001), the act of looking in this context is an act of being looked at too, an ongoing interpenetration leading to utter immersion of the viewer in the image. In Eck's depiction of the situation, 'it is precisely the image that facilitates and enhances the close relationship of the worshipper and God' (1998: p. 46). Literally replacing the divine, the image transcends itself and brings the act of seeing into the foreground. That act becomes the core of the spiritual activity.

We can map the centrality of the act of looking by paying attention to a number of South Asian practices, such as that of marking the eyes of small children with *karjal* to prevent their exposure to what is conventionally referred to as the Evil Eye. Receiving the gaze of the deity reverses this logic: again, being under that gaze is something auspicious. 'When Hindus stand on tiptoe and crane their necks to see through the crowd, the image of Lord Krishna, they wish not only to "see" but to be seen', writes Eck (p. 7). Eyes loom large in these settings: Hindu deities are conventionally depicted with big eyes, and the presence of the third eye (with its divine qualities) stands out in many depictions of Shiva and Ganesh. An even more extreme example is the depiction of Indra as the god with 'a Thousand Eyes', in an icon with eyes covering the skin in all possible places. The most striking eye-centred icon is that of Lord Jagannath. See Figure 4.5.

Worshipped mainly in India (the Orissa region primarily), Jagannath ('Lord of the Universe'), 'Juggernaut' in English, is probably the most eye-oriented

134 *Visual Studies*

Figure 4.5 Lord Jagannath amidst the crowd of worshippers. Photograph copyright Samarendra Dash.

deity that one could encounter in Hinduism. Considered to be an abstract form of Krishna, Jagannath is depicted as a log of neem wood with gigantic brightly painted eyes. He is conventionally portrayed in the company of his brother and sister (they too are characterised by the presence of large eyes). Every nineteenth year, a ritual of 'new embodiment' takes place in the temple of Puri (in Orissa), during which the old statues are replaced with new ones in a long and involved procedure. This ends with revealing the eyes of the deity. After the various processes for purifying the new materials and mourning of the old ones, the statues eventually get painted in their traditional bright colours, but the pupils of the eyes wait. They receive their paint last, from the Brahmin priest (cf. Eck, 1998); then they can finally look out at the crowds who have gathered for the annual festival, called Rath Yatra (which includes what is considered to be the oldest and largest parade of chariots also). In fact, this procedure of revealing the eyes at the end of a ritual is typical for the installation of practically all Hindu deities. The images' eyes usually are sealed with a cover of honey and ghee (purified butter), which the priest removes in the very last part of the ritual. This ritual maintains the same form over time; for instance, it was performed in January 2024 upon installation of the statue of Rama in the much-disputed new Hindu temple in Ayodhya.

Another example of the centrality of looking in Hindu practices is to be found in South India's Keralite festival of Vishu (cf. Eck, 1998). Literally marking 'the first thing seen on the day after waking', this festival celebrates the beginning of the new year. On the morning of the Vishu festival, one of the family's elders wakes you up and takes you to the shrine, which was adorned the night before with fruits, nuts, lamps, and images of favourite deities. Telling you not to open your eyes, the elder will make sure that you kneel in front of the shrine. Suddenly he will tell you to open your eyes and contemplate the god. The first time Paolo took part in this ritual, it was to his great surprise that he saw, upon opening his eyes, his own face reflected in a mirror. Celebrating the fusion of viewer and viewed, of the human and the godly, the divine and the mundane, Vishu makes material – in quite a significant way – an indigenous understanding of viewing as a spiritual act.

Principles paralleling these are visible in other cultural contexts. Travelling back in European history, we can see how the Byzantine art considered earlier in this book generated interesting dialogues between the viewer and the viewed, amid efforts to encapsulate one in the other. The use of metal assisted considerably in detaching the icon from its representation duty. Recall that, substituting for a landscape surrounding the object portrayed, it gave the image a decontextualised character while anchoring it in the lived world of the worshipper. The parallel arises especially from the surface of the thin gilt layer in which the viewers see in the aura area their own reflection and a reflection of the actual world that surrounds them. The immersive effect could be even more spectacular in Byzantine churches, which literally wrapped the worshipper in the image. Surrounded by visual details, by glittering light generated by mirroring of the candlelight off the metal and glass tiles composing the image, by the smell of incense, and by the sound of bells, worshippers would expose themselves to a full sensory experience able to bring them, through the senses, in touch with the divine.

Similar notions present themselves at the very heart of Christian art. Exploring reciprocal components in the context of icons, Florensky suggests in his book-length essay 'Ikonostas', probably written around 1920 (via its 1970 Italian translation, 'Le Porte Regali'), that icons are windows allowing the light (i.e., God) to reach the viewer. In musings that reflect his position as theologian, mathematician, and art historian, he regarded such objects of art as being two things at once when fulfilling their duty of lifting 'the conscience to the spiritual world' (Florensky, 1977: p. 61): in the absence of light they are nothing but a piece of wood and glass, but in the presence of light they are doors to 'revelation':

[W]ith the blooming of the prayers of the greatest ascetics it is not strange to notice how icons become not only a window through which the visages depicted on them appear, but also a door through which these enter the sensible world.

(p. 69)

As a 'sustained dream', art, in his view, raises the soul from earthly matters, bringing it in touch with another dimension (for him, the celestial one). Through artefacts such as the icons he contemplated, it offers a junction between the visible and the invisible world. Just as the Hindu devotional images are, icons of this sort are therefore not a mere representation of something external. They are an entry into that something.

Completing the circle back to the context central to our discussion here, we must acknowledge how the photographs of the dead seem to resonate with Florensky's understanding of the ontology of icons. They affect the viewers in a similar way. More than documents from days gone by, they are tools for acting upon the space that separates life from death (or the visible world from the invisible). Similarly to the icon, the photograph can be seen as opening windows, and through these we see, 'or at least can see, through the glasses the living testimonies of God' (Florensky, 1977: p. 58).

We have discussed how Hindu icons can be seen, as Pinney argued, as a matter of corpothetics rather than of aesthetics, underscoring the importance of an embodied, tactile way of perceiving and of being perceived. Foregrounding efficacy and presence rather than realistic representation, such visual objects (and the practices of looking that support them) seem to associate the act of seeing with that of touching. In the Hindu world, as Babb pointed out, seeing is an 'outward-reaching process' that directly engages the object seen. Seeing is a kind of material exchange between the viewer and the viewed, one involving not just the eyes but the whole body. Again as Babb suggested, one, in a sense, becomes what one sees. This action can be regarded, therefore, as exhibiting true contagion of qualities and could probably be deemed to lie within the logic of magic. What Alan Dundes called a liquid logic seems to characterise this particular way of gazing, which turns the visual act into a kind of sucking life energy from the image. It may be important to stress also that, in contexts of many rituals with worshipping before an icon, the act of looking is underlined by manifold acts of touching and the use of material engagements (such as pouring of milk, water, and purified butter; involving the smells of incense; and using the sounds of a conch shell).

This multisensory, performatively oriented approach to vision is far from unique to India. The ancient Greeks and Romans too believed that the eye had the capacity to cast rays that touch the things we see. Byzantine churches played with the same notions in their ways of creating dialogues between the human and the divine. And these ideas surface also in parts of Western visual-culture theory. Barthes, for instance, must have had this intuition when he suggested that 'in order to see a photograph well, it is best to look away or close your eyes' (1993: p. 53). With that sentence highlighting the uncanny, undecided, polysemous, ever-changing nature of photographs, he introduced the possibility that meaning is produced beyond the surface of a photograph, beyond its content and message. Ideas along related lines were put forth by Arnheim, who wrote in *Art and Visual Perception* that 'in looking at an object we reach out for it' (2004: p. 13). For Merleau-Ponty too, vision came attached to movement through the presence of the body, which is also a part of the visible world ('I only have to see something to know how to reach it and deal with it'). And this indeed leads to a series of reciprocal exchanges; one 'simultaneously sees and is seen' (1993: p. 120). Neuroscience has studied the process closely and reached a similar conclusion. In the words of Antonio Damasio:

> [n]one of the five senses alone produces a comprehensive description of the outside world, although our brains eventually integrate the partial contributions of each sense into an overall description of an object or event. The result of this integration approximates a 'whole' object description. On its basis, it is possible to generate a reasonably comprehensive image of an object or event.
>
> (2017: p. 54)

As Mirzoeff put it when summing up the potential dialogues between the social sciences and neuroscience, we must acknowledge how 'our minds and bodies are continuously interacting, forming one system' (2015: p. 87).

It is fascinating to recognise the correspondence in the insight gathered within these different spaces. Social science and neuroscience, philosophy, and many distinct forms of local knowledge all indicate that images do far more than provide viewers with a disembodied portrayal, a document that is strictly detached from those who see it. Instead they do things to us, they interact with us physically, they guide us, and they merge with us. They become part of our bodies and life-worlds – literally. This is what Alessandra acknowledged when looking at the photo of little Francesco. The photo did something physical to her (giving her the creeps) and interpellated her, looking at her in a particular, uncanny and 'strange' way.

We posit that Alessandra's approach is far from deviant or naïve. Rather, it constitutes an opening toward ways of approaching photographs that, while having been marginalised via dominant narratives based on realist representation, are still very much present among us. We are sure that just a very few of the readers may have seen someone burn or tear up a picture of a deceased family member. And how often do films portray widowers covering the picture of their departed partner on the bedside table when finally daring to enter physical intimacy with a new lover? We could think also of the portraits that were so commonly worn in lockets in preceding generations or of photos that we carry in our wallets. Are these practices not perhaps already opening the doors to acknowledging photographs as items capable of entering a reciprocal relationship with us? And what about all the 'superstitious' practices related to the Evil Eye, the blue-eyed amulets ('Nazar' in Turkish) worn by individuals all over the word, etc.? Do we really live in a truly rational and secular world?

In the aftermath of the death of his father, Paolo found this dimension of our mundane engagement with photographs and vision crystallising. He discovered that in the office of a bank his father used to visit regularly the personnel had hung the commemorative photograph distributed of the deceased above the central safe, thus making him into a kind of guard over the work landscape. 'He used to come visit us; now he looks at us from there', said one member of staff. Similarly, Dominka, a young woman who had helped Paolo care for his father in hospital, kept a picture of the departed in the kitchen, and his friend Antonio kept the same image on the passenger's-side door of his car, along with a note typed by Paolo's father on an old typewriter.

If we are to accept these practices as part of a broader culture, we are forced to rethink our conceptualisations of death too. Rather than appearing as a conclusion to the process of living, death here appears to be, as Robert Herz (1960) phrased it, a temporary suspension from life. Promptly reincorporating the absent into our lives with the aid of photographs, we show our desire to connect to the world of the dead, thereby perhaps betraying the shortcomings of our conventional notions pertaining to the relationship between life and death. This might be precisely what photographs of the dead do: they allow the dead to materialise in our lives, thus connecting these image practices to a wider anthropology of the image, as pioneered largely by Belting. In this context the image is therefore, as Merleau-Ponty posited, not a copy or a second thing; it is 'the inside of the outside and the outside of the inside' (1993: p. 126). Allowing for genuine mimesis to take place, with true fusion of the viewer and the viewed, these photographs, with their reciprocity, permit the thing represented to become you, the viewer, in repeated traversal of the boundary that separates me form the rest, from the world. Similar to poetry, these images 'crisscross the division between the living and the dead creating thereby a state of living-death' (Taussig, 2001: p. 310).

4.3.4 Some Conclusions

Images at large (and photographs more specifically) bring us into a 'being-towards-death', into a space where the meaning of the words 'life' and 'death' too needs to be rethought. More than portraying something out there, more than freezing a moment, they open up that moment – they open time to us, providing us with a passage of connection between life and death. In the experiences we described above, photographs as objects and photography as a practice come in as powerful mediators in the experience of mourning. They bring the dead back into our lives, allowing them to look at us, to touch us, to exchange gazes and stories with us. And they allow us to conjure up a sense of our destiny, a facet of living in the present while at the same time preparing ourselves for dying and, hence, for reappearance in the form of photographs. Through this powerful confluence of forces, images hence offer an inversion of some of the conventional expectations related to photographs as objects to look at and whose obvious duty is to represent. In this case, photographs instead present and act in the world. They do far more than merely representing it.

4.4 X-Rays Between Science and Popular Culture

We have made our way to a form of image-making where science, popular culture, and art meet to produce visions that quite evidently extend past what the human eye can see yet can nonetheless reveal the stuff of very concrete human desires and yearnings. These are X-ray images.

As we reflect on X-ray imagery, our first thoughts go to serious matters. Deep visions are, after all, a matter of deep truths. Many of us have, at some point in life, had an accident or a check-up that required an X-ray image to be produced. And most of us have trusted the machine's capacity to produce a factual insight, situated beyond our perceptual capacities. Our thoughts may also wander to X-ray images in the context of surveillance, those used for preventing the movement of people and goods across borders. Again, deep visions for deep truths: matters of life and death. But there is also another, more superficial and perhaps morally dubious side to X-ray imagery. This is a space of hidden desires and sexual fantasies. A space of popular culture where deep vision stands for superficial arousal. A space with its own particular politics.

In the 1970s, a series of advertisements circulated prominently in popular magazines and newspapers in Europe and elsewhere. It marketed 'X-ray glasses' (or 'X-ray specs', or 'gogs'), a commercial item that promised to make deep vision cheaply available for anyone. The item rapidly became the secret object of desire for heterosexual male buyers. Promising the power to see beyond the barriers of materiality, these specs, as visible in the ads, stimulated the fantasy of seeing beneath the clothes of women (and also, but that was secondary, through your own skin). Sold by mail-order companies, these specs were often ordered in secrecy. They were pitched at, teased and reinforced the erotic fantasies of heterosexual male audiences.

The X-ray glasses were, needless to say, a hoax. Consisting of a double layer of cardboard 'lenses' with a hole in the middle with a small feather (or lens) diffracting the light, the glasses simply showed the wearer offset images. Yet these images played with the uncanny aesthetics of X-rays with their double layer made up of a darker body (a silhouette) and a surrounding shadow image. With their cheeky, unethical and perhaps immoral nature, X-ray specs point us, however, in the direction of a dialogue between the search for knowledge and for pleasure. The modern desire to see beyond materiality (the deep vision promised by X-rays) is inevitably connected to the ruthless

140 *Visual Studies*

modern desire and pleasure for penetrating, digging, excavating for, and extracting truth (metaphors and practices that are today finally under attack in the ruling debates on the decolonisation of science and popular culture).

Before we go any further, let us ask the reader to briefly stop and meditate upon the sheer beauty of the X-ray picture. This is a special kind of image that belongs simultaneously to different image types. If we are to go back again to Mitchell's 1986 typology of the family of images, we can say that X-ray pictures are both 'graphic' and 'optical'. According to Mitchell, the former refers to visible objects such as photographs, sculptures, or drawings, the latter to those images generated within the realm of natural phenomena (via mirrors and projections of whatever sort). The X-ray image is a combination of both. It is obviously graphic (it is an image-object) but it also looks like a shadow. Like a shadow, it is ambiguous; it has unclear boundaries and is capable of overlapping a vast quantity of layered data on its two-dimensional surface. As shadows do, X-ray images seem to play with the affirmative nature of negation. An X-ray image functions according to the same visual principles that guide the design of Sufi Mausolea, where the divine (and therefore, meaning) emanates visually in the play of shadows and light that are created by the beautiful marble grids. Similarly, X-ray images, too, produce meaning through the contrast between light and darkness as it appears on the lightbox. Conventionally viewed in negative, they leave to the dark parts the duty to display the light (organs appear dark in X-ray negatives). X-ray images are, hence, existential objects, and they remind us of the uncertain continuum of darkness and light that makes up life. See Figure 4.6.

Figure 4.6 Aboriginal Australian X-Ray style rock art, Anbangbang Rock Shelter, Kakadu National Park, Australia.

Credit: Thomas Schoch, 2005.

Applications of Visual Studies 141

The visuality of X-ray images reminds us of many other works of art which depict that which seemingly lies beneath the surface. Think of the art of ancient Aboriginal Australian populations (approximately 3,000 to 4,000 years BCE) or of the mysterious visions offered by the Shroud of Turin, both forms of imagery that have much more to do with relations and forms of being in the world than with mere representation. Pushing this connection even further, let us consider the so-called anatomical machines contained in the basement of Italy's Sansevero Chapel, in Naples. Testifying to the passion for science and art of the prince of Sansevero and to his longing for seeing bodies from the inside, these are two skeletons (a man and a pregnant woman) displaying a system of red and blue arteries and veins. Made of beeswax, iron and silk, these bodies were long considered the result of magical or alchemic intervention. See Figure 4.7.

The same suspicion was also raised with regard to Giuseppe Sanmartino's *Veiled Christ* (1753), a depiction of a dead man (Christ) lying, whose every muscle and expression are visible under what looks like a thin veil of wet

Figure 4.7 Giuseppe Sanmartino's *Veiled Christ* (1753).

gauze. Rumour has it that upon delivery, Sanmartino was suspected of having embalmed a real human being and solidified a real thin veil in order to obtain this effect. This statue, along with other sculptures that surround it, defies the impenetrability of materials and displays, in a game of veiling and unveiling, a tense play of eroticism and thanatology. In the vicinity of the Veiled Christ are Corradini's *Pudicizia* ('Modesty' or 'Chastity') displays a standing naked woman covered by another thin veil, and Francesco Queirolo's *Release from Deception*, a naked man who with the help of an angel tries to free himself from a net. Just as *Veiled Christ* does, these statues testify to the prince of Sansevero's interest in entering spaces beyond the skin.

There have been many attempts at penetrating the skin of bodies and defying the materiality of surface layers. X-rays are just one more step in that journey. And this is a journey, as witnessed by the case of the Sansevero Chapel, that is also filled with dangers. We now know that X-rays are physically dangerous for the 'imaged' subject, but they pose dangers also at a symbolic level, representing a transgressive desire to penetrate reality, to defy common perception, conventions and 'normality'.

It is obvious then, that X-ray vision would also become an ability of superheroes. The capacity to see in X-ray appeared for the first time in the 1930s, embodied by female comic book superhero Olga Mesmer, who had developed a capacity to see behind walls due to exposure to X-ray radiation as a child. This quality inspired the creators of Superman, the hero who turned X-ray vision into a weapon to protect humans. Defending life from evil powers, Superman however, falls prey to the erotic temptations offered by this medium. In Superman: The Movie (1978) he inspects not only Lois Lane's lungs but also her underwear. James Bond too, who has X-ray glasses as part of his arsenal of spy gadgets does something similar in The World is Not Enough (1999). During a mission to identify concealed weapons at a casino, he cannot resist the temptation of glancing beneath the clothes of female staff members. The X-specs with which we opened these confabulations surely gathered inspiration from these scenes.

Popular culture added to the X-ray fantasies of deep vision, those of invisibility (an association born of the capacity of X-rays to make bodies transparent). In Jules Verne's The Secret of Wilhelm Storitz (written just a couple of years after the first X-ray image taken by Wilhelm Röntgen in 1895 and published in English only in 1963) the central character learns to make himself invisible and throws a whole city into panic. Put into perspective with Verne's other novels, this book offers an evident insight into the connection between (in)visibility, knowledge and depth. The novel constitutes a natural prolongation of Verne's interest for science and technology that in other novels such as his 1864 *Journey to the Center of the Earth* (the first English translation appeared in 1871) and the 1870 *Twenty Thousand Leagues under the Sea* (appearing in English in 1873) are cast into metaphor through the idea of physical depth. The world of erotic comic books too is populated by

Applications of Visual Studies 143

invisible men. In Milo Manara's *The Scent of the Invisible* (1987), a man who has discovered an ointment capable of making him unseeable, invades the intimacy of a young woman and starts an erotic relationship with her thanks to his invisibility. See Figure 4.8.

Figure 4.8 Theatrical release poster of X: The Man with the X-ray Eyes by Reynold Brown, 1963. The work of art itself is in the public domain.

Popular culture has not only played with the pleasures of deep vision but also with the dangers attached to it. In the 1963 movie X: The Man with the X-ray Eyes, Dr Xavier, is the inventor of a liquid that when dropped into the user's eye expands the spectrum of vision into the realm of ultraviolet and X-rays. Like a superhero, Dr. Xavier starts using his power for noble purposes. Very soon, however, he loses control of the drug and begins a descent into crime. The capacity to see 'through the very fabric of reality' (as the official film storyline has it) quickly becomes a tool for making money. A miracle diagnostician and a casino cheater, Dr Xavier ends up escaping to the desert where, blinded by his powers, he eventually meets an evangelist. Seeing in his deep vision the doings of the devil the priest encourages him to follow the bible's suggestion: 'If thine eye offends thee, pluck it out!'.

In Western popular culture X-ray vision is represented as a tool for transgressing the boundaries and limits of neurotypicality, of normality and morality, often in explicitly gendered and sexist ways. This urge to move beyond materiality and the sensory capabilities of our bodies is also something dangerous. It defies the border that separates life from death. Producing predictive visions of the body as it will one day look like (i.e., a skeleton), X-ray images break a taboo. They anticipate and visualise our death. As legend has it, when Röntgen's wife saw the X-ray image of her hand, she exclaimed that she had seen her own death. This predictive capacity has been the object of attention in popular culture and art. Artist Nick Veasey consciously plays with this idea in his X-ray portraits, transforming the most mundane poses and situations into extraordinary actions performed by what look like skeletons. Life and death meet in the space of Veasey's images testifying that there is something sublime to X-ray imagery. These images come very close to death, yet they never fully enter into contact with it. They witness it from a place of safety, like a Kantian observer would witness a mountain avalanche from the safety of a warm hut. X-ray images are sublime objects that consolidate the nexus between photography and death that has been central to the history of this medium. X-rays, hence, consolidate the nexus between photography and death that as we already discussed in this book, has been central to the history of this medium (Barthes, 1993). Yet, it also takes this connection further.

The photography of Lennart Nilsson surely consolidates the yearning for going beyond the surface of the human body. Showing it from the inside for the first time using an endoscopic camera, Nilsson created another space where science and popular culture meet. The 1965 close-ups of a foetus (Foetus 18 Weeks) created a degree of turmoil in society, also polarising the debate on abortion. More recently the documentary film by Lucien Castaign Taylor and Serena Paravel *De Humani Corpora's Fabrica* looks back at this history enquiring into the passages from X-ray to CT scans, MRI, etc. Inner pornography takes on a similar endeavour today, also deploying the same kind of cameras. Inverting established points of observation, it conventionally shows sexual intercourse from the inner perspective of an organ being penetrated. Today, hyperspectral cameras offer probably the most (subtle) expression of this longing. Using both visible light and invisible near-infrared light they simultaneously stay above and enter beneath the surfaces of objects. Producing patterns capable of revealing what human eyes are missing, they can, among other things, show the skin and structure of a hand together with the veins beneath it. Hyperspectral cameras offer perhaps a new 'hybrid vision' capable of simultaneously contemplating the inner and the outer, the deep and the superficial. This would be a very much-needed non-dualistic shift in discourse.

In her book *Good Looking*, Stafford enquires into the Western distrust for surfaces. A key characteristic of Western culture, she suggests, is the reduction of the perception of reality to a matter of language (1996) and hence, we may add, of thought. Is this what lures behind this yearning for and fascination with deep vision? A celebration of the (Cartesian) separation of body from mind? Of the supremacy of the mind and the soul and the (possibly erroneous) identification of the mind/soul as an 'inner' quality? Contemporary neuroscientists are today enquiring into the latter aspect. Having identified the locus for practically all types of human perception they can still, however, not identify where the sense of self (or consciousness) resides. Possibly, exactly because it is not 'inside'? Neuroscientist Niebauer (2019) asks 'What if the brain is connected to, or a part of, consciousness – rather than a possessor of consciousness?' (p. 204).

X-ray images and vision take us to these reflections because they are much more than a pure matter of hard science. They are part of a much broader narrative and represent a yearning – one for deep vision that penetrates surfaces, getting beneath them. This is a question that fascinates popular culture and culture more generally. In this desire for crawling beneath the surface of the skin, for penetrating the human body and the world, and for overcoming the limits of typical human perception, the search for knowledge coexists with that for pleasure and arousal. This is a terrain of 'visual culture', a space where scientific discourse meets cultural narratives and where the quest for advancement collides with the risks of extractivism; where sexual fantasies, with their attached forms of masculinity, encounter a quest for exploring the fundamental but thin border that separates life from death. Here, Eros meets Thanatos, and superficial desires prove to be a matter of deep truth.

4.5 Shadows: Between Light and Darkness

4.5.1 An Introduction: Peering Into the Shadows

What happens when the light is gone? When points of reference are lost and you get wrapped in the dark? You may sense being sucked up in a void that pulls you back down to Mother Earth. The reassuring and simultaneously scary condition of not being. The perception of the eye getting in tune with perception by the soul. Darkness. 'I go back to black' sang Amy Winehouse amidst her despair, visually depicting her state of mind.

But what happens if, instead of fighting it, you were to choose to enter that darkness? Eventually your eyes would begin to adjust. As they say in the theatre world, darkness doesn't actually exist. A completely dark room, a space of total invisibility, can never be created. In the deepest of darkness, you slowly start seeing again as your eyes eventually start to adjust, however little. Details emerge that tell of a different world, a world possibly made up of what no longer is. A world inhabited by ghosts.

In the midst of darkness you may begin to see shapes. You may meet your ghosts coming alive. From the past straight into your present, pointing you towards the future. You may see them dancing all around, in swirls, circles, and spirals. A choreography of present absences accompanying you during your everyday life. Shadows. Omnipresent shadows. And suddenly love may emerge through these shapes. It may appear to you in the shape of light. The light of possibility. A thin border between what actually is and what could be. 'Prospect' is the word we can use to define this light, the one that can break through the darkness. 'Prospect' is something special indeed. It is not a guarantee, it is not a plan. A prospect is just a possibility. Yet one that faithfully points ahead without actually visualising a clear path. 'Prospect' suits the darkness. It is there in potency, but it cannot really be seen. A prospect represents the clinging on to life and its beauty.

Prospect and possibilities, are, after all, all that human beings have. This is something that those of us trapped in the neoliberal capitalist tsunami tend to forget. Life is an unclear, uncertain continuum filled up as much by darkness as by light. And sometimes it is only the darkness, the blackness that can teach us to see. In the digitalised contexts of the present world, the striving for constant visibility (through social media such as Instagram and Facebook) causes us to forget that sometimes it is in the spaces of darkness, where it is impossible to see, that light can be perceived. Invisibility is a powerful communicator.

This idea, this inversion, has been at the centre of many philosophies and world views such as Buddhism, Tantrism and Sufism. It is summed up in Persian poet Rumi's suggestion that 'the wound is where the light enters your body'. Within this logic, removal, just like pain and suffering, are as important for human life as accumulation and pleasure. A strange concept for a capitalist world. In the capitalist reigns of the world we are thought to overcome, ignore, or even attack all that we attach to these dark areas. 'We' want to stick to the light, to see and be seen, believing that only in this way we are given access to clarity and knowledge. 'Enlightenment' is after all the core motto of Western civilisation, although its failures started becoming heavily debated after the Second World War.

Yet, the spaces of darkness and those of suffering, weakness, defeat, and death can show us the way too. In the darkness we can learn to connect life with death, love with hate, pleasure with pain. The Indian philosopher Jiddu Krishnamurti explained this very clearly when he said that death is the

Applications of Visual Studies 147

ultimate state of enlightenment. That is when humans empty themselves of all they assumptions. And only in this emptiness can they learn to see things clearly. And this is an act of cleansing of the mind. In 1966, Krishnamurti said the following at a public talk held in Saanen:

> I wonder how you see things. Do you see them with your eyes, with your mind? Obviously, you see things with your eyes, but you see with the mind much more quickly than with the eye. You see the world much more quickly than the eye can perceive. You see with memory, with knowledge, and when you so see things, that is with the mind, you are seeing what has been, not what actually is.

The relativity of these notions can be visualised also in the different associations that can be found in the world between colour and death. To give a simple binary, while the West addresses death with black, for Hinduism it is white. White is the colour to be worn during funerals and mourning. As we know, white is after all the result of the merging of all colours in light. Also, if you paint a wheel with all colours and let it spin quickly, white is what you will see. All colours merge into it, as they do if you make a long exposure photograph of the sea early in the morning. The deep blue, emerald and turquoise sea will turn into a foamy white. And indeed, this idea fits well with the overarching notion of reincarnation. According to Hinduism, every individual is in fact nothing but a collection of particles connected to the Universe. The individual spirit (the *purusa*) is nothing but part of the broader *Purusa*, the spirit of cosmos, God. At the end of a human life the spirit is split up into many different particles that recompose within the Universe. According to this view, the end is therefore always the beginning of something else. Hence, death is life. Black is white. Darkness is light. All the elements come together. During a cremation ritual you can learn to detect the changing colours of flame. As the flame crawls down to the body the colour changes, reacting to the life of a decaying body. The love for the dead is the love for life. It all comes down to white ash that, at the end, will be thrown back into the world by the wind.

So, the possibility is that darkness can be seen as more than a space of absence, negation, danger. And it is quite evident that in the West there has been little attention to the shifting meanings (and to the lightness) of black. As the history of cinema has told us, film chemicals were produced to capture the subtle shades of white skin but never of black skin. The same debate popped up recently also with regard to smartphone cameras and Instagram filters. So how to enquire deeper into the materiality and ontology of darkness?

4.5.2 Entering the Shadowlands

The shadow is probably the best metaphor and phenomenon for entering and unpacking this terrain. In the shadowlands, black and white, light and darkness, life and death meet and merge, they dance with each other, inverting positions and meanings. Let us enter the question of darkness from this particular angle. The shadowlands are a space revealing the coexistence and co-dependence between the opposite extremes that make up the human experience. Shadows are, in fact, quintessential possibilities. They mark that thin boundary between darkness and light. Between presence and absence. Between black and white.

Have you ever tried exploring that moment in the late afternoon when nature attempted to retreat into invisibility? Those moments when the electric bulb, the prosthetic prolongation of the human eye, gradually takes over and dominates the cityscape? The effect of the bulb is impressive then. Through its presence the single, majestic source of light of the sun is split up into a plethora of micro-suns. Electricity transforms the city into a new landscape, a world of pluralities and contradictions. Under the light of a street lamp, you may witness how your body gets split into various micro-bodies, into many shadows, many possibilities and prospects. By the night's city lights, an individual shadow is morphed into a multiplicity of shadows, with choreography of shadows dancing and moving as you move – all around, like the ghosts of life. Have you ever paid attention to this? In the city lights you may become unsure of who you are. Like Peter Pan (see below) you may fear of having lost your shadow and, along with that, your sense of self. Unlike Peter Pan, though, you may also enjoy the loss. If it is true that, as Rabindranath Tagore made us understand, becoming oneself is, as Hanif Qureshi phrased it so beautifully, something that we always do in company, then shadows are a good indicator of that. Shadows are always in company and the night, with its darkness, is a provider of wisdom.

And, we wonder, have you ever tried chasing shadows in the early morning? Try being out on the streets before the city really comes to life. Explore the moment of the day when the electric light gives way to the sun, again. When the prosthetic-electric makes room for nature again. During that precious, transformative moment, the multiple selves that the night helps scatter around recompose into one. The multiple shadows of the city lights slowly merge into one singular shadow. The sun invites you to return to 'yourself'; you become yourself again, an in-dividual (non-divisibility being another culturally relative notion), heedless of contradictions and ready for another productive day.

4.5.3 Shadows and Selves

The play of shadows is, hence, more than an optical matter. It speaks to our vision of the self, to our constant labour of identity-making. Shadows are transformative presences that allow us to discover the other side of ourselves. The shadow is the thin membrane that separates us from the world of darkness. Separating day and night, blackness and light, it offers us a renewed way of looking at the world.

Shadows have indeed nurtured the fantasies of writers and artists alike. In Western civilisations the shadow carries somewhat uncanny and most often negative connotations. Shadows are conventionally associated with fear, with notions of danger and loss; they are dark and worrisome. Shadows speak of removal and absence, of superficiality and negative forces. Shadows are proverbial figures that hunt the living and stand for the dark side of life. We therefore speak of 'shadow government' or 'shadow economy', suggesting that the shadow stands for something somewhat mysterious and unethical. 'When small people start casting big shadows it is time for sunset' says the proverb. The shadow also becomes synonymous with the ghost (as in the 'ghost writer') aligning itself with all that is invisible and scary. Like ghosts, shadows are not good things in Western culture. Think of the scary shadows of German Expressionism and of American horror movies. 'The Curse of the Fires and of the Shadows' was the title William Butler Yates gave one of his short stories.

Freud elaborated on the shadow in his writings on 'the uncanny' (1919). Building upon Otto Rank's work on the multiple connections between shadows, mirrors, guardian spirits, and the figure of the 'double' (the Doppelgänger), he suggested that the shadow after all represented nothing but an ongoing struggle between humans and death. The double, like the shadow, he said, enters the experience of human beings at their childhood as an insurance 'against destruction to the ego' or to use Rank's words, an 'energetic denial of the power of death'. Yet, as the child grows up the double takes on a different meaning: from having been an assurance of immortality, he becomes 'the ghastly harbinger of death'.

Regardless of the point of entrance, we plunge again into an association here between shadows, darkness, and fears. The shadow is the omen of something scary, threatening, and dangerous. As described with the case of Peter Pan and some of the legends mentioned above, in Western fantasies fears of losing the shadow amount to fears of loss of the self. In 'Pendulum', a song about the inevitability of death, the American band Pearl Jam sings 'My shadow left me long ago'.

But in the West shadows are also considered to be the true side of the soul. This can be found in many myths, folk legends, and superstitions. 'Don't trust people with no shadow!' says another famous popular maxim. A sense that the shadow is connected to the true side of an individual is hence there in the West too. And it is no coincidence that in that civilisation, which is guided by notions of in-dividuality, the shadow is always in singular form. We have one, not many shadows and we are, unlike in other civilisations, one self, not many.

The tale of Peter Pan concretises this idea. We introduced this above but let us now look deeper into it. In J.M. Barrie's novel, Peter loses his shadow one night while visiting the house of Mrs. Darling. The latter, finding the shadow, treats it as a mundane object. She washes it, dries it, and stores it in a drawer. It will be Wendy, later on, who will try to stitch it back onto

Peter's feet, thereby allowing him to reconnect with his other litigious side. In Disney's film, in fact, Peter keeps flying back and forth in a room lit artificially in the night as he tries to catch his own shadow, thus re-enacting, albeit in reverse, a play with which many children entertain themselves: trying to run away from or jump away from their shadow. Peter Pan's experience with his shadow can be easily read as a part of his ongoing struggle against growing up ('growing up is the beginning of the end' recites the novel), a struggle between his various selves. The shadow in this context can be easily read as the alter ego of normality (the life of a middle-aged man), a tool helping humans to bring their own life into a critical perspective. The shadow is not where we should be. Shadows in fact are ambiguous, at once superficial and deep, true and fake. They are mundane objects that can be washed, dried, and stored in a drawer.

Shadows sum up some qualities that are considered to stand in conflict with Western rationality and morality. In the first place, as anyone can easily observe, a shadow is a pure surface. Shadows skim upon, morph and adapt to whatever they encounter on their path. A shadow is a pure trace without depth and meaning. Like a caress, it does not correct, it leaves what it seeks untouched. Kids discover the wonder of shadows as they try to run away from them, failing to do so. The shadow always wins. Like their conscience, the shadow always comes back to them. Like a gaze, a shadow, if we may borrow the words of Florensky, 'tenderly caresses and cuddles the surface of the reality that amazed the philosopher' (2011: p. 76). Yet again, surfaces too are somewhat scary in Western culture. Surfaces are the negation of the true depth of human beings, which, from Greek philosophy onwards is meant to reside in the soul, in the inner invisible parts of humans. And the shadow is its total negation, it is pure ephemerality. You might recall how Stafford's writings on surfaces castigate the 'totemisation of language as a godlike agency' that characterises Western culture. She suggests in particular that Saussure's schema 'emptied the mind of its body', reducing images to 'encrypted messages requiring decipherment' (1996: pp. 5–6). Western culture builds on the principle that surfaces are devoid of meaning and substance.

But indeed, the roots of these ideas are to be found further back in time. Through the cave experiment Plato instilled in Western culture the pervasive idea that shadows (and along with them images) are deceivers. They negate truth and knowledge, subjugating human beings to false myths. This notion was indeed reinforced by Descartes with his dualistic hierarchy of body and mind (that we addressed earlier in this book). His vision of the senses as part of the fallible human body and of the intellect (which according to him was connected to the soul) as the ultimate 'interpreting judge of sensory perception' (cf. Mirzoeff, 1999: p. 43), further highlighted this distinction.

A second dimension of shadows that is worth addressing here is that they are also somewhat contradictory. While being a physical object, a phenomenological fact, they are indeed also deprived of materiality. Shadows do exist but they cannot be touched, grabbed, directed (this is where the defying force in Peter Pan lies). As such they are a part of our life-world, of our experiences, but in a very uncomfortable, troubling way. We are never sure how to approach them and what to do with them. And this problem has grown even stronger given the many transformations that shadows, as ontological things, have been exposed to through human intervention (with the discovery of first fire and later the invention of electricity). At the most basic level, shadows are always in motion but tend to appear to us, as a result of the interaction of physical bodies with the light of the sun, as fairly stable. Yet, in the presence of fire, or of a candle, they at once show their dynamic nature. Shadows flicker, achieving a capacity to animate themselves, to move and make the environment around them change accordingly. Even more so, in the presence of electric light (as discussed above) shadows become uncanny figures, multiplying their presence in our life-worlds. Shadows populate our cities and our mundane urban experience of the night. Sometimes they anticipate our movements, sometimes they guard us from behind. At the end of every day, as the 'natural' shadow abandons us, the artificial ones (note the plural form) come to the fore. If shadows are, as myths would have it, an emanation of our true self, then our self is a multiplicity, split into parts. When primitive people learnt to produce light by means of fire, they also managed to craft their own artificial shadows, filling up the gap created by that big shadow that we call the night. After all, the night too is nothing but one big shadow created by the constant interplay between the Sun and the Earth.

Shadows may constitute a threat against key pillars of Western thought and science, with that persistent preoccupation with dualism, clear-cut lines, linear narration, and separations (something running as an unbroken thread from Descartes to Renaissance perspective and the construction of nation-states, from Christian cosmology to the fundaments of capitalist ideology). Porous, ephemeral, ever-changing, immaterial, ungraspable, shadows challenge dichotomies and separations. Where exactly does the line between light and dark run in a shadow? Where does the shadow begin and where does it end?

Moving in space and time we cannot but notice the extent to which shadows have been addressed by other civilisations in a more positive manner helping us realise that, paraphrasing Casati (2004), shadows not only hide, they also reveal. The productive aspect embedded in a shadow can, for instance, be detected in the invention of the sundial, which reads the time of day on the basis of the shadow projected by the sun on a stick. Shadows are also useful for characterising space. To give one example, author Ruesch (1977) called the land in which the Inuit lived 'the land of long shadows'. Defining the unicity of the long sundown and dawn that can be found in the northern part of the Northern hemisphere, over time this term was adopted for describing all lands of the North.

Shadows are also at the core of the invention of photography, as the first images produced were sort of shadows imprinted on paper or metal plates.

And even before that, they were used to make portraits through the famous method of the silhouette, an important precursor of modern visual identification methods, as well as those methods used to remember one's loved ones. And they were also deployed extensively for entertainment purposes with the shadow theatres, which are still popular in many parts of Asia (and not only there). The Romans too consciously incorporated the use of shadows for the construction of immersive environments, using them to blur, as we saw earlier in this book, the distance between the physical word and the world as it was perceived by humans. As we noted in the case of Rome's Altar of Augustan Peace, shadows are fundamental to the creation of a sense of depth that confuses the viewers with regard to their position in space. The Romans exploited the shadows to act upon the perception of physical space.

Shadows do have a capacity to blur our conventional experience of space. Think of how the projection of the shadow of a tree can gently fall upon, and merge with, the sleek marble surface of a modern building or a monument. They can help bring the human-made environment and nature in contact with each other.

Just like love, shadows are generous and have an immense capacity to accumulate and overlap. 'Two shadows can occupy the same space without bothering one another', says Casati (p. 41). The shadow is like love, like transcendental love, always capable of more.

We have to remain in 'Eastern' parts of the world if wishing to genuinely acknowledge the generative capacity of shadows. The dialectic between darkness and light is what characterises the design and architecture of many Sufi Mausolea. See Figure 4.9.

Figure 4.9 Tomb of Hazrat Nizamuddin, New Delhi.

Source: Photograph by Paolo SH Favero.

In visiting, for instance, the tomb of Sufi saint Hazrat Nizamuddin, of his disciple, the poet Amir Khusrau, or of another more recent poet Mirza Ghalib in Nizammuddin, the Sufi Islamic neighbourhood in South Delhi, the passing of time causes continuous movement of light across the beautiful marble grids that decorate the walls surrounding the tombs. In the absence of a human representation of God – in Sufism, as in all Islam, God, who is also denoted by means of the word 'Love', can never be visually portrayed – God enters the space of the living in the shape of a play between shadow and light. Here the shadow highlights the role of light, just as in Rumi's poems. It exploits the principle of inversion. This dialectic can be detected also from observing a cat playing with shadows. The cat runs in all directions, almost seeming possessed by the shapes projected on the floor through the hands and objects waved by the people around her. And, indeed, what she follows is the light, not the shadow. The latter only helps to create room for the light to be properly engaged with and enjoyed.

As many other Sufi poets have, Rumi (2010), writing in the thirteenth century, often referred to the notion of the shadow in his writings. For him, the shadow, as much as darkness, was never a matter of absence or of the loss of something (of light, vision, understanding, etc.). On the contrary, it was the very essence that made humans appreciate the true meaning of light, visions, and knowledge – in other words, of Life and of Love, and hence of God. In an inversion typical of much Sufi poetry and art, Rumi wrote: 'You must have shadow and light source both' and that 'both light and shadow are the dance of Love [...]. Lover and loving are inseparable and timeless'. In his poem 'Wetness and Water' he states:

How does
A part of the world
Leave the world?
How does wetness
Leave water?
Don't try to put out fire
By throwing on more fire!
Don't wash a wound
With blood.
No matter how fast you run,
Your shadow keeps up.
Only full, overhead sun
diminishes your shadow.
But that shadow has been serving you.
What hurts you blesses you.
Darkness is your candle.
Your boundaries are your quest.

Notes

1 For a feminist discussion of modes of Instagram image editing by lifestyle content creators, see Roivainen 2024.
2 The original is held by the Spencer Museum of Art, in Lawrence, Kansas. One may also consult the Draper Collection, in the photographic-history materials of the Smithsonian Institution's National Museum of American History (Gillespie, 2012: p. 243).
3 It has even been suggested that Draper's interest in the process of daguerreotypy and less on the results of his processes had an impact on many of the scientific discoveries visible in those results (e.g., from his lunar photography) remaining less known in his lifetime (Gillespie, 2012).

5 Conclusions

We wrapped up the vignettes with which we opened our book with two short poetic extracts. One is from a song in which Joose Keskitalo tells us that now, as the night has anointed us, it is our time to see visions. The song asks its listener to give careful attention to a specific painting, to focus on its details, especially a group of people depicted in it in a classical style (whatever the meaning of 'classical' might be here). We are told that, if observing the painting in such a way, listeners will realise who they are. The conclusion extends to the analysis of images. This self-transformation, enacted by means of careful observation, encompasses recurrent, awareness-rich use of images. Images get used because they change the world – they change us and also the social relations in which we are embedded. In the song, the night and the darkness are deemed especially important for bringing on transformation. The darkness is present, again as an agent of transformation, also in the second excerpt opening the book, from the poem of Rumi, with whose work we ended the previous chapter. Darkness stimulates growth, calling us to overcome barriers ('Darkness is your candle / Your boundaries are your quest') in what is yet another process of transformation.

Both examples point toward the intricacies of images and visions, their subtle nature, and their complexity. What do we see with our eyes, and what is seen with our imagination and memory? Is there anything beyond the immediate visible world? What are images about? And who are 'we' when we see images? What is the self that is supposedly formed via these images, if a self exists at all? And do we need darkness if wishing to see?

We have sought to offer you a thoughtful yet practical perspective for analysing images and visuality, stressing their importance in human life. The book has devoted attention to the role that images and vision in general, fill in our ways of thinking, perceiving, acting on, and inhabiting our beloved Earth. We have pointed out a need to pause for a moment, to wait, before moving from our observations to analytical suggestions. The gradual unfolding of our journey in this book mirrors a progressive discovery of how vision and visuality are tightly interwoven with the most profound and the

DOI: 10.4324/9781003084549-5

most detailed ways of thinking. In many languages, this weave is visible in the etymological links between forms of knowing and the ability to see.

The core implication for our situated social scientific approach to visual cultures is that our ways of knowing are closely bound up with our ways of thinking about vision. For studying this web of nuanced interrelation, we have recommended a focus on various forms of mediation. Since we lack direct access to perception, we must study vision and ways of looking via mediating mechanisms; therefore, throughout this book, we have identified visual media that humans have created across historical and contemporary thresholds. We have suggested that the histories and genealogies of these diverse media may be studied well by attending to specific visual media, examining their interrelations, and engaging in juxtapositions. Our perspective implies also that images emerge only within interactions; images are always a temporally unfolding event. Depending on how we look, for how long, with what kinds of interests and intentions, the images we see start to shift and change.

Finally, our approach spotlights images as much more than mere representations. Providing us with an opening to the world of the senses and of affectivity, they can be understood as our co-travellers, our companions. Each of us lives life in the presence of images and is guided by them in attending to and acting within the world. Hence, a book such as this holds some relevance for everyone. It is our hope that our analyses delving into matters of vision, images, and looking have provided our readers with useful starting points for investigation and theory-building for a wide range of deep explorations within the area of visual studies.

References

Ahmed, S. (2004). *The Cultural Politics of Emotion*. New York: Routledge.
Aiello, G., & Parry, K. (2019). *Visual Communication: Understanding Images in Media Culture*. London: SAGE.
Akomolafe, B. (2017). *These Wilds Beyond Our Fences: Letters to My Daughter on Humanity's Search for Home*. Berkeley: North Atlantic Books.
Alpers, S. (1984). *The Art of Describing. Dutch Art in the Seventeenth Century*. Chicago, IL: University of Chicago Press.
Altaratz, D., & Schoch, P. (2021). Sentient Photography: Image-production and the Smartphone Camera. *Photographies*, 14(2), 243–264.
Anderson, B. (1991). *Imagined Communities: Reflections on the Origin and Spread of Nationalism*. London: Verso.
Argan, G.C. (2008). *Storia dell'Arte Italiana: Dall'Antichita' al Medioevo* [History of Italian Art: From Antiquity to the Middle Ages]. Milan: RCS Libri.
Arnheim, R. (2004). *Art and Visual Perception*. Berkeley, CA: University of California Press.
Babb, L.A. (1981). Glancing: Visual Interaction in Hinduism. *Journal of Anthropological Research*, 37(4), 387–401.
Bakewell, L. (1998). Image Acts. *American Anthropologist*, 100(1), 22–32.
Banet-Weiser, S., & Higgins, K.C. (2023). *Believability: Sexual Violence, Media, and the Politics of Doubt*. Hoboken, NJ: John Wiley & Sons.
Barthes, R. (1967). *Elements of Semiology* (Translated by A. Lavers & C. Smith). New York: Hill and Wang.
Barthes, R. (1972). *Mythologies*. New York: Hill & Wang.
Barthes, R. (1977). *Image – Music – Text*. London: Fontana Press.
Barthes, R. (1993). *Camera Lucida* (Original Version as Translated by R. Howard). London: Vintage.
Batchelor, S. (1998). *Buddhism Without Beliefs: A Contemporary Guide to Awakening*. London: Penguin.
Batchelor, S. (2015). *After Buddhism: Rethinking the Dharma for a Secular Age*. New Haven, CT: Yale University Press.
Bazin, A. (1967). *What Is Cinema*. Berkeley/Los Angeles/London: University of California Press.

Behdad, A. (2016). The Orientalist Photograph: An Object of Comparison. *Canadian Review of Comparative Literature*, 43(2), 265–281. https://doi.org/10.1353/crc.2016.0023

Belting, H. (2005). Toward an Anthropology of the Image. In M. Westermann (ed.), *Anthropologies of Art* (in the Series Clark Studies in the Visual Arts) (pp. 41–58). Williamstown, MA: Sterling and Francine Clark Art Institute.

Belting, H. (2011). *An Anthropology of Images: Picture, Medium, Body* (Translated by T. Dunlap). Princeton, NJ: Princeton University Press.

Belting, H. (2011). *Florence and Baghdad: Renaissance Art and Arab Science*. Cambridge, MA: Harvard University Press.

Belting, H. (2014). *Faces. Eine Geschichte des Gesichts* ['Faces: A Story of the Face'] (2nd ed.). Wemding, Germany: C.H. Beck.

Benjamin, W. (1999). *The Storyteller: Reflections on the Works of Nikolai Leskov*. Berlin: Schocken Books.

Berger, J. (1972). *Ways of Seeing*. London: Penguin.

Berger, J. (2013). *Understanding a Photograph*. London: Aperture.

Böhme, G. (2013). *Atmosphäre: Essays zur neuen Ästhetik*. Frankfurt am Main: Suhrkamp.

Bräunlein, P.J. (2004). Bildakte. Religionswissenschaft im Dialog mit einer neuen Bildwissenschaft. In B. Luchesi & K. von Stuckrad (eds.), *Religion im kulturellen Diskurs: Festschrift für Hans G. Kippenberg zu seinem 65. Geburtstag* (pp. 195–231). Berlin: Walter de Gruyter.

Bredekamp, H. (2015). *Der Bildakt* ['The Picture Act']. Berlin: Verlag Klaus Wagenbach.

Buci-Glucksmann, C. (1994). *Baroque Reason. The Aesthetics of Modernity*. Thousand Oaks, CA: SAGE.

Buczek, I. (2014). The Immersive Dome Environment (IDE): Old Concept in a New Light or a New Hybrid Medium to Enhance Human Cognitive Faculty? *Technoetic Arts: A Journal of Speculative Research*, 10(2–3), 247–254.

Bühler, K. (1965). *Sprachtheorie. Die Darstellungsfunktion der Sprache*. Jena: Gustav Fischer Verlag.

Bundesen, C., & Habekost, T. (2008). *Principles of Visual Attention: Linking Mind and Brain*. Oxford: Oxford University Press.

Buolamwini, J., & Gebru, T. (2018). Gender Shades: Intersectional Accuracy Disparities in Commercial Gender Classification. 1st Conference on Fairness, Accountability and Transparency. Proceedings of Machine Learning Research (pp. 77–91). New York.

Burnett, R. (1995). *Cultures of Vision*. Bloomington, IN: Indiana University Press.

Carrier, J.G. (1995). *Occidentalism: Images of the West*. Oxford, UK: Oxford University Press.

Casati, R. (2004). *Shadows: Unlocking Their Secrets, from Plato to Our Time*. London: Vintage.

Casetti, F. (2013). What Is a Screen Nowadays? In C. Berry, J. Harbord, & R. Moore (eds.), *Public Space, Media Space* (pp. 16–25). Basingstoke, UK: Springer. https://doi.org/10.1057/9781137027764_2

Casetti, F. (2015). *The Lumière Galaxy. Seven Key Words for the Cinema to Come*. New York, NY: Columbia University Press.

Chalfen, R. (2008). Shinrei Shashin: Photographs of Ghosts in Japanese Snapshots. *Photography and Culture*, 1(1), 51–71.

Chateau, D., & Moure, J. (2016). Screen, a Concept in Progress. In D. Chateau & J. Moure (eds.), *Screens: From Materiality to Spectatorship – A Historical and Theoretical Reassessment* (pp. 13–22). Amsterdam: Amsterdam University Press.

Chaudhary, Z.R. (2012). *Afterimage of Empire: Photography in Nineteenth Century India*. Minneapolis: University of Minnesota Press.

Chun, W.H.K. (2008). The Enduring Ephemeral, or the Future is a Memory. *Critical Inquiry*, 35(1), 148–171.

Chun, W.H.K. (2016). *Updating to Remain the Same: Habitual New Media*. Cambridge, MA: MIT Press.

Clanton, C. (2016). *Uncanny Others: Hauntology, Ethnography, Media* [PhD thesis]. Goldsmiths' College, University of London, London.

Cohen, L. (1998). *No Aging in India: Alzheimer's, the Bad Family, and Other Modern Things*. Berkeley: University of California Press.

Collins, R. (2005). *Interaction Ritual Chains*. Princeton, NJ: Princeton University Press.

Crary, J. (1990). *Techniques of the Observer: On Vision and Modernity in the Nineteenth Century*. Cambridge, MA: MIT Press.

Crary, J. (1992). *Techniques of the Observer: On Vision and Modernity in the Nineteenth Century*. Cambridge, MA: MIT Press.

Crosby, K. (2020). *Esoteric Theravāda: The Story of the Forgotten Meditation Tradition of Southeast Asia*. Boulder, CO: Shambhala Publications.

Damasio, A. (2017). *The Strange Order of Things. Life, Feeling, and the Making of Cultures*. London: Pantheon.

Davis, R.H. (1997). *Lives of Indian Images*. Princeton, NJ: Princeton University Press.

Deleuze, G., & Guattari, F. (2004). *A Thousand Plateaus*. London: Continuum.

Descartes, R. (1988). *Descartes: Selected Philosophical Writings*. Cambridge, MA: Cambridge University Press.

Descola, P. (2013). *Beyond Nature and Culture*. Chicago, IL: University of Chicago Press.

Despret, V. (2021). *Our Grateful Dead: Stories of Those Left Behind*. Minneapolis, MN: University of Minnesota Press.

Didi-Huberman, G. (2003). *Images in Spite of All: Four Photographs from Auschwitz* (Translated by Shane B. Lillis). Chicago and London: The University of Chicago Press (translation of the original work).

Didi-Huberman, G. (2015). *Il passo leggero dell'ancella. Sul sapere eccentrico delle immagini*. [The Light Steps of the Maiden. On the Eccentric Knowledge of Images]. Bologna: EDB.fkam.

Divino, F. (2024). *The Apparent Image: The Phenomenon, the Void, the Invisible*. Padova, Italy: Edizioni Diodati.

Dolezal, L. (2009). The Remote Body: The Phenomenology of Telepresence and Re-embodiment. *Human Technology*, 5(2), 208–226.

Draper, J. W. (1840). XXXII. On the Process of Daguerreotype, and Its Application to Taking Portraits from the Life. *The London, Edinburgh, and Dublin Philosophical Magazine and Journal of Science*, 17(109), 217–225.

Dunbar, R. (2010). *How Many Friends Does One Person Need? Dunbar's Number and Other Evolutionary Quirks*. Cambridge, MA: Harvard University Press.

Dundes, A. (1980). *Interpreting Folklore*. Bloomington: Indiana University Press.

Durkin, K.F. (2003). Death, Dying, and the Dead in Popular Culture. In C.D. Bryant (ed.), *Handbook of Death & Dying* (pp. 43–49). Thousand Oaks, CA: SAGE.

References

Easwaran, E. (1978). *Meditation: Commonsense Directions from an Uncommon Life*. London: Routledge.

Eck, D.L. (1998). *Darsan: Seeing the Divine Image in India*. New York: Columbia University Press.

Eder, J., & Klonk, C. (2016). Introduction. In *Image Operations: Visual Media and Political Conflict* (pp. 1–22). Manchester: Manchester University Press.

Edwards, E. (2006). Photographs and the Sound of History. *Visual Anthropology Review*, 21(1–2), 27–46.

Edwards, E., & Bhaumik, K. (eds.) (2009). *Visual Sense: A Cultural Reader*. Milton Park, UK: Routledge.

Elkins, J. (1999). *The Domain of Images*. Ithaca, NY: Cornell University Press.

Elsaesser, T. (2013). The 'Return' of 3-D: On Some of the Logics and Genealogies of the Image in the Twenty-First Century. *Critical Inquiry*, 39(2), 217–246.

Evdomikov, P. (1970). *Teologia della Bellezza: l'arte dell'icona* [Theology of Beauty: the art of the icon]. Milan: Edizioni San Paolo.

Faris, J.C. (2002). The Gaze of Western Humanism. In M.K. Askew & R.R. Wilk (eds.), *The Anthropology of Media: A Reader* (pp. 77–91). Malden, MA: Blackwell.

Farocki, H. (2004). Phantom Images. *Public*, 29, 12–22.

Favero, P.S.H. (2017). The Transparent Photograph: Reflections on the Ontology of Photographs in a Changing Digital Landscape. In RAI Photography Committee (ed.), *Anthropology & Photography* (Vol. 7) (pp. 1–16). London: Royal Anthropological Institute.

Favero, P.S.H. (2018). *The Present Image: Visible Stories in a Digital Habitat*. Basingstoke, UK: Palgrave Macmillan.

Favero, P.S.H. (2019). A Journey from Virtual and Mixed Reality to Byzantine Icons via Buddhist Philosophy. *Anthrovision*, 7(1). https://journals.openedition.org/anthrovision/4921

Favero, P.S.H. (2020). Notes on Blackness, Darkness, and Shadowlands. In N. Haq & P. Gielen (eds.), *The Aesthetics of Ambiguity: Understanding and Addressing Monoculture*. Amsterdam: Valiz.

Favero, P.S.H. (2021). *Image-Making-India: Visual Culture, Technology, Politics*. London: Routledge.

Favero, P.S.H. (2022). It Begins and Ends with an Image: Reflections on Life/Death across Autobiography and Visual Culture. *Anthropological Journal of European Cultures*, 31(1), 72–87.

Favero, P.S.H. (2024). Deep Visions and Superficial Desires: X-rays As Science and Popular Culture. In S. Khosravi (ed.), *The Gaze of the X-ray: An Archive of Violence*. Bielefeld, Germany: Transcript Verlag.

Feiersinger, L., Friedrich, K., & Queisner, M. (2018). Image – Action – Space: Situating the Screen in Visual Practice. In L. Feiersinger, K. Friedrich, & M. Queisner (eds.), *Image – Action – Space* (pp. 7–10). Berlin: De Gruyter.

Florensky, P. (1967). The Reverse Perspective. Retrieved November, 2019, from https://monoskop.org/images/1/11/Florensky_Pavel_1967_2002_Reverse_Perspective.pdf

Florensky, P. (1977). *Le porte regali*. [The Royal doors] (Translated by E. Zolla). Milan: Adelphi.

Florensky, P. (1993). *Lo spazio e il tempo nell'arte* [Space and Time in Art]. Milan: Adelphi.

Florensky, P. (2002). *Beyond Vision: Essays on the Perception of Art*. London: Reaktion Books.
Florensky, P. (2011). *Florensky, Pavel A. 2011. Stupore e dialettica*. [Marvel and Dialectics]. Macerata: Quodlibet.
Flusser, V. (2005). *Lingua e Realidade*. [Language and Reality] (originally published in 1963). São Paulo: Annablume
Flusser, V. (2006). *Per una filosofia della fotografia* [For a Philosophy of History]. Milan: Mondadori.
Foster, H. (1988). *Vision and Visuality*. New York, NY: Dia Art Foundation.
Foucault, M. (1960). *The Birth of the Clinic: An Archaeology of Medical Perception*. Presses Universitaires de France.
Foucault, M. (1988). Technologies of the Self. In P.H. Hutton, H. Gutman, & L.H. Martin (eds.), *Technologies of the Self: A Seminar with Michel Foucault* (pp. 16–49). Amherst: University of Massachusetts Press.
Foucault, M. (1995). *Discipline and Punish: The Birth of the Prison*. London: Vintage.
Foucault, M. (2020). *Discipline and Punish: The Birth of the Prison*. London: Penguin.
Fraser, N. (1990). Rethinking the Public Sphere: A Contribution to the Critique of Actually Existing Democracy. *Social Text*, 25–26, 56–80.
Frazer, J.G. ([1890] 2009). *The Golden Bough: A Study of Magic and Religion*. Auckland: The Floating Press.
Freedberg, D. (1989). *The Power of Images: Studies in the History and Theory of Response*. University of Chicago Press.
Freud, S. (1919). The Uncanny. In *The Standard Edition of the Complete Psychological Works of Sigmund Freud* (Vol. XVII). London: The Hogarth Press.
Frosh, P. (2015). The Gestural Image: The Selfie, Photography Theory, and Kinesthetic Sociability. *International Journal of Communication*, 9(22), 1607–1628.
Gabrys, J. (2019). Sensors and Sensing Practices: Reworking Experience across Entities, Environments, and Technologies. *Science, Technology, & Human Values*, 44(5), 723–736.
Gallese, V. (2009). Mirror Neurons, Embodied Simulation, and the Neural Basis of Social Identification. *Psychoanalytic Dialogues*, 19(5), 519–536.
Gell, A. (1998). *Art and Agency: An Anthropological Theory*. Oxford: Clarendon Press.
Gibson, J.J. (1979). *The Ecological Approach to Visual Perception*. Boston, MA: Houghton Mifflin.
Gilardi, A. (2002). *Storia della fotografia pornographica* [The History of Porographic Photography]. Milan: Mondadori.
Gillespie, S. K. (2012). John William Draper and the Reception of Early Scientific Photography. *History of Photography*, 36(3), 241–254.
Goffman, E. (1966). *Behavior in Public Places: Notes on the Social Organization of Gatherings*. New York, NY: Free Press.
Goffman, E. (1978). *Gender Advertisements*. New York, NY: Macmillan.
Goodwin, C., & Goodwin, M.H. (1996). Seeing As a Situated Activity: Formulating Planes. In Y. Engeström & D. Middleton (eds.), *Cognition and Communication at Work* (pp. 61–95). Cambridge, UK: Cambridge University Press.
Gramsci, A. (1971). *Selections from the Prison Notebooks of Antonio Gramsci*. London: Lawrence & Wishart.
Grasseni, C. (2004). Skilled Vision: An Apprenticeship in Breeding Aesthetics. *Social Anthropology*, 12(1), 41–55.

References

Grau, O. (1999). Into the Belly of the Image: Historical Aspects of Virtual Reality. *Leonardo*, 32(5), 365–371.

Gunthert, A. (2008). Digital Imaging Goes to War: The Abu Ghraib Photographs. *Photographies*, 1(1), 103–112.

Gupta, A. (1998). *Postcolonial Developments: Agriculture in the Making of Modern India*. Durham, NC: Duke University Press.

Habermas, J. (1990). *Strukturwandel der Öffentlichkeit. Untersuchungen zu einer Kategorie der bürgerlichen Gesellschaft*. Frankfurt am Main: Suhrkamp.

Hall, E.T. (1969). *The Hidden Dimension*. Garden City, NY: Anchor Books.

Hansen, M.B.N. (2004). *New Philosophy for New Media*. Cambridge, MA: MIT Press.

Haraway, D. (1985). *A Cyborg Manifesto*. Minnesota, MN: University of Minnesota Press.

Hauser, A. (1999). *The Social History of Art: From Prehistoric Times to the Middle Ages* (Vol. 1) . London: Routledge (originally published in 1951).

Hausken, L. (2024). Photorealism versus Photography. AI-Generated Depiction in the Age of Visual Disinformation. *Journal of Aesthetics & Culture*, 2024, 1–13.

Heidegger, M. (1962). *Being and Time*. London: Harper and Row Publishers;

Heidegger, M. (1977). The Age of the World Picture. In *The Question Concerning Technology and Other Essays* (pp. 115–154). Translated and with an Introduction by William Lovit. New York: Harper.

Helmreich, S. (2007). An Anthropologist Underwater: Immersive Soundscapes, Submarine Cyborgs, and Transductive Ethnography. *American Ethnologist*, 34(4), 621–641. https://doi.org/10.1525/ae.2007.34.4.621

Hertz, R. (1960). *Death and the Right Hand*. Glencoe, IL: Free Press.

Hjorth, L., & Pink, S. (2014). New Visualities and the Digital Wayfarer: Reconceptualizing Camera Phone Photography and Locative Media. *Mobile Media & Communication*, 2(1), 40–57.

Hockey, J., & Collinson, J.A. (2006). Seeing the Way: Visual Sociology and the Distance Runner's Perspective. *Visual Studies*, 21(1), 70–81.

Hoffman, D. (2019). *The Case against Reality: Why Evolution Hid the Truth from Our Eyes*. New York: W.W. Norton & Company.

Howes, D. (2003). *Sensual Relations: Engaging the Senses in Culture and Social Theory*. Ann Arbor: University of Michigan Press.

Howes, D. (ed.) (2005). *The Empire of the Senses: The Sensual Culture Reader*. Oxford, UK: Berg.

Huhtamo, E. (2016). The Four Practices? Challenges for an Archaeology of the Screen. In D. Chateau & J. Moure (eds.), *Screens: From Materiality to Spectatorship – a Historical and Theoretical Reassessment* (pp. 116–124). Amsterdam: Amsterdam University Press.

Husserl, E. (1989). *Ideas Pertaining to a Pure Phenomenology and to a to a Phenomenological Philosophy*. New York: Springer.

Ierodiakonou, K. (2014). On Galen's Theory of Vision. *Bulletin of the Institute of Classical Studies*, suppl. 114 ('Philosophical Themes in Galen'), 235–247.

Ingold, T. (2000). *The Perception of the Environment: Essays on Livelihood, Dwelling and Skill*. London and New York: Routledge.

Ingold, T. (2010). Ways of Mind-Walking: Reading, Writing, Painting. *Visual Studies*, 25(1), 15–23.

Ingold, T. (2011). Worlds of Sense and Sensing the World: A Response to Sarah Pink and David Howes. *Social Anthropology*, 19(3), 313–317.
Ings, S. (2008). *The Eye: A Natural History*. London: Bloomsbury.
Ito, M. (2005). Intimate Visual Co-Presence. Retrieved August 26, 2024 from www.itofisher.com/mito/archives/ito.ubicomp05.pdf
Jackson, M. (2012). *Lifeworlds: Essays in Existential Anthropology*. Chicago, IL: Chicago University Press.
Jappy, T. (2013). *Introduction to Peircean Visual Semiotics*. London: Bloomsbury.
Jay, M. (1988). Scopic Regimes of Modernity. In H. Foster (ed.), *Vision and Visuality* (pp. 3–23). Seattle: Bay Press.
Jay, M. (2011). *Essays from the Edge. Parerga and Paralipomena*. Charlottesville, VI: University of Virginia Press.
Jay, M. (2012). Scopic Regimes of Modernity Revisited. In I. Heywood, & B. Sandywell (eds.), *The Handbook of Visual Culture* (pp.102–114). London: Bloomsbury.
Jovanovic, N. (2001). Eyes Full of Soap: Soap Opera, Phantasm, Ideology. Retrieved from www.mediaonline.ba/mediaonline/attach_eng/2784.pdf
Kandinsky, W. (1989). *Lo spirituale nell'arte* [Concerning the spiritual in Art] (Translated by E. Pontiggia). Milan: Brossura.
Kember, S., & Zylinska, J. (2012). *Life after New Media: Mediation as a Vital Process*. MIT Press.
Kittler, F. (2010). *Optical Media*. Cambridge, UK: Polity.
Knorr Cetina, K. (2014). Scopic Media and Global Coordination: The Mediatization of Face-to-Face Encounters. In K. Lundby. *Mediatization of Communication* (pp. 39–62). Berlin: De Gruyter. https://doi.org/10.1515/9783110272215.39
Knott, K. (1999). *Induismo*. Torino: Einaudi.
Koch, C. (2019). *The Feeling of Life Itself*. Cambridge, MA: MIT Press.
Komalesha, H.S. (2008). *Issues of Identity in Indian English Fiction: A Close Reading of Canonical Indian English Novels*. Bern, Switzerland: Peter Lang.
Krämer, S. (2006). The Cultural Techniques of Time Axis Manipulation: On Friedrich Kittler's Conception of Media. *Theory, Culture & Society*, 23(7–8), 93–109.
Kromm, J., & Bakewell, S. B. (2010). *A History of Visual Culture: Western Civilization from the 18th to the 21st Century*. London: Berg.
Kuper, A. (1988). *The Invention of Primitive Society: The Transformation of an Illusion*. London and New York: Routledge.
Lannoy, R. (1975). *The Speaking Tree*. London: Oxford University Press.
Latour, B. (1986). Visualization and Cognition: Drawing Things Together. In H. Kuklick (ed.), *Knowledge and Society Studies in the Sociology of Culture Past and Present* (Vol. 6, pp. 1–40). London: Jai Press.
Latour, B. (1999). *Pandora's Hope: Essays on the Reality of Science Studies*. Cambridge, MA: Harvard University Press.
Latour, B. (2005). *Reassembling the Social*. Oxford University Press.
Lehmuskallio, A. (2016). The Camera as a Sensor Among Many: The Visualization of Everyday Digital Photography as Simulative, Heuristic and Layered Pictures. In E. Gómez Cruz, & A. Lehmuskallio (eds.), *Digital Photography and Everyday Life*. Empirical Studies on Material Visual Practices (pp. 243–266). New York, NY: Routledge.

Lehmuskallio, A. (2019). The Look As a Medium: A Conceptual Framework and an Exercise for Teaching Visual Studies. *Journal of Visual Literacy*, 38(1–2), 8–21. https://doi.org/10.1080/1051144x.2018.1564607

Lehmuskallio, A. (2020). The Camera As a Meeting Place for Decision Making. In A. Cox Hall (ed.), *The Camera As Actor: Photography and the Embodiment of Technology* (pp. 17–28). New York, NY: Routledge.

Lehmuskallio, A. (2021). Keeping Distance: Notes on Video-Mediated Communication during the Covid-19 Pandemic. *Inquiries into Art, History, and the Visual*, 21(3), 161–175.

Lehmuskallio, A., & Haara, P. (2023). The Passport As a Medium of Movement. In C. Eisenmann et al. (eds.), *Varieties of Cooperation: Mutually Making the Conditions of Mutual Making* (pp. 137–165). Wiesbaden, Germany: Springer Fachmedien.

Lehmuskallio, A., Häkkinen, J. & Seppänen, J. (2019). Photorealistic Computer-Generated Images are Difficult to Distinguish from Digital Photographs: A Case Study with Professional Photographers and Photo-Editors. *Visual communication*, 18(4), 427–451.

Lehmuskallio, A., & Meyer, R. (2022). Experimental Indices: Situational Assemblages of Facial Recognition. *The Journal of Media Art Study and Theory*, 3(1), 85–112.

Leroi-Gourhan, A. (1993). *Gesture and Speech* (Translated by A.B. Berger). Cambridge, MA: MIT Press.

Levin, B., Ruelfs, E., & Beyerle, T. (eds.). (2022). *Mining Photography. The Ecological Footprint of Image Production*. Leipzig: Spector Books.

Lindberg, D.C. (1981). *Theories of Vision from Al-Kindi to Kepler*. Chicago, IL: Chicago University Press.

Lindsay Opie, J. (2014). *Nel Mondo delle Icone: dall'India and Bisanzio*. [In the world of icons: from India to Byzantium]. Milan: Jaca Books.

Lippit, A.M. (1999). Three Phantasies of Cinema – Reproduction, Mimesis, Annihilation. *Paragraph*, 22(3), 213–214.

Lutz, C.A., & Collins, J.L. (1993). *Reading National Geographic*. Chicago, IL: University of Chicago Press.

MacDougall, D. (1997). The Visual in Anthropology. In M. Banks & H. Murphy (eds.), *Rethinking Visual Anthropology* (pp. 275–295). New Haven, CT: Yale University Press.

MacDougall, D. (1999). Social Aesthetics and the Doon School. *Visual Anthropology Review*, 15(1), 3–20. https://doi.org/10.1525/var.1999.15.1.3

Mack, A., & Rock, I. (1998). *Inattentional Blindness*. Cambridge, MA: MIT Press.

Mäenpää, J. (2022). Distributing Ethics: Filtering Images of Death at Three News Photo Desks. *Journalism*, 23(10), 2230–2248.

Manghani, S. (2013). *Image Studies: Theory and Practice*. New York, NY: Routledge.

Manghani, S., Piper, A., & Simons, J. (eds.) (2006). *Images: A Reader*. Thousand Oaks, CA: SAGE.

Marci, T. (2014). *Codificazione artistica e figurazione giuridica: Dallo spazio prospettico allo spazio reticolare*. [Artistic codification and legal figuration: From perspective space to reticular space]. Turin: G. Giappichelli Editore.

Margolis, E., & Pauwels, L. (eds.) (2011). *The SAGE Handbook of Visual Research Methods*. Thousand Oaks, CA: SAGE.

Marks, L. U. (2000). *The Skin of the Film. Intercultural Cinema, Embodiment, and the Senses*. Durham, NC: Duke University Press.

Mayne, J. (2000). *Framed: Lesbians, Feminists, and Media Culture*. Minneapolis, MN: University of Minnesota Press.
McLuhan, M., & Fiore, Q. (1967). *The Medium Is the Massage*. London: Penguin Books.
McQuire, S. (1997). *Visions of Modernity* (1st ed.). SAGE.
McQuire, S. (2013). Photography's Afterlife: Documentary Images and the Operational Archive. *Journal of Material Culture*, 18(3), 223–241.
Merleau-Ponty, M. (1962). *Phenomenology of Perception* (Translated by C. Smith). London: Routledge & Kegan Paul.
Merleau-Ponty, M. (1964). Eye and mind. In J. M. Edie (ed.), *The Primacy of Perception, and Other Essays on Phenomenological Psychology, the Philosophy of Art, History and Politics* (pp. 159–190). Evanston, IL: Northwestern University Press.
Merleau-Ponty, M. (1993). Eye and Mind. In B.M. Smith (ed.), *The Merleau-Ponty Aesthetics Reader* (pp. 121–149). Evanston, IL: Northwestern University Press.
Metz, C. (1982). *The Imaginary Signifier: Psychoanalysis and the Cinema*. Bloomington, IN: Indiana University Press.
Meyer, R. (2019). *Operative Porträts. Eine Bildgeschichte der Identifizierbarkeit von Lavater bis Facebook*. Konstanz University Press: Konstanz.
Milgram, P., Takemura, H., Utsumi, A., & Kishino, F. (1994). Augmented Reality: A Class of Displays on the Reality-Virtuality Continuum. *SPIE, Telemanipulator and Telepresence Technologies*, 2351, 282–292.
Mirzoeff, N. (1999). *An Introduction to Visual Culture*. London: Routledge.
Mirzoeff, N. (2011). *The Right to Look: A Counterhistory of Visuality*. Durham, NC: Duke University Press.
Mirzoeff, N. (1999). *An Introduction to Visual Culture*. London: Routledge.
Mirzoeff, N. (2015). *How We See the World*. London: Pelican.
Mitchell, W.J.T. (1984). What Is an Image? *New Literary History*, 15(3), 503–537.
Mitchell, W.J.T. (1986). *Iconology: Image, Text, Ideology*. Chicago, IL: University of Chicago Press.
Mitchell, W.J.T. (1992). *The Reconfigured Eye: Visual Truth in the Post-Photographic Era*. London: MIT Press.
Mitchell, W.J.T. (1994). *Picture Theory: Essays on Verbal and Visual Representation*. Chicago, IL: University of Chicago Press.
Mitchell, W.J.T. (1995). Interdisciplinarity and Visual Culture. *Art Bullettin*, LXXVII(4), 540–544.
Mitchell, W.J.T. (2006). *What Do Pictures Want?: The Lives and Loves of Images*. Chicago, IL: University of Chicago Press.
Mitchell, W.J.T. (2015). *Image Science*. Chicago, IL: University of Chicago Press.
Mulvey, L. (1975). Visual Pleasure and Narrative Cinema. *Screen*, 16(3), 5–18. https://doi.org/10.1093/screen/16.3.6
Mulvin, D. (2021). *Proxies: The Cultural Work of Standing In*. Cambridge, MA: MIT Press.
Nancy, J.-L. (2005). *The Ground of the Image*. New York: Fordham University Press.
Niebauer, C. (2019). *No Self, No Problem: How Neuropsychology Is Catching Up to Buddhism*. San Antonio, TX: Hierophant Publishing.
Niederer, S., & Colombo, G. (2024). *Visual Methods for Digital Research. An Introduction*. Cambridge, UK: Polity.
Niemelä-Nyrhinen, J., & Seppänen, S. (2020). Visual Communion: The Photographic Image As Phatic Communication. *New Media & Society*, 22(6), 1043–1057.

References

Osborne, H. (2001). Camera Obscura. In H. Brigstocke (ed.), *The Oxford Companion to Western Art*. Oxford University Press. Retrieved from www.oxfordreference.com/views/ENTRY.html?subview=Main&entry=t11 8.e445

Panofsky, E. (1991). *Perspective as Symbolic Form*. Zone Books.

Panofsky, E. (1992[1927]). *Tomb Sculpture Four Lectures on Its Changing Aspects from Ancient Egypt to Bernini*. New York, NY: Harry N Abrams Inc.

Parks, L. (2020). *Cultures in Orbit: Satellites and the Televisual*. Durham, NC: Duke University Press.

Parks, L., & Schwoch, J. (eds.) (2012). *Down to Earth. Satellite Technologies, Industries, and Cultures*. New Brunswick, NJ: Rutgers University Press.

Pascal, B. (1897). *Les pensées de Pascal: Reproduites d'après le texte autographe, disposées selon le plan primitif et suivies des opuscules* (Vol. 1). Paris: P. Lethielleux.

Pauwels, L. (2017). *Reframing Visual Social Science: Towards a More Visual Sociology and Anthropology*. Cambridge, UK: Cambridge University Press.

Peirce, C.S. (1988). *The Essential Peirce. Selected Philosophical Writings. Volume 2 (1893-1913)* (Edited by the Peirce Edition Project). Bloomington, IN: Indiana University Press.

Pencheva, B. (2010). *The Sensual Icon: Space, Ritual, and the Senses in Byzantium*. Pennsylvania: Pennsylvania State University Press.

Pencheva, B. (2013). *The Sensual Icon: Space, Ritual, and the Senses in Byzantium*. University Park, PA: Pennsylvania State University Press.

Peters, J.M.L.P. (1961). *Visuele communicatie en visueel onderwijs: over de rol van beelden in het communicatieproces en over het gebruik van audio-visuele hulpmiddelen*. Harlem: Stam.

Peters, J.D. (1997). Seeing Bifocally: Media, Place, Culture. In J. Ferguson & A. Gupta (eds.), *Culture, Power and Place: Explorations in Critical Anthropology* (pp. 75–92). Durham, NC: Duke University Press.

Peters, J.D. (2015). *The Marvelous Clouds: Toward a Philosophy of Elemental Media* (Kindle edition). Chicago, IL: University of Chicago Press.

Peters, J.D. (2020). A Cornucopia of Meanwhiles. In J.D. Peters, F. Sprenger, & C. Vagt (eds.), *Action at a Distance* (pp. 25–50). Lüneburg: Meson Press in collaboration with University of Minnesota Press.

Pink, S. (2010). The Future of Sensory Anthropology / The Anthropology of the Senses. *Social Anthropology*, 18(3), 331–340.

Pink, S. (2011). Sensory Digital Photography: Re-Thinking 'Moving' and the Image. *Visual Studies*, 26(1), 4–13. https://doi.org/10.1080/1472586x.2011.548484

Pinney, C. (1997). *Camera Indica: The Social Life of Indian Photographs*. London: Reaktion Books.

Pinney, C. (2001). Piercing the Skin of the Idol. In C. Pinney & N. Thomas (eds.), *Beyond Aesthetics* (pp. 157–179). London: Bloomsbury Academics.

Pinney, C. (2004). *'Photos of the Gods', The Printed Image and Political Struggle in India*. Chicago, IL: University of Chicago Press.

Pinney, C. (2006a). Four Types of Visual Culture. In C. Tilley, W. Keane, S. Küchler, M. Rowlands, P. Spyer (eds.), *Handbook of Material Culture*. London: SAGE.

Pinney, C. (2006). The Body, Materiality and the Senses. In C. Tilley et al. (eds.), *Handbook of Material Culture*. Thousand Oaks, CA: SAGE.

Plato. (2000). *The Republic* (Translated by Tom Griffith). Cambridge, MA: Cambridge University Press.

Prakash, C., Stephens, K.D., Hoffman, D.D., Singh, M., & Fields, C. (2021). Fitness Beats Truth in the Evolution of Perception. *Acta Biotheoretica*, 69(3), 319–341. https://doi.org/10.1007/s10441-020-09400-0

Prieto-Blanco, P. (2016). (Digital) Photography, Experience and Space in Transnational Families: A Case Study of Spanish–Irish Families Living in Ireland. In A. Lehmuskallio & E. Gómez Cruz (eds.), *Digital Photography and Everyday Life* (pp. 122–140). New York, NY: Routledge.

Ramachandran, V.S., & Hirstein, W. (1999). The Science of Art: A Neurological Theory of Aesthetic Experience. *Journal of Consciousness Studies*, 6 (6–7), 6–7.

Rancière, J. (2008). *The Future of the Image*. London: Verso Books.

Rettberg, J.W. (2023). *Machine Vision: How Algorithms are Changing the Way We See the World*. Hoboken, NJ: John Wiley & Sons.

Ritchin, F. (1990). *In Our Own Image: The Coming Revolution in Photography*. New York: Aperture.

Rizzolatti, G., & Sinigaglia, C. (2006). *So quel che fai. Il cervello che agisce e i neuroni specchio* [I Know What You Are Doing. The Actin Brain and the Mirror Neurons]. Milan: Cortina Raffaello.

Roivainen, I. (2024). 'How I Edit My Instagram Images': Investigating Skilled Vision in the Work of YouTube's Lifestyle-Content Creators. *Visual Studies*, 1–17 (Online First).

Rose, G. (2022). *Visual Methodologies: An Introduction to the Interpretation of Visual Methods* (5th ed.). London: SAGE.

Roth, L. (2009). Looking at Shirley, the Ultimate Norm: Colour Balance, Image Technologies, and Cognitive Equity. *Canadian Journal of Communication*, 34, 111–136.

Ruesch, H. (1977). *Back to the Top of the World*. London: Pocket.

Rumi, J. (2010). *The Big Red Book: The Great Masterpiece Celebrating Mystical Love and Friendship*. San Francisco: HarperOne.

Said, E.W. (1978). *Orientalism*. New York: Pantheon Books.

Sardar, Z. (1998). *Postmodernism and the Other*. London: Pluto Press.

de Saussure, F. (1974). *General Course in Linguistics*. New York: Philosophical Library.

Schreiber, M. (2017). Audiences, Aesthetics and Affordances Analysing Practices of Visual Communication on Social Media. *Digital Culture & Society*, 3(2), 143–164.

Schutz, A. (1973). *The Structures of the Life-World*. Evanston, IL: Northwestern University Press.

Sendler, E. (1985). *L'Icona: Immagine dell'Invisibile*. Milan: Edizioni San Paolo.

Seppänen, J. (2006). *The Power of the Gaze: An Introduction to Visual Literacy*. New York: Peter Lang.

Seth, A. (2021). *Being You: A New Science of Consciousness*. London: Faber & Faber.

Shaw, J.L. (1978). Negation and the Buddhist Theory of Meaning. *Journal of Indian Philosophy*, 6(1), 59–77.

Sheikh, G. (1997). The Making of a Visual Language: Thoughts on Mughal Painting. *Journal of Arts and Ideas*, 30–31, 7–32.

Sheikh, G. (2013). Viewer's View: Looking at Pictures. In E. Edwards, & K. Bhaumik (eds.), *Visual Sense: A Cultural Reader*. London: Blooomsbury.

Shiva, V. (2010). *Staying Alive: Women, Ecology, and Development*. London: Zed Books.

Siegert, B. (2015). *Cultural Techniques: Grids, Filters, Doors, and Other Articulations of the Real*. New York, NY: Fordham University Press.
Simons, D.J., & Chabris, C.F. (1999). Gorillas in Our Midst: Sustained Inattentional Blindness for Dynamic Events. *Perception*, 28(9), 1059–1074.
Sloterdijk, P. (2011). *Bubbles: Spheres Volume I: Microspherology (Semiotext(e) / Foreign Agents)* (Translated by W. Hoban). Cambridge, MA: MIT Press.
Sontag, S. (1977). *On Photography*. London: Penguin Books.
Sontag, S. (2003). *Regarding the Pain of Others*. New York: Farrar, Starus & Giroux.
Spencer, J. (1995). Occidentalism in the East: The Uses of the West in the Politics and Anthropology of South Asia. In J.G. Carrier (ed.), *Occidentalism: Images of the West*. Oxford: Clarendon Press.
Spivak, G.C. (1985). The Rani of Sirmur: An Essay in Reading the Archives. *History and Theory*, 24(3), 247–272. https://doi.org/10.2307/2505169
Stafford, B.M. (1996). *Good Looking: Essays on the Virtue of Images*. Cambridge, MA: MIT Press.
Starosielski, N. (2015). *The Undersea Network*. Durham, NC: Duke University Press.
Sturken, M., & Cartwright, L. (2009). *Practices of Looking: An Introduction to Visual Culture* (2nd ed.). Oxford: Oxford University Press.
Taussig, M. (2001). Dying Is an Art, Like Everything Else. *Critical Inquiry*, 28, 305–316.
Thielmann, T. (2018). Early Digital Images: A Praxeology of the Display. In L. Feiersinger, K. Friedrich, & M. Queisner (eds.), *Image – Action – Space* (pp. 41–54). Berlin: Amsterdam University Press. https://doi.org/10.1515/9783110464979-004
Tiidenberg, K., & Gómez Cruz, E. (2015). Selfies, Image and the Re-making of the Body. *Body & Society*, 21(4), 77–102.
Toister, Y. (2024). Seeing and Sensing. *Media Theory*, 8(1), 259–276.
Tucci, G. (1992). *Storia della filosofia Indiana* [The History of India Philosophy]. Bari, Italy: Laterza.
Turner, J.H. (2002). *Face to Face: Toward a Sociological Theory of Interpersonal Behavior*. Redwood City, CA: Stanford University Press.
Turner, V. (1974). *Dramas, Fields, and Metaphors: Symbolic Action in Human Society*. Ithaca, NY: Cornell University Press.
Turkle, S. (2011). *Alone Together. Why We Expect More from Technology and Less from Each Other*. New York, NY: Basic Books.
van Gennep, A. (1960). *The Rites of Passage*. Chicago, IL: University of Chicago Press.
Van Lier, H. (2007 [1983]). *Philosophy of Photography*. Leuven: Leuven University Press.
Venema, R., & Lobinger, K. (2017). 'And Somehow It Ends Up on the Internet.' Agency, Trust and Risks in Photo-Sharing among Friends and Romantic Partners. *First Monday*, 22(7).http://dx.doi.org/10.5210/fm.v22i17.7860
Verhoeff, N. (2012). *Mobile Screens: The Visual Regime of Navigation* (in the MediaMatters series). Amsterdam: Amsterdam University Press.
Vertesi, J. (2015). *Seeing Like a Rover: How Robots, Teams, and Images Craft Knowledge of Mars*. Chicago, IL: University of Chicago Press.

References

von Amelunxen, H., Iglhaut, S., Rötzer, F., Cassel, A., & Schneider, N.G. (eds.) (1996). *Photography after Photography: Memory and Representation in the Digital Age*. Amsterdam: G+B Arts.

von Glasenapp, H. (1967). *Indiens Religioner* [The Religions of India]. Lund, Sweden: Studentlitteratur.

Wittgenstein, L. (2009). *Philosophical Investigations* (4th ed.). Hoboken, NJ: Wiley–Blackwell.

Yarbus, A.L. (1967). *Eye Movements and Vision* (Translated from Russian by Basil Haigh). New York: Plenum Press (originally published in 1965).

Zelizer, B. (2010). *About to Die: How News Images Move the Public*. Oxford: Oxford University Press.

Zuckerkandl, V. (1969). *Sound and Symbol, Volume I: Music and the External World*. Princeton, NJ: Princeton University Press.

Zylinska, J. (2015). The Creative Power of Nonhuman Photography. In J. Zylinska (ed.), *Photographic Powers* (pp. 132–154). Helsinki: Aalto University.

Index

Note: Page locators in **bold** represent figures. Endnotes are indicated by the page number followed by "n" and the note number e.g., 154n3 refers to note 3 on page 154.

3D cinema 106–7
3D laser-mapping 107

abduction, theory of 72–3, 75
Aboriginal Australia 53, 59, 98, 141
Abrahamic religions 50
advertising campaign 81; in London 84; against sexual harassment 82–3
agent–patient relationships, Gell's theory of 72
Agrigento 21
Alberti, Leon Battista 31
al-Haytham, Ibn (Alhazen) 10, 31; *Book of Optics, The* (1021) 25; as the creator of the *camera obscura* 26–7; experiments on behaviours of light 25–6; theory of the functioning of the eye 25
al-Kindi, Abu Yusuf 22–3, 25, 29; philosophy of radiation 25; on role of light in functioning of vision 25
Altar of Augustan Peace (*Ara Pacis Augustae*) 37
American horror movies 149
analogon 48, 56–7
analogue–digital continuum 93
anamorphism, use of 34
Antiquity, knowledge of 24, 44
aqueous humour (watery fluid inside the eye) 28
Ara Pacis case 106
Argan 37–8
Aristotle 22–3, 26; notion of the phantasm 24
Arnheim, Rudolf 51

Art and Visual Perception (Arnheim, 2004) 51, 137
artificial intelligence (AI) 67, 73, 93, 97
associated viewing practices 93
Atget, Eugene 127
ATR Institute, in Kyoto, Japan 70
attention, cultivation of 75
augmented reality (AR) 34, 93, 95
Augustine, Saint 103–4
automatic licence-plate readers 121

barite photographic paper 67
Barrie, J.M. 149
Barthes, Roland 48, 117
basal expressions 113
Beato, Felice 127
Bentham, Jeremy 42
Berger, John 30
bifocal vision, notion of 85–6
biometric information, diagrammatic depiction of 68
biometric technologies 116
bodily spacing 103
Book of Optics, The (al-Haytham, 1021) 25
Bourbaki Panorama (Lucerne, Switzerland) 39, **39**
bourgeois society, establishment of 128
Bredekamp, Horst 61
British Transport Police 81
Brunelleschi, Filippo 31
Buddhist double negation 108
Byzantine art 40, 135
Byzantine churches 135–6

Byzantine icons 40, 53–4, 94
Byzantine paintings 59

Calugareanu, Ilinca 71
camera-based surveillance 90
camerae obscurae 10–11, 13–14, 16, 26–8, 54, 102, 121
cameras 12; 360-degree 103; function as sensors 121; hyperspectral 145; proliferation of 130; as sites for decision-making 122; surveillance cameras 84–7; technologies 119; and their environments 122–6; use of 119–20
Capa, Robert 127
Cartesian perspectivalism 33, 40, 75
Cartesian separation, of body from mind 42
Casetti, Francesco 90
Castres, Edouard 39
central nervous system 51
Chabris, C.F. 14
chemical-film-based visual practices 54
Christian art 135
Chun, Wendy 88
Church of St Ignatius of Loyola 34, 38
classical theory of vision 21–4; extramission *vs.* intramission theories 21–3; representation 23–4
communication technologies, digitisation of 87
communities of practice 7, 15, 54, 55, 75–6, 80
computer-generated image 66, 70, 73
computer-learning systems 66
computer screens *see* digital screens
computer vision 121
computing, story of 5
corpothetics 49, 58, 98, 136
Crary, Jonathan 10
crystalline lens 28
cultural constructs 16
cultures, across time and space 6

Daguerre, Louis 124
daguerreotypy, process of 124, 154n3
darsan, concept of 16, 59, 98, 133
da Vinci, Leonardo 27–8; *Last Supper, The* 33, **33**
death masks, production of 127
death, visual culture of 126–39; cultural history 128–32; images and 126–8; photographs of the dead 130, 132–8

decision-making 119–22; automated forms of 121; cameras as sites for 122; modes of 28
deep learning 70, 73–4
deep vision 139, 142, 144–5
Democritus 21–2, 34
Descartes, René 2, 10, 29–31, 150–1
de Tracy, Antoine Destutt 62
device-borne communication 91
digital cameras 67–8
digital computation 122
digital image-making 95
digital imagery, indexicality of 67
digital images 67, 70; reflections on 95–9
digital screens 87–9; emergence of 90; human–screen relations 87–8; interactions based on 89–92; meanwhile structures 91; for social interactions 92; used for human-to-human interactions 87; used in in video-mediated communication 91
digital technologies 67, 96, 98
digital visualities, materiality of 48
Dionysian initiation ritual 37, 105
Discourse on the Method (1637) 29
docile bodies, notion of 63
Draper, John William 122, 124
Draw Mm Close 111n8
Dunbar, Robin 92
Dundes, Alan 136
Dürer, Albrecht 32–3, 102

Eck, Diana 15–16
Eder, Jens 121
Edwards, Elisabeth 48, 131
ekphrasis, of images 50, 61
electric circuitry 96
Elsaesser, Thomas 107
Empedocles 21–2
Enlightenment, notion of 146
ethnic identity 62
Etruscans 37
Euclid 23
expanded reality (XR) 92, 93, 95–6, 110
extramission, principle of 21–2
eye: aqueous humour (watery fluid inside the eye) 28; connection with brain via optical nerve 28; crystalline lens 28; movements of 9; pupil of 28; theory of the functioning of 25
eye-tracking technology 16; development of 13–14; experiments by Yarbus 47

Facebook 10, 95, 146
face engagement, forms of 83
faceless gaze 42
faces: immutable mobiles 118; mediation into operative images 118; significance of 112–17; structured and unstructured 117–18
facial expressions 11–12, 79, 113–14
facial images: exteriorisations of 12; visual orders in 117
facial muscles 116
facial-recognition technology 114, 116, 118, 121
Farocki, Harun 117, 121
Favero, Anna Maria 129
Feiersinger, Luisa 88
Fenton, Roger 127
film canons, decolonisation of 94
fitness beats truth (FBT) 46
fixation points 13–14
Florensky, Pavel 34, 52, 59, 98, 109, 135–6, 150
focused interactions 81
Foster, Hal 3
Foucault, Michel 20, 42
Francesca, Piero dell 39
Franco-Prussian War of 1871 39
Freud, Sigmund 10, 101, 149
Friedrich, Kathrin 88
funerals, visual display of 130
Future of the Image, The (Rancière, 2008) 51

Galla Placidia mausoleum, in Ravenna 106
Gandhi neurons 51
Garbo, Greta 56
gaze, notion of 62
Gell, Alfred 72; theory of agent–patient relationships 72
Gender Advertisements (1978) 76
generative adversarial networks 66, 67
Generative Pre-trained Transformer 3 model 70
genetic indexes 15
geometrical viewing, principles of 107
German Expressionism 149
ghost writer 149
Gibson, James Jerome 88
glass-plate film 12
Goffman, Erving 76, 81, 87
Golden Age of Islam 24
good images 119–20, 121; ethics and moral values 120; importance of 120; qualities of 120; social and moral expectations related to 125
gorilla test 14
Gramsci, Antonio 56
graphic communication, rules of 96
graphic media 50
Grasseni, Cristina 15
Greek Orthodox church 38, 106
Guardian, The (British newspaper) 100
Guevara, Che 53
Gupta, Akhil 62

Hall, Edward T. 76, 80, 87–8
Hediger, Heini 88
Heidegger, Martin 40, 57, 61, 103–4, 132
Helmreich, Stefan 117
Herschel, John 124
Hindu devotional practices 98, 133
Hoffman, Donald 46
House of Mysteries (*Villa dei Misteri*) 37
Huhtamo, Erkki 87
human–animal relationships 66
human anticipation, importance of 22
human–machine relations 70
human-made images 96
Husserl, Edmund 57–8, 104
hyperspectral cameras 145

icon and the index, tension between 63–75; analysing a photograph 69–71; awareness of agency 72–3; debating of indexicality 74–5; Peirce's theory 64–6; photorealism 66–9; studying photographers 73–4
'icon, index, symbol' triad 75
'Ikonostas' essay (Florensky, 1920) 135
illusion 24
image analysis 63, 68, 73, 121
image creation 29, 114
image-origin discrimination 75
image-processing algorithms 70
images: *in corpore* 77, 84, 116, 118; and death 126–8; dependence on the ways in which we look 12–14; in effigy 116; emerging in between 45–6; family of 47–50; functions of 52–4; geometrical perspective of 31–5; of Hindu icons 136; human-made 96; immersive viewing 92–110; meaning of 44–5; moving from signs to 57–60; photographic 13, 48; proceeding from experience to politics 60–3; relations and the senses 50–2; retinal 27–9;

satellite images 49, 54; as signs 55–7; social interaction, role of 75–92; for strengthening of social ties 12; study of 54–5; vision when we focus on 16–20; Western approaches to the world of 95; *see also* good images; photographic images
image-sharing practices 95
image-viewing 95
Imagined Communities (Benedict Anderson) 91
imaging technologies 103
immersion, sense of 105
immersive viewing: Buddhist philosophy on 101; from Byzantine icons to virtual reality 92–110; immersive desires 93–5; immersive longings 105–10; reflections on digital images 95–9; reframing viewing 102–5; VR/MR art and documentary forms 99–102
immutable mobile 118
inattentional blindness 14
inattentional blindness attests, phenomenon of 18
indexical interrelations, between images and the objects 65
indexicality, idea of 67, 74–5
infrastructural interrelations 9
Ingold, Tim 8, 11, 30, 44–6, 50, 103–4
Ings, Simon 20
Instagram 112, 146, 147, 154n1
interactions, focused and unfocused 81
interdisciplinary indiscipline 61, 63, 92
intramission, theory of 22
intuition, Plato's theory of 23
Ishiguro, Hirohito 70–1, 73
Ito, Mizuko 95

Jacobs, Ken 107
Jay, Martin 31
journalistic photograph 119
Journey to the Center of the Earth (1864) 142
Jung, Carl 50

Kandinsky, Wassily 94
Kant, Immanuel 103
Kepler, Johannes 27–8, 30
Keskitalo, Joose 2, 155
Khusrau, Amir 153
Kittler, Friedrich 10
Klonk, Charlotte 121

Koch, Christoph 46
Krishnamurti, Jiddu 146–7
Kuper, Adam 62

Lacan, Jacques 24
langue 56
learning, to pay attention 15
lidar 67
light, importance of 29–31
light-sensitive materials, use of 27
Lindberg, David C. 28
Lippit, Akira Mizuta 106–7
liquid-crystal displays 67
look, as a medium 5–16; images 12–14; looking as a skilled practice 14–16; vision 7–11; visual media 11–12
Louis XIV, King 34, 41
Luckmann, Thomas 57

MacDougall, David 2
machine-vision systems 68
Mackenzie, Adrian 117
male gaze, concept of 9, 54, 62–3
Manara, Milo 143
Marx, Karl 10
mass media 23, 102
material mediations, role of 54, 119
Mausoleum of Galla Placidia 38
maya, notion of 23
McLuhan, Marshall 96
McQuire, Scott 40
mediaeval Islam, theories on vision 24–7; *camera obscura* 26–7
mediated staring 84–7
mediation, theory of 72
medical gaze 54
meditation, practices of 104
memory-driven vision 17
'mental' images 50
Merleau-Ponty, M. 11, 46, 51, 57, 104, 110, 137–8
Mesmer, Olga 142
meta-language 117
micro-saccadic movements 13
mirror neurons, discovery of 51
mirrors, roles of 54
Mirzoeff, Nicholas 27–8
missiles guidance 121
Mitchell, W.J.T. 43, 92, 96
mixed reality (MR) 93, 95
Mobile World Congress (Shanghai) 5, **6**
Morse, Samuel F.B. 124
Mughal paintings 37, 41

Multimedia Messaging Service (MMS) 95
Mulvey, Laura 54, 62

Nancy, Jean-Luc 51, 59–60
National Geographic 13
networked camera technologies 87
neuroscience accords 51
new images, model of 96
Nietzsche, Friedrich 132
Nilsson, Lennart 144
nonhuman photography 61
non-representative images 68
non-visual sensory stimuli, visual strength of 51
non-Western epistemologies 24

oil paintings 49, 71
open stories 131
operative images 68, 117, 120–2
optical-camera-origin photograph 67
optical illusions 34
optical media 10, 50, 73–4, 81
optical nerves 22, 25, 28
Oriental gaze, concept of 9, 54
Orientalism 61–2, 75
Orientalist imaginaries 62
Orientalist paintings 36, 62
'Oriental' societies 62
Orthodox religious icons 93

Painter's Manual, The (Dürer, 1525) 102
painting: Bourbaki Panorama (Lucerne, Switzerland) 39, **39**; depicting Greek culture 37; European 39; Mughal approach to 37, 41; oil paintings 49; 'Oriental' painting 36; religious 49
Panofsky, Erwin 35, 60, 67
Pan, Peter 148–51
Paravel, Serena 144
parole 56
Pascal, Blaise 2
pattern recognition 121
Peirce, Charles Sanders 45, 56, 64–6
Pencheva, Bissera 108–9
Pennetta, Francesca 100
perception, theory of 88
'perceptual' images 50
perceptual psychology 31
Perrault, Charles 39
person's gaze 13
Peters, Jan-Marie 48, 91
Peters, John Durham 10

phantasm, Aristotle's notion of 24
phenomenological scholarship 57
photogrammetry 67
photographic cameras *see* cameras
photographic devices *see* cameras
photographic images 13, 48; centrality of 53; of corpses 128; dimension of analysing 57; of funerals 130; iconic quality of 73; journalistic 119; nonhuman 61; role among Australian Aboriginal communities 48–9, 53
Photographs and the Sound of History (2006) 48–9
photography, forms of 119
photorealism, notion of 66–9
photorealistic computer-generated images 66, 73
photorealistic iconicity 66–7; specificity of 67
phototherapy 120
Pierre, Abbè 56
Pink, Sarah 90
Pinney, Christopher 49, 51, 58, 98–9, 133
Plato 2, 21–3; *Republic* (2000) 24
Platter, Felix 28
Plexiglas 89
pneuma 22
political disobedience 34
Pompeii's Villa dei Misteri (House of Mysteries) 105
pornographic imagery 106
portrait photography 71, 122, 126
post factum observation 85
post-traumatic stress disorder 105
Pozzo, Andrea 38
press photographs 48
proxemics 79–80; significance of 88
punctum 57

Queisner, Moritz 88
Qureshi, Hanif 148

'racial' identities 62
radiation, philosophy of 25
Rancière, Jacques 51
Rath Yatra 134
reincarnation, notion of 147
religious chromolithographs, Pinney's analysis of 58
religious icons, study of 53
religious paintings 49

Renaissance, politics of 61, 96, 110
retinal images 27–9
Roman art 37
Roman Catholic church 38, 106
Roman Empire 37
Roman stucco work 38
Röntgen, Wilhelm 142, 144
Rumi (Persian poet) 2

Said, Edward 61
Sanmartino, Giuseppe 141–2
SARS-CoV-2 pandemic 87, 129
satellite images 49, 54, 67
Scent of the Invisible, The (Manara, 1987) 143
Schütz, Alfred 57
screen-based spaces 88
self, sense of 145, 148
self-transformation 155
Sendler, Egon 109
Sengupta, Shuddha 103
senses, Western distinctions of 6
sensory perception 31
sexually motivated stare 83
shadow economy 149
shadow government 149
shadow images 25; for the dark side of life 149; entering the shadowlands 147–8; between light and darkness 145–53; and selves 148–53
Sheikh, Gulam Mohammed 36
signs and symbols: moving to images as experienced 57–60; pragmatist theory of 56; study of 55–7
Simons, D.J. 14
skilled vision (per Grasseni), notion of 75
Snapchat 114, **115**, 116
social aesthetics 80–1
social agents 72
social conversation, realm of 80
social interaction, role in imaging 75–92, 90, 118; focused and unfocused interactions 81; involvement 78–9; mediated staring and 84–7; proxemics 79–80; screen-based interactions 89–92; screens 87–9; staring 81–4
socially shareable knowledge 119
social media: algorithm-driven 88; Facebook 10, 95, 146; Instagram 112, 146, 147, 154n1

social order 114, 129, 131
social space 80–1, 90
social ties, strengthening of 12
societal gaze 86
solar eclipses 27
Sontag, Susan 127
spectator gaze, concept of 9
Stafford, Barbara Maria 98
still images 13
storytelling, simulation-based 100
studium 57
surveillance, banalisation of 116
surveillance cameras 84–7, 114; players 86; uses of 85

tactile visuality 109
Tagore, Rabindranath 148
Tammi, Maija 70
Tannahill, Jordan 99
Taylor, Lucien Castaign 144
technological determinism 86
Theon of Alexandria 20
Thielmann, Tristan 87
tilets 130
time axis manipulation 85
Tomb of Hazrat Nizamuddin, New Delhi **152**, 153
Tomb of the Leopardi, in Tarquinia 37
topoi 47, 54
transducts 116
transformative viewing 107–10
trigesima Mass 131
Turkle, Sherry 88
Twenty Thousand Leagues under the Sea (1870) 142

Uccello, Paolo 39
underwater telecommunication cables, laying of 54
Unexpected Visitor (Ilya Repin) 13
unfocused interactions 81

Veasey, Nick 144
Veiled Christ (Sanmartino, 1753) 141–2
Verhoeff, Nanna 87–8
Verne, Jules 142
Versaille, theatre of **41**
video-mediated communication 88, 90–2; use of digital screens in 91
Viola, Bill 107
virtual reality (VR) 42, 107; immersive viewing and 92–110

Vishu festival 135
vision 7–11; classical 21–4; dominant theory of 99; geometrical perspective of 31–5; history of 16–42; and mediaeval Islam 24–7; memory-driven 17; new model of 96; parallel visualities 35–40; politics of perspective 40–2; role of light in functioning of 25; visual renaissance 27–31; western conceptions of 20–42; when we focus on an image 16–20
visual ascesis 109
visual co-presence 95
visual cultures 94, 114; of death 126–39; interdisciplinary indiscipline 61, 63; self-theorizing 61; study of 3–4, 54
visuality of icons 107, 110
visual media 6–7, 54; creations of 11–12; exhibitions of 55; forms of media as 11; infrastructure of 49; role in humanity's development 11; surface qualities of 54
visual orders: of facial images 117; potential of 75, 81, 93
visual perception, sense of 17, 23
visual spirits 22, 28
visual-studies scholarship 6

visual technologies 4, 19, 29, 54, 74, 81, 85–6, 89
vraisemblance, use of 34
VR goggles 99–100

Warburg, Aby 60
Western civilisation 2, 26, 62, 146, 149
Western hegemonic visuality 94
Western pictorial illusionism 36
Western societies 128
Western visual culture 10, 110
What Do Pictures Want?: The Lives and Loves of Images (2006) 52
Wittgenstein, Ludwig 47

X-ray imagery 112; capacity to make bodies transparent 142; fantasies of deep vision 142; in popular culture 144; between science and popular culture 139–45; visuality of 141

Yarbus, A. L. 13, 18; eye-tracking experiments 47
Yates, William Butler 149

Zahn, Johann 25; Oculus Artficialis by **26**
Zylinska, Joanna 61, 97